"One cannot keep the grim reality of gun violence at arm's length after reading this book. Taylor brings it close. She writes about trauma with honesty and compassion. Regardless of one's political views or personal stance on gun ownership, Taylor's research provides a practical and compelling case for gun reform. This book is for any Christian concerned with our biblical call toward neighbor love."

Rachel Joy Welcher, author of *Talking Back to Purity Culture: Rediscovering Faithful Christian Sexuality*

"On my thirty-fifth birthday I witnessed the close-range shooting of a police officer by a felon. My story is not the same as Taylor's, not as tragic for me nor as potent to tell, but it became a story that changed my life in more ways than I can count. In the months and years after my experience, I wanted to find comfort and solace in the church, and I couldn't. Most church folks I knew had only thoughts and prayers for survivors but no plans, personally or politically, to reconsider any Second Amendment reform. I needed allies like Taylor, who understands what only victims of gun violence understand: something *must* change."

Lore Ferguson Wilbert, author of *Handle with Care: How Jesus Redeems the Power of Touch in Life and Ministry*

"It's hard to think of a more polarizing topic than gun control, but *When Thoughts and Prayers Aren't Enough* reminds us that before we talk policy, we need to listen to people's stories. As a shooting survivor, Taylor Schumann invites us into her story before inviting us to consider broader policy issues and the responsibility of Christians to address the well-being of our neighbors. The result is a poignant and clarifying book that will help facilitate a much-needed conversation."

Kristin Kobes Du Mez, author of *Jesus and John Wayne: How White Evangelicals Corrupted a Faith and Fractured a Nation*

"*When Thoughts and Prayers Aren't Enough* is an urgent, thoughtful, and painful book. It hurts to see the realities of gun violence laid bare before us. And yet Schumann, by looking at both the personal and systemic impacts of gun violence, does what seems impossible. She models for us the prophetic work of allowing suffering and statistics to change our hearts and minds toward real action regarding gun violence in the United States. I wish this book wasn't so achingly necessary, but since it is, I will be encouraging everyone to read it. May our prayers for peace be turned into real laws that protect the most vulnerable among us."

D. L. Mayfield, activist and author of *The Myth of the American Dream: Reflections on Affluence, Autonomy, Safety, and Power*

"There are two things that are abundantly clear in *When Thoughts and Prayers Aren't Enough*. The first is that there are few things more important than the power of one's story, and the second is that we should all care about gun violence and the havoc it wreaks on its victims. Not only does Taylor Schumann humbly ask us to consider the impact of gun control legislation through well-researched, thorough, and illuminating information; she does so by first inviting us on her honest and raw journey of trauma, faith, and survival."

Kat Armas, host of *The Protagonistas* podcast and author of *Abuelita Faith: What Women on the Margins Teach Us About Wisdom, Persistence, and Strength*

"Compulsively readable, *When Thoughts and Prayers Aren't Enough* presents a practical guide to changing our minds about guns. The view into the continued difficulty of Schumann's life as a gun violence survivor gives readers reasons and permission to reexamine our views on guns. She has laid out hopeful, doable action that can follow our collective knee-jerk instinct to give thoughts and prayers. As Schumann suggests, prayer can actually be the beginning of our work and not the end."

Hayley Morgan, author of *Preach to Yourself*

"I don't say this lightly: this is a book that will change minds. Taylor's personal story is heartbreaking and compelling, but it is her passion for justice, her well-researched arguments, and her empathy for different perspectives that make this book so powerful. I am confident that *When Thoughts and Prayers Aren't Enough* will inspire many people, but I am even more confident that it will guide and inform real conversations that we desperately need to have in our families, churches, and communities."

Kaitlyn Schiess, author of *The Liturgy of Politics*

"This book is a rallying cry for a culture that has simply not cared enough to tackle the problem of gun violence. Taylor Schumann invites us into her pain, then guides us toward thoughtful consideration and practical, long-haul action. Vulnerably told, packed with both data and empathy, our list of excuses ends within these pages."

Shannan Martin, author of *The Ministry of Ordinary Places* and *Falling Free*

"By sharing the gritty reality of her own journey, Taylor Schumann offers us all a complex understanding of gun violence that we simply can't get from the latest headlines. Even when thoughts and prayers are given with the best of intentions, Taylor shows us that what survivors need isn't sympathy offered from a distance but connection from a place of curiosity and care."

Sarah Stewart Holland, cohost of *Pantsuit Politics* and coauthor of *I Think You're Wrong (But I'm Listening): A Guide to Grace-Filled Political Conversations*

"In *When Thoughts and Prayers Aren't Enough*, Taylor Schumann tells a story and makes an argument. With wisdom and heart, Taylor not only unpacks the scourge of gun violence in America but provides a model for Christians who ought to be moved by experience and compassion into the public square to advocate for the common good."

Michael Wear, founder of Public Square Strategies and author of *Reclaiming Hope: Lessons Learned in the Obama White House About the Future of Faith in America*

"What America's gun debate needs is credibility, and Taylor Schumann brings it in spades. She's both a survivor of gun violence and a writer who can strip the bitter partisanship from the issue. Schumann makes it clear: the vast majority of Americans want simple, achievable reforms that will prevent tens of thousands of Americans from needlessly dying each year. Her book is a testament to the chance for change, giving hope to survivors and all the rest of us who desperately want the violence to end."

Seth Moulton, congressman from Massachusetts

"I live in a state that has more mass shootings per capita than almost anywhere in the United States. The day before I finished reading Schumann's book, there was a mass shooting just thirty-five minutes from my home. *When Thoughts and Prayers Aren't Enough* is the honest conversation and tear-stained lament our nation desperately needs. Through haunting and hopeful story-telling, Schumann gives a human face to the casualties of gun violence. By combining compelling research and reflection, Schumann lights a way forward through the darkness of American individualism."

K.J. Ramsey, licensed professional counselor and author of *This Too Shall Last: Finding Grace When Suffering Lingers*

"More than thirty-six thousand people are dying each year from gun violence. Taylor Schumann shows grace, passion, and leadership in *When Thoughts and Prayers Aren't Enough*. Some of us lead because we want to; Taylor has decided to lead because she has too. This book is a must-read for my college students who have grown up in the era of school shootings, but it is relevant to every Christian looking to love their neighbor and seek justice."

Heather Thompson Day, author of *It's Not Your Turn*

"A powerfully personal story of gun violence and the process of healing. Grounded in faith, Taylor makes a clear case for common-sense gun safety laws. I can't wait to share her book with others who are willing to engage in the tough but critical conversations needed to ensure we reduce gun violence in our country."

Amy O'Rourke, wife of former congressman Beto O'Rourke

"*When Thoughts and Prayers Aren't Enough* should be required reading for anyone desiring to fulfill Jesus' command to love our neighbor. When the American church is complicit in propagating the carnage resulting from gun violence, we must find a better way forward. Schumann's personal narrative as both a victim and survivor of gun violence lends credence to her impassioned plea to engage with the often-divisive topic of gun control and to our spiritual imperative to value commandments more than amendments. While statistics may seem abstract, her story of survival is visceral and absorbing. When victims' experiences are discounted, the facts are sobering. Schuman expertly offers us both while challenging us to contend with the cost of our 'rights' and the love of our neighbor."

Alia Joy, author of *Glorious Weakness: Discovering God in All We Lack*

"One of my greatest passions is coaching women to use what they've got for the good of others + the glory of God. A lot of what we have to use is our story, and unfortunately it's not usually our easy stories that make the most impact. I wish my friend Taylor didn't have this story; I wish no one had her story. But Taylor's bravery, wisdom, insight, and compassion are just some of the components that make her an incredible leader, and make this a book not to miss out on. It's the book I wish we didn't have to read but the one we need. Thank you, God, for my friend who is using what she's got for the good of others + the glory of God."

Jess Connolly, author of *You Are the Girl for the Job* and *Breaking Free from Body Shame*

WHEN THOUGHTS AND PRAYERS AREN'T ENOUGH

A SHOOTING SURVIVOR'S
JOURNEY INTO THE REALITIES
of GUN VIOLENCE

TAYLOR S. SCHUMANN

An imprint of InterVarsity Press
Downers Grove, Illinois

InterVarsity Press
P.O. Box 1400, Downers Grove, IL 60515-1426
ivpress.com
email@ivpress.com

InterVarsity Press® is the book-publishing division of InterVarsity Christian Fellowship/USA®, a movement of students and faculty active on campus at hundreds of universities, colleges, and schools of nursing in the United States of America, and a member movement of the International Fellowship of Evangelical Students. For information about local and regional activities, visit intervarsity.org.

Cover design and image composite: David Fassett
Interior design: Jeanna Wiggins
Images: smoke curls: © Jasper James / The Image Bank / Getty Images
    rifle casing: © gsagi / iStock / Getty Images
    smoke: © Henrik Sorensen / DigitalVision / Getty Images
    girl silhouette: © Nikola Spasenoski / iStock / Getty Images
    smooth white paper: © Nenov / Moment Collection / Getty Images

ISBN 978-0-8308-3170-8 (print)
ISBN 978-0-8308-3171-5 (digital)

Printed in the United States of America ∞

Library of Congress Cataloging-in-Publication Data
Names: Schumann, Taylor S., 1990- author.
Title: When thoughts and prayers aren't enough : a shooting survivor's
    journey into the realities of gun violence / Taylor S. Schumann.
Description: Downers Grove, IL : InterVarsity Press, [2021] | Includes
    bibliographical references and index.
Identifiers: LCCN 2021008046 (print) | LCCN 2021008047 (ebook) | ISBN
    9780830831708 (hardcover) | ISBN 9780830831715 (ebook)
Subjects: LCSH: Schumann, Taylor S., 1990- | Violence—Religious
    aspects—Christianity. | Gun control—United States. | Christianity and
    politics—United States. | Victims of violent
    crimes—Virginia—Christiansburg—Biography. | School
    shootings—Virginia—Christiansburg.
Classification: LCC BT736.15 .S38 2021 (print) | LCC BT736.15 (ebook) |
    DDC 362.88/293092 [B]—dc23
LC record available at https://lccn.loc.gov/2021008046
LC ebook record available at https://lccn.loc.gov/2021008047

| **P** | 22 | 21 | 20 | 19 | 18 | 17 | 16 | 15 | 14 | 13 | 12 | 11 | 10 | 9 | 8 | 7 | 6 | 5 | 4 | 3 | 2 | 1 |
| **Y** | 40 | 39 | 38 | 37 | 36 | 35 | 34 | 33 | 32 | 31 | 30 | 29 | 28 | 27 | 26 | 25 | 24 | 23 | 22 | 21 | | |

For every person who has been

affected by gun violence.

You are seen.

CONTENTS

INTRODUCTION

AFTER I GOT SHOT ON APRIL 12, 2013, as I was hiding out in a closet praying for rescue, I remember thinking, *This happened to me. A shooting happened to me, and now it will never have not happened to me.* I knew that my life would forever be divided by that moment—before the shooting and after—and on the other side of surviving it, everything would be different.

Despite growing up in a post-Columbine world—the 1999 high school shooting took place when I was eight years old—I never imagined something like it would happen to me. I never imagined turning around to see a person point a gun at me. I never imagined getting shot. I certainly couldn't have foreseen becoming an activist for gun reform. And while I always hoped I would write a book someday, I never imagined a world in which it would be about this.

My life took an unexpected turn that day and everything changed. On a beautiful spring morning in April, a student decided to walk into his school with a gun, and I was forced into a world I only saw from the comfort of my living room with the television screen separating me from tragedy. After that day, I understood what it was like to see the worst experience of your life on the national news and the front of the newspaper. I felt the physical pain of a bullet ripping my body apart. I woke up from nightmares constantly through the night and started sobbing at sudden noises. Contending with physical and emotional trauma resulting from the attack became my life. I found myself joining a club of shooting survivors who lived all of their days like this long before I did. Despite the fact we strongly oppose adding new members—since none of us want to be in this club in the first place—our membership number goes up every day.

Before it happened to me, it was easy to see shootings in the news, feel sad, offer my thoughts and prayers, maybe add one of those little ribbons to my Facebook profile picture, and then move on with my day. I didn't have to stare at the suffering. I didn't have to think about it if I didn't want to. It wasn't my problem. I didn't have to acknowledge the fact that in America, more than 36,000 people die every year because of gun violence.[1] Or that the gun suicide rate in America is ten times higher than other high-income countries.[2] Or that for children and teens in America, firearms are the second leading cause of death.[3] None of this affected me. Until it did.

Maybe this is you too. Perhaps gun violence hasn't affected you in a direct way. It makes you sad, of course, and after mass shootings you sincerely offer your thoughts and your prayers, and hope that it doesn't keep happening. But beyond that, you don't think about it. Maybe you even feel a little guilty about it, but what can you do? You wouldn't know where to start.

I get it, I really do. I lived it. Can I let you in on a little secret? I don't really want to think about it either. I would love to be able to go through a day without a memory trying to take me down, or panicking when I hear an ambulance siren, or feeling tears collect in the bottom of my eyes when I hear news of an active shooter. I would love to live my life that way, but I can't. I don't have the option anymore. And in some ways, I'm actually thankful for that. Because here's the thing: people are hurting and suffering. Survivors are retraumatized daily as more and more people become victims themselves. Gun violence is wreaking havoc on our country, and the effects ripple out farther than we can possibly know or imagine. We, all of us, have to look at it head-on. We have to stop turning away.

I spent a lot of days feeling forgotten. In the weeks and months after the shooting, most of my friends and people in my life were able to move on with their lives. Things went back to normal for them, but I was drowning, trying to figure out what my life was supposed to look like. Surviving a shooting is a whole thing. Getting shot is a whole other thing. Living in the aftermath of the trauma and trying to make a life for yourself in the midst of the surviving is, for lack of a better term, *messy*. It baffled me how every morning people got up and had their coffee and went to work like nothing ever happened, while I laid in my bed struggling to find a reason to get out of it.

Most painful of all was the realization that those who turned away, who remained silent, were the ones I most expected to see on the front lines—leaning into my pain, joining with me to call out for healing, justice, reform. I expected to see my fellow Christians, the church body as a whole, rally around the issue of gun violence and fight for a better, more peaceful, more loving vision for our nation. I expected to see the church loudly proclaim that lives of our fellow human beings are worth more than guns. I had been following Jesus almost my whole life, and everything I knew and believed about him told me that as believers, we are to love our neighbor as ourselves, plead the cause of the hurting, and defend the least among us. We are even instructed to only seek the good of others instead of our own good. Yet as I became more involved in advocating for gun reform, I saw very little of that, sometimes none at all, and the greater the silence from the church rang in my ears. Seeing my fellow Christians remain silent as violence ripped at the fabric of our communities and survivors were wielded as political footballs increased my pain exponentially. To those who should have seen me most deeply, I felt invisible.

That's why I don't want to look away from the pain of other victims, survivors, and families. This pain deserves to be seen. Someone has to look and really see. Someone has to remember because no one should feel forgotten. Someone has to decide that enough is enough. This pain has to be used to propel us to a better future.

I'm grateful for the people who have chosen not to look away. Many of these people are fellow survivors, and I am honored to call them my friends. Many have lost their people to gun violence. And many are just people who realized we don't have to live this way, but, in order to do that, we have to choose not to turn away.

So, I'd like to invite you in. I'd like to offer you a chance to look at the pain, to sit with it, and to resist the urge to turn away. I want to ask you to fight against that nagging thought telling you that gun violence is too divisive an issue, too hard a problem to be solved, that it can't be stopped, so it's not worth it. There are absolutely things that we can do, but we have to decide it's a problem worth fixing if we have a fighting chance at all.

This book isn't just about gun violence, though. It's about surviving in the aftermath of trauma, about suffering, healing, grief, hope, faith. It's about my journey with God: my struggle to believe his promises, my fears that my life wasn't worth saving, and how he continues to sustain and restore me. Most of you reading this book haven't survived a shooting, but you've all been through hard, even impossible things. I hope you see parts of yourself and your story in parts of this book. I hope you feel seen.

I just have one request for you as we start this journey. As you go through these pages, can I ask you to open your hearts and your hands to what you read? If you already support gun reform, I pray this book encourages you in your mission and empowers you to keep going. I hope it gives you hope in a future that reflects more of God's dream for us—life abundant. If you are hesitant to support gun reform, trust me when I tell you I know it feels uncomfortable and a little awkward to even consider changing your mind. We'll talk about that too. So I pray you'll allow yourself to unclench your fists a little and open yourself to a new way of thinking. I pray you'll receive these words in the spirit of compassion and grace that they're intended. I pray that we can move toward a place of respectful dialogue, even if we don't agree on everything.

Wherever you're coming from, thank you for being here and opening yourself to hear my story. Thank you for sitting with me. We're in this together.

A NOTE TO GUN OWNERS

If you are a gun owner, whether you have one gun or twelve, I want to thank you for picking up my book. Maybe you know me personally, so you felt obligated to buy it but weren't really planning to read it. Maybe you're curious about what I have to say. Or maybe you are planning to just read the personal stuff and skip over the gun stuff. No matter your motives, I appreciate that you choose to purchase a book that may disagree with your personal beliefs. I know that's not always a comfortable choice.

I come from a family of gun owners and for many years of my life existed as a pro-gun, staunch supporter of the Second Amendment. I know many advocates for gun ownership want to protect people from gun violence just as I do. I hope by the end of this book, you will see a place for yourself in the conversation around gun reform. We need gun owners who understand the gravity of owning one and the responsibility that comes with it. I can talk all day long about the realities of surviving gun violence and the havoc it is wreaking in our communities. It is you, however, who can speak to those on the opposite side of where I sit, and who can help bridge the gap between us and find common ground. I hope that at the least, you become acquainted with what guns can do to people who find themselves unjustly on the barrel end of one, and that it may influence your beliefs as you move forward.

I once wrote in an article for *Christianity Today* that I have a complicated relationship with thoughts and prayers. I believe in the power of prayer like I believe the sun will rise and set again tomorrow. I believe that through prayer, we can seek God and allow him to reveal himself to us, and through that, we may have our eyes opened to his vision for how we can love and serve one another. At the same time, I'm tired of prayer being the end of our work and not the beginning. God has given us access to him through prayer. He also gave us hands and feet to do the work of bringing a little of his heavenly kingdom to his people here on earth. There is so much we are missing when we let prayer be the period on our concern for gun violence. There is so much God can do in us and through us when we ask him to break our hearts for what breaks his and to use us for the mending.

Thoughts and prayers are not enough, but they were never supposed to be. There is more for us to do. Let's figure it out together.

PART 1

A SURVIVOR'S JOURNEY

1

SURVIVING

I STARED DOWN THE BARREL of a shotgun, two feet away from me, pointed at my head. I was going to die.

It was the most terrifying moment of my life—and yet all I could think was, "Doesn't he know he can't bring guns to school?"

My therapist later would explain to me that this was a natural reaction; my brain was quickly trying to make sense of what was happening, and "You are about to get shot" happens to be low on the list of likely possibilities. The thought briefly passed through my mind that maybe the boy just forgot this rule and I would tell him and he would take the gun back to his car.

That wouldn't happen, of course.

I looked at him. He was young, a student probably, I thought. He was wearing a T-shirt and a zip-up sweatshirt. No trench coat or mask or battle gear to give away his intentions. He was calm, but he seemed unsure of himself. Maybe, I thought in a moment that seemed to last an eternity, he'll give up, maybe he doesn't really want to do this. But he did. I was looking evil directly in the eyes. He was going to shoot me. He wanted to kill me. And there was nothing I could do about it.

● ○ ●

It started like any other day. I had my morning coffee and got ready for work with the news playing on the TV in the background. I half-listened to a report of a possible shooter on the campus of a university in North Carolina. The reports would ultimately be unfounded, but I paused to whisper a prayer and a version of "I can't even imagine."

April 12, 2013, was a Friday. For me, it was a particularly special Friday because my bridal shower was scheduled for the next day. My friends were coming into town to spend the weekend with me, and I was anxious to get through the day and get the festivities started. I even wrote a Facebook post that morning when I got to work: "Beyond excited to have so many of my dear friends together in one place this weekend—my heart is already so happy."

My fiancé, Eric, and I were just a few weeks out from our May 25 wedding, and we couldn't wait to get married. Eric and I met in the summer of 2010 when mutual friends introduced us at a birthday party. He immediately intrigued me. His hair fell just above his eyes, and he had a motorcycle, so he was obviously very cool—probably too cool for me. It was immediately apparent how smart he was. And so funny. We laughed the whole party. Thankfully, he was interested in me too, and we began dating a few months later. We dated for two years before Eric asked me to marry him in May 2012, the day before I graduated from college. I thought he was messing with me when he got down on one knee and opened the ring box, letting the sun reflect off the diamond band. I am grateful he was not, in fact, messing with me.

Eric had recently been accepted into pharmacy school in spring 2013, and in between wedding and honeymoon details, we were planning our move to a town in Tennessee eight hours away from where we currently lived in Virginia for him to attend school. Life wasn't perfect, of course. I mean, is it ever? But things were falling into place for us. We were happy and hopeful, and life felt like it was just beginning.

I arrived at New River Community College's mall campus in Christiansburg, Virginia, at 10 a.m. with my coffee in hand. I greeted my coworkers Debbie and Carrie. Debbie and I had the same job title, administrative specialist, and we were both in our early twenties, so we became good friends in the months we'd been working together. Our boss, Carrie, was an older woman who exuded a warm, comforting presence. I was always happy when she decided to spend some time with us at our desk instead of working in her office.

Since I worked at the front desk, I was the first person a visitor encountered when they entered the school. The desk was in a big L shape, with a gate to enter into the administrative area. A small closet bordered it where we kept office supplies, the copy machine, and testing materials. I'd been working at the community college for about three months, and I enjoyed the collegial atmosphere and working with students. That day, I spent my morning answering phone calls and emails, and filing tests for the distance education program. Not many classes were scheduled for Friday mornings, so things were slow and quiet.

A couple of hours into work, Debbie asked if we could switch our lunch breaks. "Do you mind if I take the first one? I have a few calls I need to make." I agreed; I was in the middle of responding to some emails and was happy to wait until 2:15.

Debbie got up to take her break around the same time our IT specialist, Brian, arrived. He had come to take a look at my computer monitor, which had been acting up. Wanting to continue working, I decided to log in on Debbie's computer, the one closest to the front door.

Focused on the task at hand, I wasn't paying much attention to the rest of the office until, just before 2:00, I heard Carrie stand up. Glancing up from my desk, I saw Carrie slowly moving backward from her chair as she faced toward the door. Her face turned to a shade of white I can only describe as ghostly. Her voice was shaky and panicked as she pointed at something over my shoulder and started saying, "No. No. No." Something was terribly wrong. I don't know what I expected to see when I turned around, but I do know probably last on my list was a man about two feet away with a shotgun pointed at my face.

● ○ ●

Everything felt urgent, yet moving in slow motion at the same time. When the reality of the situation sunk in, and I realized that this wasn't a student who'd forgotten to leave his gun in his car but someone who intended to harm us—a realization that took seconds but felt like much longer—and I ducked underneath my desk. I knew this wasn't the best location to hide, but I didn't know where to go or what to do. I was panicking and really regretting mindlessly clicking through the active-shooter training I had taken months earlier.

Carrie and the IT tech, Brian, ran out from behind the gate, sprinting to find an escape. Out of the corner of my eye I could see the shooter follow after them. This was my chance. It felt like my body was on autopilot; even while I was still trying to decide what to do, I was already running into the supply closet a few feet behind my desk. I don't remember deciding to do it. It felt like God just picked me up and moved me.

I ran in and slammed the closet door shut, just as I heard the gun go off. I made it. I slowly looked down and noticed blood dripping onto the floor. Whose blood is that?

And then I realized that it was mine. I didn't yet know where I was shot, and I was too scared to look. This cannot be real.

I didn't feel anything yet. That thing where people say they don't realize they've been shot at first? I didn't believe it until it happened to me. But my body did what it was supposed to do: it protected me from the initial shock and gave me a second to try and figure out what was happening before the pain overtook me.

I looked down at my left hand and could hardly believe what I was seeing. I wish I could describe it with more delicacy, but gunshot wounds are graphic. It looked like my hand had exploded. It looked ripped apart. The swelling was happening right before my eyes and I couldn't figure out where the bullet had gone in or out, but I knew it was bad. In a moment of clarity, I winced in pain as I slipped off my engagement ring from my swelling finger and put it into my pocket.

I felt a burning sensation and touched my other hand to my chest. When I pulled my hand away, it was bloodied. I also realized I couldn't see out of my left eye. I looked at the door behind me: there was a hole the size of a baseball where the bullet went through, sending shards of wood into my eye, face, and chest.

Then I remembered: the door doesn't lock from the inside and my key is in my desk. I was trapped in a room with a door that I couldn't lock, and a man with a gun stood on the other side. I slid down to the floor with my back against the door as I tried to keep it shut. The burning smell of gunpowder drifted into the room. I had no idea where the shooter had gone, but I could hear the sound every time the gun fired.

Boom. Boom. Boom.

Some people think the sound of a gun is "bang," but in my experience it's more of a "boom." It was loud and deafening, and the sound carried throughout the whole building. Boom. And then another boom. And another. My mind reeled as I imagined who was on the other end of each of those shots. How many of us were going to be killed? How many injured?

I looked down at my hand again. The blood was pouring out but I couldn't tell the full extent of the injury at that point. I didn't want to look at it anymore. It was so mangled and I was worried the bullet cut through the artery at my wrist. If it had, then I wouldn't have much time. This cannot be happening to me. I cannot die here. I cannot die this way. I didn't want to be there anymore. I wanted it to be over, but there was no way out. I was trapped in that room, alone, waiting to die.

I thought about my fiancé, Eric, who was working just a few minutes up the road. He was so close, and it hurt me to think that he had no idea what was happening to me, how his life was about to change. I thought about the wedding and the life we would never get to have. I wondered if he would be okay without me. He needs me. I thought about my parents and my sister. Would they ever recover from the death of their daughter and sister? I thought about our dogs and our cat. It was too much for me. Too heavy. I can't do this. That's when the tears came, along with my first coherent prayer.

God, I can't sit here and wait to die. If you're going to take me, please just take me quickly. Please. Please. Please.

It is a surreal experience, praying to die quickly.

In that moment, I heard the Lord speak to me clearer than I ever had in my life. I knew he was telling me: "Today is not your day. There is more for you to do."

Sitting there in that closet with my back against the door, I didn't know what to pray. I was terrified. The tears were streaming down my face faster than I could wipe them away. My body was fighting against rapidly intensifying pain and my mind was still struggling to grasp the reality of the situation. This was too much.

Just when I thought my mind and body were failing, I felt the Spirit of God interceding on my behalf, and I remembered the words of Romans 8:26: "Likewise the Spirit helps us in our weakness. For we do not know what to pray for as we ought, but the Spirit himself intercedes for us with groanings too deep for words" (ESV). I knew that I was experiencing this. I knew these words and had read them many times before. But now I knew what it meant. I can still feel it deep in my soul even today what it was like to remember that I didn't need the right words, or any words. He was with me. And he was working.

So I decided to live. Well, I decided to do my best to try and live. Pull it together, Taylor. I knew if I was going to survive, I needed to stop the bleeding. By this point, just a couple of minutes later, the shock had worn off and I very much knew I was wounded. Grabbing my left hand with my right, I had to stop myself from screaming out in pain. I lifted my hands above my head. That's about as much first aid as I remembered, but thankfully it was enough.

As I lifted my arms up, I heard another gun shot. Boom. My body jerked forward away from the door. I looked back and saw another hole in the door where my right arm had been. He was coming back for me, I realized, to make sure I was dead.

I slid myself across the floor as quietly as I could. I didn't want him to hear me or see me through the holes in the door. What was I supposed to do? Casting my eyes frantically around the small space, I saw the copy machine. I could push it over to block the door, but would that make too much noise? Was my best chance to play dead instead? Or was that a mistake too? I recalled hearing that sometimes shooters would shoot people in the head to make sure they were dead. I preferred to not be shot in the head. Every option terrified me. So I hid in the corner of the room, paralyzed. Waiting.

After more agonizing indecision, I concluded that if he came in the room, I would try to fight. Maybe I was going to die, but I wasn't going to let him kill me that easily. I got into some sort of fighting stance—what I imaged a boxing stance looked like, I suppose. It would almost be laughable, if it wasn't so terribly serious: me, crouched like a boxer, trying to muster up my courage to take down a man with a gun who wanted to kill me. I don't think of myself as a tenacious person usually. I'm an entry-level pacifist with limited athleticism and low self-confidence when it comes to matters of self-defense. But when it counted, I decided I could at least try to take this person down. In the worst moment of my life, when it all felt hopeless, I stood ready, with resolve.

I realized everything had gone quiet. I'm not sure how long the silence lasted, but eventually I heard voices. I couldn't make out what they were saying, but the sound of voices instead of gunshots seemed like a good change. I edged closer to the door. That's when I heard it, the words that took my breath away.

"It's okay! You can come out! Is anyone hurt?"

It was over. I made it. Even as I began shaking with relief, I pulled up short: Didn't shooters sometimes say things like this to try to get people to come out of hiding and then kill them? This is the kind of information you retain when you grow up in the world after Columbine. I couldn't take a chance. Crouching, I peered through the hole in the door. I saw an older man who I didn't recognize standing in the lobby looking around. He didn't have a gun, and I knew he wasn't the shooter. I also saw a student with a book bag standing with him, terror and relief mingled on his face. This wasn't a trick.

I slowly opened the door and stuck my wounded hand out so that they would know I was there, and injured, and not another shooter. I fell to the floor. It's over, I survived. I repeated these words over and over in my head in disbelief. It felt like I was stuck in that closet for hours, and was absolutely shocked to find out it had only been five minutes.

But now I was safe. I was overwhelmed again, but this time by relief and the whiplash of surviving something just after resigning myself to death. I would get to see Eric again. I would be able to get married. I would see my family again. I would get to live the rest of the life that just seconds earlier I felt slipping through my hands.

The man who had called out approached the closet. This man, who I later found out was named Jim, had a calmness and a kindness about him I felt immediately. He was an older man, with white hair and a mustache, and even in my state of shock I found myself thinking he looked a bit like Santa Claus. (Imagine my delight when I found out later that he often volunteered to play Santa at local community events.) Jim picked me up and helped me get to my feet. I was shaking, and he put his arm around me and held me up as we walked out through the front doors of the school. I suddenly felt scared to leave the building, a feeling that came as a surprise to me. All I had wanted just moments earlier was to be able to leave that place. Now though, as I looked at the same parking lot I parked in every day fill with emergency vehicles, life was undeniably different. In a matter of minutes, the world became a more dangerous place, and I wanted desperately to go back to 1:54 p.m., before any of this had happened.

I blinked in the sunlight. Looking around, I could see police officers running around and the flashing red and blue lights of their cars. I could hear the ambulance sirens getting closer. People were frantic, cellphones held to their ears as they tried to relay the situation to loved ones. I had watched this same scene unfold on the news many times following other school shootings. Students gathered in a line, hands above their heads. People consoling one another as tears streamed down their faces. It was all familiar, except now it was happening to me, to my school.

The pain began to overwhelm me, and Jim helped me lie down on the sidewalk as the EMTs rushed over to help. They were calm but acted with swift urgency.

"Were you shot anywhere else?" one asked.

"I don't know. But I can't see out of my eye," I said.

"Okay. We need to cut off your shirt so we can make sure you don't have any other injuries."

I lay on the sidewalk, exposed to the world, as they cut off my clothes. I hadn't even thought to be embarrassed until I saw someone take photos with their cellphone. Even today, I'm not sure what happened to those pictures of me on the sidewalk; I suppose they're out there somewhere. Lying there in shock, the main thought running through my mind was that I wore my sister's black cardigan to work that day without asking her permission. But I was confident she would understand why I would be unable to return it to her.

I waited on the sidewalk for what felt like forever as the EMTs looked me over and examined my injuries. There was shrapnel from the door embedded in my eye, which was why I couldn't see. It was in my chest too, which explained why it felt like my chest was on fire. Finally they loaded me into the ambulance, and I heard them say over the radio: "En route. GSW to the hand."

GSW. Gunshot wound. That was me. I felt the awful, defining weight of those words. This happened to me. And I could never go back to life before it did.

The EMT in the ambulance with me tried to keep me calm as we drove to the hospital. We were students at Virginia Tech at the same time, we learned. He asked me about my job and my plans for the future. He kept me talking as I patiently asked for something for the pain. His eyes were glossy from trying to hold back tears. I finally felt like I wasn't alone; someone else was carrying this pain with me. I wish he hadn't needed to.

We arrived at Montgomery Regional Hospital in Blacksburg, Virginia, just a five-minute drive from the college. They wheeled my stretcher into the trauma room, and I looked around. There were nurses and doctors everywhere. There must be dozens of us coming, I thought to myself.

"How many of us are there?" I asked the nurse.

"It's just you," she said.

She went on to tell me there was one more victim, a student named Kristina, who was taken to a different hospital. Everyone else was safe, at least physically. In that moment I never felt so relieved and so lonely at the same time.

● ○ ●

My memories after arriving at the hospital are fuzzy. In my mind, things happened in a different order than I would later learn they actually did. Even after talking to people who were there who told me how things unfolded, my brain remembers it differently. I've learned this is normal after a traumatic event. But I do remember the kindness of the nurses who took care of me. I asked if they could get my engagement ring out of my pants pocket for me. I asked if they could pull my hair up for me to get it out of my face. No one had a hair tie but one of the nurses gently pulled back my thick blonde hair and tied it up with a rubber band they found in the room.

At some point, Eric arrived. I will never forget the image as long as I live: Eric walking in, tears streaming down his face, as two people held him up by his arms. He rushed over to my hospital bed and touched his forehead to mine. I don't remember what we said to each other. I just remember sobbing uncontrollably and not wanting to let him leave my side. I told him I was okay and tried to find the words to tell him what happened, but they weren't coming. People were rushing around on all sides of me trying to take care of my wounds and discern next steps.

After x-rays were done, it was quickly determined that I needed immediate surgery with an orthopedic surgeon. The doctors decided to transfer me to a larger hospital about forty-five minutes away that was better equipped to deal with my injuries. Being wheeled out of my hospital room to the ambulance, I was shocked to see dozens of my friends and loved ones who had made their way to the hospital to be with me. They lined the hallway, standing vigil. As I passed by, they broke into tears and hesitant smiles when they saw I was alive. I could see the fear in their faces though, and wanted to assure them that I was okay. Even then, I was realizing how hard it was going to be to help people understand the gravity of what happened to me.

◉ ◎ ◉

My parents and sister met me at the larger hospital since it was near where we lived. Seeing my family for the first time was incredibly emotional for all of us. They enveloped me in hugs as my sister cried, looking terrified. "I'm going to be okay," I insisted.

My mom did what I needed my mom to do and began to comfort me, fluffing my pillows and pushing the hair out of my face. My dad did what I needed my dad to do; he took charge, as he often does, by asking the nurses to make sure I was getting proper pain medicine and asking who my surgeon would be and ensuring he was qualified to take care of his daughter.

We waited. At some point, I was taken into a trauma room in the emergency department to meet with a forensic nurse from the police department. I had never heard of a forensic nurse before. She explained to me that it was her job to care for victims of assault, abuse, neglect, and violent crimes while collecting evidence to help the police and even provide expert testimony in a court case. She was going to ask me questions about the crime and try to get as many details as possible for the police.

I didn't want to do it. I was so tired and in so much pain. Seeing the police in the corner of every room I was taken to and speaking to this nurse really made me realize none of this would be over anytime soon, and it felt like too much. But she explained to me that the earlier they do it, the more accurate the information would be. It went on and on until I couldn't answer any more questions.

Do you know what kind of gun it was?

No.

Do you remember what he looked like?

Yes.

Do you remember what he was wearing?

Yes.

Do you know who he is?

No.

Did he say anything to you?

No.

Do you know why he did this?

No.

How many times did he fire his weapon?

A lot.

Finally, I met my surgeon, Dr. Cay Mierisch. He was a tall, thin German man with hair to his shoulders that was slicked back on his head. He was matter of fact, as surgeons often are, but I could tell he cared about what happened to me, and I never doubted that I was in capable hands. "We're ready to take you back in to surgery," he told me.

I asked to see my x-rays. When Dr. Mierisch put them up on the screen, though, I had no idea what I was even looking at. It didn't look like a hand. What was left of it looked like gravel. My fingers were there, but my thumb was internally severed, and everything else looked like a bomb went off inside my hand.

Dr. Mierisch explained to me that they were going to try to repair everything as best they could but weren't sure what the outcome would be. Everyone who spoke to me did so with a deep sympathy and caution: "We're going to do our best to fix your hand, and we are so sorry this happened to you." They weren't positive I would ever be able to use my hand again. It was a strange feeling to go into surgery with no idea what the end result would be. Worst-case scenario was that I would lose my hand. The best-case scenario seemed to be keeping my hand, but only for decorative purposes.

I was in too much pain to decide which was preferred. I just wanted it to be over.

◉ ◎ ◉

When I woke up from surgery, I was alone in a recovery room. I couldn't feel my hand or even my arm. They had to cut it off, I thought to myself. I immediately started coming to terms with the idea that I would no longer have a hand. I can do it. Lots of people live their lives with only one hand. It's fine. I'm alive.

Finally, the anesthesiologist came in the room. He was soft spoken and gentle as he sat next to me and put his hand on my right hand. "How are you doing?" he asked.

"I'm okay," I said, my voice scratchy. I swallowed. "Where is my hand?"

He laughed a little and pointed above my head. "It's right here." He explained that they put a nerve block in at my shoulder to help with the pain level, which was why I couldn't feel anything. They'd elevated it above my head to help with the swelling and blood flow.

I had never been so relieved. I still have my hand. The doctor stayed with me and talked for a little while. I will never forget the concern he showed for not only my physical well-being but my mental and emotional well-being as well. He held back tears as he asked me how I was doing and apologized for what happened to me. He asked if he could send the hospital chaplain to see me during my hospital stay, and I told him I would love that. Up until that point, everyone's focus was on my physical needs, and understandably so. And yet in the midst of this trauma I knew I needed to process all of this with someone who could guide me spiritually as well. The idea of being able to talk with someone I could be honest and open with brought me comfort.

Eric was waiting for me when they finally moved me from the recovery area to my own room. I was extremely sick from the anesthesia, and he was by my side as the nurses took care of me. After I was able to get settled, my family came to check on me and see how the surgery went. My mom told me about all the people who came to the hospital when they heard the news and were praying for me in the waiting room.

"I'm sure they'd love to see you. Are you up for visitors?" she asked.

I nodded without hesitation. "Yes."

Looking back, I don't know why I decided to have visitors. I was tired and in pretty bad shape. But only hours before, I had imagined never seeing any of my loved ones ever again, and now I was getting to see all these people who I loved so dearly. I didn't even ask who all was there; I just wanted to see their faces.

They came into the room one by one, I'm sure. But what I remember is looking up and seeing a sea of people in my hospital room all at once. These were people who I loved deeply and who came to support my family and me in our time of desperate need. They sat with Eric and our families, praying and comforting them. They offered to get drinks and meals and bring things to the hospital. This was the body of Christ at work, being his hands and feet. *I can do this,* I thought as I viewed this vast network of love and support. *I will survive this.*

I'm glad I had that moment of resolve and peace on the night of April 12 because the next days, weeks, and years would often feel like absolute hell.

2

EVEN IF NOT

ON THE DAY OF THE SHOOTING, I spent hours lying on a hospital bed with my left arm propped up on a stack of pillows. Every so often the nurse would come and switch out the blood-stained top pillow for a new fresh white one. The smell of gunpowder still lingered around me as I watched doctors and nurses methodically move around the room whispering things to each other. Everything felt like it was happening around me and not to me, like I was watching it from somewhere else. I felt the pain and I saw the damage, but it hardly felt real. Occasionally someone would ask me a question, bringing me back to the reality of what was happening.

"Can you rate your pain on a scale from one to ten?" a nurse would ask. I wondered if she knew how ridiculous it felt to be asked that as I looked at the two gaping holes in my hand.

Through tears I would reply, "One hundred?"

One hundred was not presented as an option, but ten was what I had rated my kidney stone pain a few years prior and this felt, at minimum, ten times worse than that. I wish I'd counted how often I was asked that question throughout this entire experience. Most of the time I would say ten, but sometimes I worried that if I said ten every time they would stop taking me seriously. So occasionally I would say eight or nine in order to leave some room for more excruciating pain that would surely come.

Before I went in for my first surgery, I was told by the surgeon they were going to do everything they could to save my hand and put it back together. Afterward, my surgeon looked at me with all the kindness he could muster up and said to me, "You will never regain full use of your hand, and you probably won't get much function back at all." He went on to explain I would need a lot of occupational hand therapy, and it was going to be hard and painful work. There is a special cruelty in experiencing an intense trauma at the hands of someone else and then realizing you'll be paying for it the rest of your life. I remember thinking to myself, *I didn't ask for any of this. I don't want any of this.* I wanted to go back in time and not go in to work. I wanted to go to sleep and wake up twenty-four hours earlier. That couldn't happen, of course, no matter how much I wanted it to.

I was discharged from the hospital on Monday, April 15, and I was terrified to go home. At the hospital, I was safe. Police officers were stationed outside my room for much of my time there, and the hospital wasn't allowed to tell anyone I was there. So even though I felt scared, I knew I was safe. The world outside the hospital? It didn't feel safe anymore. Any control I ever felt over my life and my safety or the safety of people I loved had disappeared. I held tightly to Eric's hand as a nurse pushed my wheelchair down the halls and outside to the car. As my mom helped me get comfortable and buckled my seatbelt, my dad turned on the radio and we heard the first reports of what we would come to know as the Boston Marathon bombing.

I let the tears come quietly and roll gently down my cheek. I tried to stifle my sniffles so no one would hear me crying. But then the sound faded and I realized the radio was turned off. I think it occurred to all of us in that moment, maybe subconsciously, that these public tragedies would feel different to us now, closer and more personal. We were initiated into a club we did not ask to join and could not leave.

● ◎ ●

The pain management side of things was harder. The doctors who cared for me after surgery did their best to come up with a way to manage the pain, but nothing was effective. Eric kept a clipboard and documented every pain pill I took in order to keep me on a schedule. I had to wake up every two hours to take more medicine or risk getting behind and not being able to manage the pain. After a week of no sleep and excruciating pain, with the help of a few family pharmacists, we figured out a way to manage the pain better.

A week after the shooting, we drove back to the hospital for my first follow-up appointment with my surgeon. I was taken back to a room where my bandages needed to be removed before the x-rays could be taken. The nurse began to undo the bandages and as he pulled on them, I realized that they were stuck to my hand because of all the dried blood. He would pull and I would scream in pain. My mom had to leave the room because she just couldn't bear it anymore. This went on and on as they kept pulling and pulling. I sat in excruciating pain begging them to figure out a better way.

When I look back on the physical pain I experienced after the shooting, this ranks as the second most painful day of my life. Later we found out they should have used a solution to help soften and dissolve the bandages, making them easier to remove, but they didn't, and I suffered tremendously for it. Every single time we had to go back to the hospital after this, I was terrified of reliving this part. No matter how much I tried to calm my mind, my body always remembered.

I'll never forget seeing the x-rays for the first time that day, with the image of the metal pins holding together the tiny fragments of bone that had been turned into gravel by the bullet. The good news was that the surgery had gone better than the surgeon hoped. We still didn't know what recovery would or could look like, but for the first time, I was given a tiny sliver of hope and was going to cling to it with everything I had.

Before we left the hospital, everyone was given strict instructions on how to care for me at home. Since the surgical bandages were now removed, there was a lot more to manage. The bullet wounds were too big to be closed surgically, so someone needed to clean my wounds and replace my bandages a few times every day. The pins also needed to be cleaned daily with alcohol so they wouldn't get infected and need to be removed early. Because of the pins, I was restricted from trying to move my hand or any of my fingers on my own. To avoid losing any more mobility, someone else had to move and stretch my fingers for me multiple times a day. Eric did it for me while I held a pillow against my face to stifle the cries and hide the tears running down my face. I will never be able to know how hard this was for Eric to do. He knew every time he touched my hand that he was about to cause me great pain. But he also knew if he didn't, I would lose more and more function of my hand. Every day he served me in ways that I truly could not quantify or explain.

Everyone around me served me in ways I needed. My mom and my sister helped me shower, fix my hair, and tie my shoes. My dad managed all communication with the detectives, my employer, and anything else that needed to be done so that I wouldn't have to worry about it. He and my (future) mother-in-law, Susy, fought together to make sure I got approved for worker's compensation, something that ended up being much harder than any of us anticipated. My friends brought me coffee and care packages full of cozy pajamas, snacks, and all sorts of things to bring comfort. They came over and just sat with me while we watched movies or reruns of *Parks and Recreation*. They all did their best to make sure I was cared for and wasn't alone.

Two weeks after the shooting, I walked back into the same hospital and checked in with the receptionist at the occupational therapy office who would come to know me quite well over the next year. Eric had his hand resting gently on my lower back, my left arm rested inside a sling, and I protectively cradled it with my right arm as each step took me closer to the occupational therapy wing. I was incredibly nervous. I didn't know what exactly I would be doing, but I knew it was going to hurt, and anticipating pain is its own sort of torture.

Looking back, I recognize that I was also nervous to *hope*. I had to hope to get through it, or else it would feel like I was putting myself through the pain for nothing. But hope felt like a risk when it seemed all the odds were against me. I'll never forget walking into the small therapy room and meeting Patti, who would be by my side for the next year. Patti seemed to be around my mom's age, with dark hair just above her shoulders. She had kind eyes, and I felt safe in her presence. When you are walking through the worst season of your life and are constantly overwhelmed with fear and uncertainty, every person you meet offering kindness and safety leaves an indentation on your heart. These people became my people, and Patti was my person.

She guided me to a chair at a small table and took the seat opposite me. She began to ask me questions about what had happened to me but assured me that I didn't have to answer if it was too hard to talk about. I couldn't tell you now what all we did that day or what we talked about, but I remember the gentleness with which she cared for my hand, slowly unwrapping the bandages and cleaning the wounds and pins with caution. I remember feeling the genuine empathy she had for me and my circumstance. I knew then I could trust her with my wounds, both physical and emotional.

I began seeing Patti three times a week, and she became a constant and a support in my life. She was with me before and after my surgeries, celebrating the smallest ounce of progress, encouraging me when I felt defeated, and honoring my grief when the results weren't what I hoped they would be. Right before my wedding, she helped make me a splint for my hand using the wedding colors so I could match our wedding party. I rarely looked forward to occupational therapy, but I always looked forward to seeing Patti. In the beginning our time was mostly spent with her massaging my hand to encourage blood flow, and her stretching and moving my fingers to help reduce loss of movement and muscle. We slowly moved up to harder exercises and more complicated rehabilitation. I was starting from scratch and having to learn how to use my hand and my fingers all over again. I would make some progress and then find out I needed another surgery. It was like starting over again each time.

Each time the surgeries didn't work, it became harder to hope for better results the next time I needed one. I was desperate to figure out how to hope just enough to get through it. With each surgery came more anesthesia that was wreaking havoc on my body, new incisions to be cared for, more scar tissue that would try to take over my bones and muscles, new stitches needing to be taken out later, and an influx of new pain medications I would have to eventually wean off of. Turns out no matter how carefully you try to come off of pain medication, you'll inevitably experience withdrawal symptoms that make you wish you would've avoided them all together. Every time we tapered my pain medicine, I got sick. Stomach aches, headaches, and full body jitters accompanied the pain of the bullet wounds, and I wondered if I really had to stop.

I'll tell you this, the empathy I have gained for people who become addicted to pain medication has increased by about 200 percent since my injury. It's hard to understand it until you go through it five times in one year. Without the strong support system I had of people to help me through it, I could easily have ended up as a statistic. Pain medicine feels good when it works. You go days of being in excruciating pain, and suddenly feel relief? Sign me up. In those moments, it's not about feeling the "high" of the medicine. It's simply being able to breathe or think without worrying how bad it will hurt.

Each surgery required intensive occupational therapy. I was going once a week before, and now I was going three or four times. Between the medicine and the pain, I lost a lot of weight each time and was probably the unhealthiest I've ever been. One day I passed out during a therapy session, only to pass out again later that day. My whole body had been through intense trauma, and each surgery took me through it again. After some time for recovery, I would have new x-rays and sit across from my surgeon only to be told it didn't work this time either. This meant being sent back to occupational therapy to keep working at getting back any function I could.

After a year of surgeries and occupational therapy and second opinions that only confirmed the first, I finally had to accept that there was nowhere else to go and nothing else to do. This was it. An evaluation by a physical therapist told me I had regained 20 percent use of my hand and 53 percent use of my arm—numbers still difficult for me to stomach. I cried when I walked out of the occupational therapy office for the last time. I knew I would miss Patti and her support, and I have. She gave me strength and courage, and even on my most discouraged days, she gave me hope. Now I would be on my own, attempting to navigate this world as a newly minted disabled twenty-something. People asked me if I was excited to be finished with therapy, but I wasn't. This didn't feel like a graduation, celebrating a goal achieved. It felt like a funeral, accepting the reality I would always feel like something was missing. It's one thing to be discharged because you are healed. It's another thing to be discharged because you aren't, and you won't be.

When I think back on it, I went from trying to accept that my hand would be amputated to feeling discouraged about having only 20 percent use of my hand pretty quickly. I worked my behind off for every single percentage point I gained back and I am grateful for each one because every day I put them all to good use. The thing is, though, for my entire life I believed in a God who could and would heal me completely should the need arise. And here we were. The need was there, and there he was, choosing not to heal me. Who was this God? This God, who had all the power to take away my pain and suffering, but wasn't. I didn't know this God.

I spent years growing up in church hearing stories from speakers and preachers about the God who healed their cancer, took away their drug addiction, saved them from a failed abortion, or repaired their broken marriage. These people were rescued, healed, saved. God gave them a victory story. So when it was my turn, I anticipated a victory story for the ages—one worthy of books and Christian conferences and viral articles. I survived, and I couldn't understand why God would save me from almost certain death and not heal me. Wouldn't he want to show his power and glory through a victory? Where did I, a broken and bruised person, fit into the victory narrative I knew? Where did a story of a lack of healing fit into the kingdom? Who would be brought closer to God by hearing about how he didn't fix it? These questions swirled around in my head long enough to make me dizzy. It never occurred to me that his glory and power could be shown through a life of pain, hurt, and quiet suffering. This, right here, was the beginning of relearning God and at the same time relearning myself.

I never lost my faith in God. Though if I'm being honest, there were times in the heaviest moments and deepest pains, I considered leaving it all behind. It is hard and heavy work to reconcile your faith with your circumstances when your life looks different than you thought it would. It's especially hard when "different" is mostly a lot of trauma and pain. Asking God questions like, "Why did you allow this to happen to me?" "Why didn't you heal me?" "What am I supposed to do now?" and "What does this say about who you are?" is scary. You don't know what the answers are going to be or even if you're going to get the answers, much less understand or be satisfied by them. Asking the questions is a vulnerable act of opening yourself to hearing answers that might cause even more hurt and confusion. In those moments, the thought of saying, "Thanks for the good times God, but I'm out" and just chalking it all up to chance of the universe seemed almost easier. Maybe if I could blame it all on chance, I thought, it wouldn't hurt so bad. It wouldn't feel so personal.

And yet, even through all these doubting thoughts, I still prayed every single day. Maybe not in the traditional, head down and eyes closed kind of way. My prayers began to sound like the simple words and phrases my toddler uses now. *Please. Help me. Where are you?* Each day I cried out to God while I was in pain. I called out to him during the night when the nightmares haunted any hope of sleeping dead in its tracks. I begged him to take the fear away and to "just please let me sleep, Lord." I thanked him for saving my life and asked him what he wanted me to do with it.

I knew I wasn't actually going to abandon my faith. It was all talk; all bark and no bite. I think perhaps I just wanted to make him sweat a little about it and make sure he knew that I did not support what happened to me and was a little bit mad about it. Maybe I just wanted an apology. God was supposed to be caring for and protecting me, after all. What about all the plans not to harm me but to give me a future and a hope à la Jeremiah 29:11? Letting me get shot sure seemed like a failure in this regard. But I knew better. I knew in my core that what happened to me did not negate God's love for me. I knew he had never abandoned me. Even in that closet as I let tears fall silently down my cheek and watched the blood run down my arm, he was with me, and he didn't forsake me.

I was grateful to God for saving me, but also angry about it happening at all. I couldn't make all these feelings fit together. It was only when my counselor explained to me about how I was living in contradictions that I would begin to understand my apparent crisis of faith. I was thankful to be alive, and mad I had been shot. I was grateful to still have my hand, but frustrated that it no longer worked the way I needed it to. I loved God, but I was a little mad at him too. Happy and sad, grateful and mad. Hopeful, but discouraged. I felt all of it and I didn't know how to hold all of these emotions at the same time.

There were many days when I wondered how I was going to survive the pain and exhaustion. I was only twenty-two years old when I was shot, and the thought of having to spend the rest of my life living like this made me feel like I was trapped in that room again. I couldn't think about it all at once. So I started telling myself "one day at a time" and I told other people to remind me of that too. I didn't have to live the rest of my life *that day*; I just needed to live that day. Sometimes I doubted it was possible, and yet, day after day I woke up and made it through. Day after day, God sustained me. God became true to me in this way: he promised to sustain me and he did. And every day he did gave me the strength to believe he would do it again the next day too. This was the God of victory. This part, the being sustained by him, was the victory story.

I thought the healing was going to come in a physical and miraculous way. I imagined having my hand x-rayed after one of my surgeries and the images showing an inexplicable healing of all injuries. I daydreamed about suddenly having full range of motion back and amazing everyone with my recovery. Doctors would look at my hand, stunned, and ask each other, "But, how? How did this recovery happen?" And I would be able to respond "Jesus! Jesus healed me!" and I would give God the glory for the miracle and people all over would hear the good news of a God who rescued and healed a young woman from her gunshot injuries. Can you picture it? I certainly could. *What a testimony it would be,* I would think to myself.

Here I sit, almost seven years later, trying to type this book after a restless night spent doing some crying because the pain in my hand was so intense. Here I sit after over seven years of trying everything under the sun for pain: seeing a pain management specialist, getting regular nerve blocks put in my arm, massage therapy, essential oils, CBD cream, lidocaine patches, TENS units, and more. There isn't a lot I haven't tried, and the trying has taken over much of my life. Every day there is a running list in my head of the things I couldn't do or had a lot of troubling doing. These days, the list is long, as I'm trying to figure out how to physically care for my never-stationary toddler and spend hours typing every day. Each thing added to this very depressing list feels like a little needle prick at my heart and tempts my spirit to lean toward bitterness. At the same time, each thing feels like a nudge pushing me to remember that my pain, my frustration, and my suffering is never out of the sight of the God who loves me.

For myself, and other victims of gun violence, the physical scars are a constant reminder of what we've been through and it still isn't over. I can look at the scars as a physical reminder of my trauma and feel the pain as an ever-present indication of my lack of healing; or I can see and feel each of these as reminders that I am still here and God sustains me every single day. Sometimes I do both of these in the span of five minutes. It often felt, and still does, like I was getting whiplash from going back and forth. It was only when I began to learn I could do both of these things, hold them both in my hands at the same time, that I began to find a peace I could cling to.

My faith in God never felt broken. I never had any indication in my pre-shooting life that I was missing something. It was only afterward that I began to see the one-dimensional relationship I had with God. It was very much a pray, receive, move on type of relationship. Don't get me wrong, I had been through some difficult things in my life, but nothing that daily left me in need of being sustained and held by a Savior in every sense of the word. I prayed, and I worshiped, and I did all the "right" things, but I didn't have to do them like my life depended on it. And I surely couldn't have known the sweetness and tenderness that would come with doing those things in the midst of pain and suffering and uncertainty. God became more real to me than I ever experienced before. He didn't give me a choice other than believing with everything in me that he was good and wanted good things for me even when the world felt like it was going to collapse around me.

I don't know why some people get healed and others don't. I don't know why I was spared and other people die. I don't know why this needed to happen to me or why the shooter decided to do what he did. As much as I wish I did, I don't have any answers. Sometimes I feel like I should be disqualified from sharing my story because I don't have answers. And yet, when I was really in the thick of walking this journey, I didn't want to talk to people who had the answers, and if they did have answers, I didn't really want them to tell me. I wanted to talk to people who could sit with me and say, "I don't understand, either, but I'm with you and I see you." As much as we crave answers and believe they would help us move on or heal or whatever it is we are hoping for, I think if we really think about it, we would realize there isn't an answer to satisfy our questions. I still got shot, your Mom still died, your husband still lost his job, the cancer still came back. Even the best answer doesn't change those things. We still have to go through all the stages of grief and all the steps of healing regardless of the why.

My broken faith was patched up and repaired before I realized how cracked it actually was. I could have gone my entire life in the way my faith looked before a bullet ripped through my hand and my mind. I could have continued going to church on Sundays and lifting my hands in worship, offering prayers to friends throughout the week, reading and doing all the right things. I would have believed and proclaimed God was good. It would have been fine and nice and tidy. It would have been true. But I would have missed out on so much God had for me beyond the bullet. God kept me close and gave me space all at the same time: to ask the questions, to express my anger, to tell him I didn't understand. He didn't, and doesn't, hold it against me or use it to manipulate me into belief. God used this horrific, awful, inexcusable thing that happened to me to replace my shallow faith with one that could, and did, persist through anything. It doesn't mean the pain hurts any less, or that my disability doesn't still affect my life every single day. It doesn't even mean the PTSD and the anxiety and fear come any less often. It does mean when those things come and I wonder if I can keep going, he holds me and sustains me.

The answer to our prayers does not always mean God heals us of the suffering. Sometimes, it means we are sustained through it.

3

GRIEVING THE
SHOULD HAVE BEENS

OUR WEDDING WAS PLANNED for May 25, a short six weeks after the shooting. We thought briefly about asking the hospital chaplain to marry us right there in my room, but we had spent eleven months planning and dreaming and waiting, and we still wanted to have our day. It felt even more important to celebrate with a big wedding and all our loved ones with us. Those weeks before the wedding were supposed to be full of events I had been looking forward to for months: my bridal showers, bachelorette party, dress fittings, and final wedding preparations. But none of it would be the same now. Even the best-laid plans are not exempt from tragedy.

My bridal shower that was supposed to happen the day after the shooting was rescheduled for a couple of weeks later. My mom asked me repeatedly if I was sure I was up for it and I said yes, because I really wanted to be. I sat in a chair as my sister styled my hair for me, something that was impossible for me to do for myself. The dress I bought for the occasion was hanging in my closet and I stared at it as my hair fell against my back, warmed from the straightening iron. I felt my eyes well with tears. It wasn't supposed to be like this. I wiped them away. I picked another dress to wear.

Eric was my pain medicine manager and helped time all my pain medication so that I would be as comfortable as possible at the shower. The car ride alone exhausted me, and I wondered for the entire thirty-minute drive if it was a bad decision to go through with it. Overwhelmed at the thought of being in a room with forty people at once, I worried if I couldn't handle it. When we arrived, though, and I walked into a room full of people who loved me, I was only overwhelmed with gratitude. I was there with my people. We were celebrating. It was good. As the day went on, though, waves of pain would come, and fatigue seemed to have its grip firmly around me. My left arm was in a sling, wrapped with as much padding as we could fit inside, and I held it tightly to my chest with my right arm.

Eric sat next to me and opened the gifts one at a time. As he took the wrapping paper off each one, I remembered having carefully picked out each thing when I added them to our registry. I remembered dreaming about using the serving dishes to host guests and putting the crisp white sheets on our bed. That was before, when I didn't know I was going to get shot. The gifts each signified things I pictured for the future yet were somehow already tainted by the past. I was feeling increasingly more vulnerable and I tried to shove all the negative thoughts down. I was there, after all. I survived. I got to live and got to attend this shower, and I was going to get married. Why couldn't I just be grateful for that?

Everything felt like this: trying to make each event feel as normal as possible even though nothing was normal anymore, and trying to push every negative feeling away because it made me feel ungrateful. After all, I was still getting to do it all, right?

A few weeks after the shower, I woke up with more pain than usual in my hand. I was scheduled to have my bridal portraits taken later that day and was hoping it wasn't anything serious enough to derail the photo shoot. I didn't want to have the photos taken away. I was already feeling extremely aware of the scarring on my chest and all the bandages wrapped around my hand. I didn't feel like myself, and I wasn't sure that I wanted to remember myself that way. We took the bandages off and noticed that around each of the pins my skin was red and swollen. Eric called the doctor and I went in to have them evaluated. The pins were supposed to stay in for at least another month to help the bones heal correctly, but once I arrived at the doctor they told me that the area around the pins was getting infected and they had to be removed immediately.

I sat in a chair in the exam room waiting for the physician's assistant to come back and remove them. She walked in holding a pair of pliers like the ones my dad kept at home, and that's when I found out these suckers were getting pulled out with pliers—and without numbing. She stood across from me, put her leg on my chair to manufacture more force, and pulled the pins out with pliers, one by one. I squeezed Eric's hand each time I felt the pain go through me like a lightning bolt, or like getting metal pins pulled out of your bones. He and his hand were thankful for my profound lack of upper body strength.

After leaving the doctor's office I went home and my mom did my hair and makeup. Then we headed to the wedding venue to have my portraits taken. I got into the dress and put on my best smiling face because this was supposed to be a happy, smiling thing. We took a lot of pictures with me in certain poses in an attempt to hide my hand. I was afraid that every time I saw the pictures, my eyes would only see the brace around my hand and the scars on my chest. Every glance down at my hand was a reminder that none of this was as it should be.

Our photographer, Jeremy, was a good family friend and knew my fears. He was sensitive to my request to hide my hand when possible. But then he encouraged me to take some pictures with it showing. "Some days, you'll look at these pictures and see your hand, and it won't be sad. It will just remind you how strong you are, and that you survived."

He was right. Some days all the wedding pictures make me sad. Some days they don't. But every day, I'm thankful to have all of them.

THE WEDDING

The days leading up to the wedding were busy and full of living the contradictions. I was so excited that we were still able to have the wedding and that we were going to be married. At the same time, I was acutely aware of how different things were. Most brides aren't worrying about how they'll hold their bouquet with one hand in a sling or where to stash their pain medicines in the reception venue for the inevitable time of need. There was no way to pretend it was normal, so I found ways to lean into the differences.

If you've ever planned a wedding, you know all the things that have to be done in the lead up to the big day: last minute seating chart changes, gathering all the decor, tying up all the logistical details, and of course doing the decorating the day before. There were a lot of things I simply couldn't help with. My mom, being the amazing mom that she is, gathered the troops and recruited a whole mess of people who volunteered to make sure everything was perfect. My friends stepped up and ran errands, picking up last minute decorations and dropping things off at all the places they needed to be. A handful of family friends, along with my parents and Eric's parents, worked for two days making the venue look like an actual dream. One friend of the family even made me a sling to match my wedding colors, with gray and yellow flowers.

I spent a lot of time during that season feeling powerless, having to let people help me with all the things I couldn't do for myself. I didn't know the extent of my desire to control things until then, but I did know about my tendency of wanting to do things myself to avoid feeling like a burden. When I moved in to my college dorm my soph-omore year, they had older students there to help us move all of our stuff. To the dismay of my dad and his back, I turned down every single person who offered to help. I didn't want to be a burden to others. Now, though, I had no choice. I had to humble myself and allow others to serve me. I had to let myself be vulnerable, believing I was not a burden, but instead recognizing that God had placed people in my life who loved me to be his hands and feet when I needed them.

When I walked in and saw the venue, fully decorated and ready for celebrating, it looked prettier than I imagined it would. Every detail had been thought of. Tears welled in the corners of my eyes as the twinkle lights shone above me. The vision I had in my mind was suddenly realized. Of course, it wasn't just about the decorations, as beautiful as they were. It was about feeling loved and cared for during a time when I mostly felt scared and alone. It was about all of these people taking time off of work and spending literal days to make sure even the smallest details that may have seemed inconsequential were attended to, for no other reason than because these things were important to me.

The night before the wedding, my bridesmaids and I had a big sleepover together. And as sleepovers often go, we stayed up way too late chatting about life and about getting married and how excited we were for the next day. I remember sitting in a circle with my dearest friends, eating popcorn and drinking water while they sipped wine. In those moments, I felt almost normal. So many parts of the wedding were changed because of what happened to me, because of my limitations. But not this part. This part was the same and it felt really good.

I woke up the next morning, after a restless night's sleep but full of adrenaline. It was my wedding day. We ate breakfast and the hairstylist arrived to start everyone's hair. We headed to the wedding venue, stopping at Starbucks along the way because are you even a bride if you don't get "Bride" written on your Starbucks cup? We spent the morning getting ready in a beautiful farmhouse. Soon our photographers arrived and began taking photos. I was determined to do my makeup myself, and I stood in front of the mirror carefully applying eyeshadow and mascara, every now and then catching a glimpse of my hand. I took a deep breath. I was doing it, this big important thing that was almost taken away—we were doing it. My bridesmaids even surprised me by wrapping their left hands in white gauze, matching mine.

Our wedding day was beautiful. The weather was perfect, no one tripped down the aisle, and no one said the wrong name at the altar. I made an effort to be as present as I could be and to enjoy every minute as much as I could. Our friends and our families made this possible, helping with anything that came up and anticipating needs before I even knew what they were. I danced my heart out and laughed with my friends and enjoyed the wedding day with my new husband.

The detectives who were working with us even came to celebrate. Despite having seats at the reception, they both stood at the doorway, observing and watching. Whenever I felt overwhelmed by the crowd of people, or felt anxiety rise up as I realized my back was to the entrance, I remembered Keith and Randy, our detectives, dutifully guarding the doors. "We don't get to see many happy endings," they told us as they congratulated us. It is still one of my most treasured memories from that day.

The day didn't come without challenges, though. Everything took constant thought and extra attention. It was hard to link arms with my dad when we walked down the aisle, and at the risk of making a Ricky Bobby reference, during the ceremony Eric and I had no idea what to do with our hands. We couldn't really hold hands plural, so Eric just held my right hand in both of his. It was the only choice really, but the pictures do look kind of silly. I was on a really rigid pain medicine schedule and was constantly having to make sure I didn't get behind. I couldn't have any alcohol because of possible interactions with pain medication, and it was sad to not be able to have that celebratory glass of champagne during the toasts.

The fatigue was an issue too. I was quite simply exhausted. Every day after the shooting, I spent large periods of time napping and the rest mostly lying in bed. So by the time we sat down to eat dinner, I was quickly losing steam. Our wedding coordinator took notice, and after all the scheduled events were finished, she quietly asked us, "Time for the exit?" I reluctantly nodded. I was sad. I didn't want to leave. But I was exhausted and in pain, and I had made it longer than I thought I would. I knew that it was time to go. As we drove away, we held hands, and I thought back to the moment in the hospital room when we almost asked the hospital chaplain to marry us, wondering if we would get to this day. We did. It was good. It was hard. I was thankful.

THE HONEYMOON

The morning after our wedding we hopped in Eric's car, with writing on the windows and the inside full of balloons announcing to all pass-ersby we were just married. We started the ten-hour drive to Orlando, Florida, for our honeymoon at Disney World. Well, what was sup-posed to be our honeymoon at Disney World. I was still way too scared to be around a lot of people and too anxious to even think about being in a crowd. I needed to see every move that every person made. I needed to be able to watch them all and make sure they weren't going to do something bad. My injuries would make rides hard too—not being able to hold on to things or being at risk for further injury.

Aside from that stuff, because of the bullet fragments remaining in my hand, the still-open wounds, and the metal pins attempting to put the bones in my thumb back together, I had to be on heavy antibiotics to prevent infections. One of the side effects of the medications was photosensitivity, essentially meaning I was at high risk of bad sunburn. Bad sunburn didn't sound like a great time to me, so this meant going to any of the parks was out of the question. All that stuff, the open wounds and pins, also meant I couldn't get my hand wet. We pur-chased tickets months earlier to go swim with dolphins during our time in Orlando. Those tickets went unused too.

We tried hard to find things that we could still do even with all the limitations. But Orlando is a tough place to have fun when you can't be outside or in the water. We did our best. We quickly discovered that there are outlet malls on every corner, so we made good use of all that refunded ticket money. I couldn't do a lot of things, but shopping? I could do shopping. We even found a beautiful indoor atrium at the Gaylord Palms Resort and spent hours walking around and exploring.

While brainstorming what to do, Eric found out Cirque du Soleil was doing shows there. I was afraid to be in a dark room with a lot of people with my back turned away from the doors, unable to know what was happening around me or who was coming and going. Eric assured me that if I got too anxious or panicked, we could leave, no problem. This arrangement, the trying and being allowed to leave guilt-free if needed, was the only way I could attempt anything. I was so afraid of ruining things, and Eric always assured me it was okay and gave me the freedom to try on my own terms. For people who are trying to recover from trauma, this is a gift.

When we arrived at the large auditorium, I felt my heart rate rise and my palms grow sweaty. Eric put my hand in his and we settled into our seats. One of the performers walked onto the stage to introduce the show. He began speaking. "If an emergency occurs during the show—" and then a loud scream, a shriek, from someone in the audience. I began panicking and wanted to crawl out of my skin. I couldn't breathe and I tried to get up and run but my legs didn't move. The woman in the audience then ran up onto the stage. She was a performer. The scream was just an act, meant to draw everyone's attention to the man who would go onto explain where the emergency exits were. Eric put his arms around me as everyone in the audience was laughing and chatting while the man pointed to each the emergency exits. It hit me in that moment, sitting in the theater waiting to watch Cirque du Soleil, that I was different now. I already knew where all the exits were, because I could no longer go through life thinking I wouldn't need to use them. I could no longer tell myself the chances of an emergency were slim and it couldn't happen to me because it did happen, and there was no guarantee it wouldn't happen again. That was the difference.

I was jealous of all those people in the theater who could go to a show and not wonder if someone would walk in through the back door and start shooting indiscriminately. I was jealous of how carefree they were. And I was angry at them for not taking it seriously. I wanted to shake them by the shoulders and say, "Don't you get it? This is real. This isn't a joke. You might have to use these exits!" Yet at the same time, I wished I could go back to a time when I believed the world was safe for me. But that was before. This was now.

After a lot of deep breaths, the panic finally settled and I was mostly able to enjoy the show. I was proud of myself for pushing through the fear, and thankful we were able to do something fun. Like so many things, though, it felt tainted. Maybe everything would feel tainted now, all happy moments pierced by a sharp pain of loss, reminding me things were not as they should be.

My newfound confidence from making it through the Cirque du Soleil show was useful when Eric asked if I wanted to try seeing a movie later that week. It was raining and he found an IMAX theater close by. Same offer: if I got uncomfortable or scared, we could leave at any time. I said yes. I wanted to go to the movies. I wanted to feel normal. And I wanted to do something Eric wanted to do. We got drinks and popcorn at the concession stands and made our way into the movie theater. I had never been to an IMAX movie before and couldn't believe how big the screen was. When we sat down, I immediately felt the fear. I glanced around the room, noting every single exit and emergency exit. I couldn't help but think about the shooting at a movie theater in Aurora, Colorado, just a year before, and I wondered if anyone else was thinking about it.

The lights began to dim and I took a deep breath, in and out. I made it through the previews. Maybe I could do this, I thought to myself. Then the movie began. This is where I tell you the movie we selected for this outing was *Star Trek Into Darkness*. I am generally very against victim blaming, but concerning this specific event, the blame is perhaps on me. The movie started, and it was a lot of space shooting and fighting and loud noises. Did I mention this was in 3D? And on the biggest screen I've ever seen in my life? It didn't go well. The loud noises and the feeling of things coming toward me overwhelmed me. I leaned over and told Eric I needed to leave. We got up and went toward one of the exits taking us into an area behind the screen. It took what felt like forever to find our way out of the building. I still wonder if people could see our shadows behind the screen of the movie.

When we got to the car, I got in and started sobbing. I was so overwhelmed and I couldn't hold it in. The noise triggered all the memories from the shooting and when we couldn't find our way out I began to feel trapped, remembering what it felt like to be stuck in the supply closet. I knew it was okay to be upset, but it felt like such a failure, and it felt like I was taking Eric down with me.

I wanted to be okay and I wanted to feel normal. I wanted everything to go back to the way it was before. Looking back, it was a lot of pressure to put on someone who had been through intense life-altering trauma just six weeks before. But we had talked about our honeymoon for a whole year. I had images in my mind of what I imagined it would be like, and none of them involved having to ask my very kind new husband if he could help shave his new wife's armpit because she couldn't hold a razor in her left hand. Or asking him to help me wash my hair or button my shorts. Yet with every failed attempt at something "normal," I was smacked hard with the reality that things weren't normal. No amount of force or pressure was going to make things go back to the way they used to be; I couldn't make my old life fit inside this new one.

After we got married in May, I was a bridesmaid in weddings in June, July, and August. I went to as many bachelorette parties and bridal showers as I could, often having to leave early or sit out certain activities. When my friends arrived home from their honeymoons, I dutifully asked how the trips were and looked at the pictures of all their big adventures. I attended bachelorette parties and watched, as the brides did not have to go change bandages covering bullet wounds. I went to bridal showers and watched the bride open gifts with two fully functional hands, not requiring an ounce of assistance. And I was pretty sure no one else was having panic attacks on their honeymoons or asking their new husbands for extensive assistance with their, ahem, personal hygiene. I was constantly having to ask my friends for help: fixing my hair, getting dressed, and cutting my food when we went out to dinner. I will never forget internally screaming as I heard a friend mention, offhandedly, that she would be "so mad" if she had to walk down the aisle with a sunburn. I stared down at my broken hand and wished for it to be replaced by sunburn. No such luck.

This was supposed to be such a special season. We were all getting married within months of each other, and for a whole year we anticipated all the fun we would have together. I was thrilled to be able to celebrate my friends and stand next to them on their big days. At the same time, it was also really hard. I was constantly confronted by the differences in our lives now. We were doing the same things, having the same experiences, but they weren't really the same. Mine was all messy and bloody. Theirs weren't. I'm not a psychopath; I didn't want them to have gotten shot too. I just wanted myself to not have gotten shot. I was so happy for my friends. I was thrilled to celebrate them and stand next to them on their big days. I have some of the sweetest memories of that time. I did my best at every event to put on a brave and smiling face. Then later on at home when the coast was clear, I let out sobs of grief over what I lost and what I would never get back. None of it was supposed to be this way.

I thought the day of the shooting was the worst day of my life. Lying in my bed with bullet holes in my hand, vision blurry from the shrapnel that struck my eye, excruciating pain pulsing throughout my body, it was impossible to imagine harder days than this. And why would I? Those were bad enough. I thought in the beginning if I could just get through those hard days, if I could be strong enough to withstand the pain, if I could work hard and recover, then I would be good to go. I got shot. It happened. But I would keep going, and I would heal. The worst was over, right?

I'm not sure exactly when I came to accept that maybe the shooting wasn't the pinnacle of worst days that I thought it was. I think maybe it was necessary to tell myself that was the worst day. Believing I faced the worst thing I would ever face and survived kept me going when things felt too hard. The anxiety of anticipating a painful day at occupational therapy could often be quelled by reminding myself I could get through a day at therapy because I had survived so much worse. The nightmares that woke me in the middle of the night were scary and jarring, but I would settle, and I would sleep again. It wasn't as bad as getting shot, I would repeat in my head. Someone tried to kill me, and I survived. I could get through anything else that was coming. It was a survival technique. There would be no point in trying or getting out of bed if the possibility of worse days than April 12 loomed in my head. No. That was the worst day. I needed that day to be the worst day.

In the first few months after the shooting there was so much going on, both medically and personally. People sent meals and gifts, and I got cards in the mail from people around the world, many of whom I didn't even know. To this day I have a hatbox taking up almost an entire shelf in our closet, full of cards and notes that were sent to me in the days following. There were doctor's appointments almost every day, and for four months there were wedding festivities and visitors. There were things to look forward to, anticipation of long-awaited events. It was all still new. People still remembered. There were plenty of things to keep me distracted. As the summer ended, though, it took with it all of our anticipated events and plans. Instead, I was left with a planner full of doctor's appointments and crossed out hopes and dreams.

That August we were supposed to be moving to another state for Eric to begin pharmacy school, but he deferred his enrollment for one year to give me time to heal and to be near our support system and my medical team. It was the right decision—the only decision really. But I cannot describe the agony I felt watching Eric give up something he worked toward for years, all while watching our friends get new jobs and move away and start their next chapter while our book slammed shut with our fingers still inside. Even when Eric went back to work, I battled pangs of jealousy. I couldn't work, and I didn't know if I would ever work again. It felt like all my losses were magnified by the people around me who got to reclaim the old parts of their lives, the before the shooting parts. Meanwhile, I was trying to claw my way out of the pit I was pushed into.

One day I was catching up with a friend and asked her how she was. She said, "I've had a really bad headache, but I probably shouldn't complain to you about a headache." Her statement took my breath away for a moment. I didn't want my friends to compare their lives with mine. I hate headaches. Headaches suck, everyone knows that. It's indisputable. I wanted the people I loved to be able to share their lives with me without feeling like it was silly or not "bad enough" compared to a shooting. If this was the scale we were using, my relationships would suffer greatly. There was room for getting shot to suck and there was room for headaches or spilled coffee or costly car repairs to suck too. I kept thinking: suffering isn't a competition. And yet, I made it a competition with myself. I was doing to myself what my friend did to me.

I was playing a dangerous game of comparison with myself. In the short-term every day, it sometimes felt helpful to compare every less than ideal experience to getting shot. It helped to keep perspective, motivated me to keep going, and to press on toward recovery. I held up every experience, every loss I grieved against April 12, reminding myself that I lived, that it could've been worse, that it could be worse. When it didn't help fix everything, because of course it didn't, I felt guilty and ungrateful. At the end of the day, pretending things weren't hard because they weren't as bad as the day of the shooting was only making it hurt worse. Shaming myself for not being grateful enough wasn't making me better, it was only making me bitter. I convinced myself, or maybe I just didn't know, I could feel two very different things at once. I could be grateful I survived and angry that it happened. I could be happy for my friends who were getting to do all the things I wanted to do, and at the same time I could recognize what I had lost.

After you survive a trauma like getting shot, you think, okay, the bad stuff is over, let's get on with the recovering now. It's not really like that, though. In the book *The Body Keeps the Score: Brain, Mind, and Body in the Healing of Trauma,* Bessel van der Kolk writes, "Being traumatized means continuing to organize your life as if the trauma were still going on—unchanged and immutable—as every new encounter or event is contaminated by the past."[1]

That's how I felt. I felt like I was living in a boxing ring. Every time I started to recover from a punch, the hits just kept coming and knocking me down all over again. I wanted to press pause or call a time-out so I could just heal and move on and go back to normal. That's not the way it works though, is it? There is no back to normal after tragedy; there is only a new normal. It's a new normal you don't quite recognize, one constantly pulling at the scabs trying to cover your wounds, sending a shock of discomfort through your body to remind you things are different.

The injuries to my hand needed to be identified in order to be healed. They needed to be found, seen, and evaluated over and over again so the doctors could figure out how to treat them. Ignoring them or covering them up with a bandage would only create more damage, causing an infection to spread throughout my body making me sicker as time went on. Over time I realized I was going to have to look at the other parts of my life the same way. I was hurting and grieving, and some days I was totally overwhelmed with loss. I was attempting to use a charade of forced gratefulness, saying things were okay when they were far from it. Pretending the hurts weren't there was making me feel alone and unseen. I didn't want to be unseen anymore. I had to start naming the injuries.

Sometimes doing it felt like digging around in my arm for a splinter. To name them, to acknowledge their existence, was to admit they were real. But they were real, after all. So it was time to start digging.

I was sad I couldn't wear my wedding rings on my left hand.

I was sad that all I could see in our wedding photos was a brace on my hand and scars on my chest.

I was sad we couldn't go to Disney World on our honeymoon.

I felt guilty that Eric couldn't start pharmacy school.

I was jealous that none of my friends had to pack whole suitcases full of medical supplies for their honeymoons.

I felt useless being unable to go to work.

I felt humiliated having to ask for help cutting my food.

I felt angry that I couldn't open a bottle of wine by myself or put toothpaste on my toothbrush without help.

I felt angry that I couldn't fix my hair or put on my makeup without someone nearby to assist me.

I was jealous of everyone around me who could go to the store, or the movies, or the mall, without having panic attacks.

I was jealous of everyone who could go on with their lives pretending the world wasn't a terrifying place.

I was envious of my friends who could sleep through the night without nightmares that felt real.

I was angry that I spent my days being exhausted by physical therapy and symptoms of PTSD that took every ounce of my strength to fight through.

I was mad that that I might never be able to care for a baby or raise children with my new disabilities.

I was mad that chronic pain was now an intimate friend who would be with me for my lifetime.

Naming these losses didn't magically fix them. It wasn't an immediate healing, but it was the start of journey toward it. I began allowing myself to grieve without guilt. It allowed me to identify the parts of me that were hurting, and it brought the freedom to invite the people around me into my experience. I allowed myself to be honest with people about how difficult living had been and share with them the things that felt hard, even if those things felt like small potatoes next to getting shot. I began to feel less isolated and lonely. I let people see all the parts and they let me grieve openly. Being honest about the losses, the anger, and the jealousy, also created the space for me to be genuinely grateful at the same time. My "fake it till you make it" method of gratefulness unknowingly made me bitter toward true gratitude. It was like when your grandmother gives you a very terrible wool sweater for Christmas, and your parents make you put it on and tell her thank you. It's itching and driving you up the wall and you say thank you, but you really just wish you could tell her how terrible of a gift this was.

So I told God how terrible this wool sweater was. Getting shot? Not a great experience for me, Lord: zero out of ten, do not recommend. I think you could've done better with your plans. And when I finally began allowing myself to sit in the pain and feel the sadness and be honest with God about how terrible things were, I was able to really thank him for the other stuff. I was able to say, *thank you God for saving me*. And I meant it.

God knew I was hurting. He knew I was in pain. I couldn't hide it from him. In the years since being shot, I've learned to be honest with God about my anger and my grief. I don't have to censor myself or try to wrap it up in a prettier package for him, something that many of us believe is required. He can take whatever I throw at him. He can hold all the weights I hand to him. I don't have to prove to him that I am grateful I survived and thankful he saved my life. He knows my heart and he sees my pain. He can handle both. For that, I am only grateful.

I felt so many little deaths in my life that I tried to pretend weren't there, hoping that if I just focused on the good things, I wouldn't have to feel the emptiness they left behind. But, there can't be gratefulness for life without recognizing of the reality of death. We can do both. We have to do both. And while I am not always thankful for the reason, I'm thankful to be learning how.

4

A NEW NORMAL

WHEN I WAS A LITTLE GIRL, I imagined myself becoming a lot of things—a writer, a teacher, a wife, and a mom. I never imagined myself becoming a shooting survivor.

I grew up in Salem, Virginia—a lovely small town that I still love quite tenderly. I lived a storybook small-town life with my family and friends. It easily could have fit into some sort of Disney Channel show. My parents, Brenda and Gerry, created a safe and loving home for my younger sister and me to grow up in. We faced hard times, like many people do, but we were always loved beyond belief and always cared for. And we laughed, a lot. My childhood memories are filled with family movie nights, complete with huge bowls of popcorn and weekly viewing of *Angels in the Outfield*, a family favorite. I was raised in church and committed my life to Jesus when I was just six years old. He has had my heart since then. I had a great group of friends at church but was never popular at school, like, at all. You might be surprised to discover the girl who shows up for the first day of high school with streaks of hot pink through her hair and a shirt that reads "Jesus is my homeboy" is not often a first-round draft pick during friend group selection. I also was not a great student. I tried, but not as hard as I could have. I was much more interested in music than academics and poured my time into voice lessons with my amazing voice teacher, Susan, and into leading worship at church. I loved to read books and write stories. Those things felt worthwhile to me, and they made me feel like myself—something that remains true to this day. I had a great childhood full of wonderful memories. My family is one that anyone would be envious of. I love them dearly.

In all those years of growing up and dreaming about what my life would be like when I was older, I can certainly say that out of all the things I hoped I would become someday, "shooting survivor" was never on the list. In all the years of becoming close to the Lord, asking him what his plans for me were, I couldn't have seen any of it coming. The life I entered into on the morning of April 12, 2013, was worlds different from any of the ones I imagined for myself. Things would never be the same after that. I would have to find a new normal.

It was a hot August night, and the noise came from the downstairs of our townhouse and echoed all the way upstairs. It was around ten o'clock at night, and Eric and I were lying in bed when we heard it. We had only been living there for a few days after moving out of my parents' house five months after the shooting and with the same amount of time living in the upstairs of my childhood home under our belts. We finally felt we could live without the extra day-to-day help from my family after my doctors had cleared me to drive. I'd been struggling to sleep since we moved into this new place away from the safety of the home I had known, the one that had kept me safe after the shooting. I looked to Eric for comfort and assurance that this noise was just in my head, but he seemed to have heard it too.

I started crying and immediately crouched beside our bed. I was convinced someone was in our house and was going to hurt us. Eric decided he would go check out the noise and come right back. I pulled on his arm and begged him to stay with me. I couldn't protect him if he left me. I couldn't know what was happening if he left our bedroom and was out of my sight. "I'll be fine, I'll be right back," he said to me as I sat sobbing beside the bed. He shut the door behind him, and I could hear echoes of him walking down the steps and moving through the house. I was rocking back and forth with my knees folded up to my chest and my arms wrapped tightly around my legs. I could hear him coming back up the stairs calling to me that it was okay, no one was there. But it was too late by then. I was gasping for breaths that felt like they were never going to come. My mind had already been filled with images of someone in our house, and I couldn't shake them. The panic took over my whole body, and I didn't know how to get it to relinquish its control.

Eric sat down beside me trying to help me calm down, telling me to take deep breaths, that everything was fine. He told me that no one was there, that we would be safe, that we weren't in danger. I don't remember how long he sat there with me on the tan carpet, holding me and telling me everything would be okay. I just know he did it as long as it took. When I started to calm down, we got back into bed and I took some antianxiety medicine to help me sleep. Eric pushed our tall dresser in front of the door to make me feel better. If I needed to get up in the middle of the night to use the bathroom, he would get up and move the dresser, wait for me to come back, and slide it back to its place in front of the door. He did this every night for a week, without complaint, until I felt safe in our home again.

This wasn't my first panic attack after the shooting, but it was the first one I had that helped me to understand what my trauma did to me on a deeper level and what it took away from me. This is the one etched in my brain and my body. I can remember the panic. I can feel the fear when I remember that day. For the first time, I had to acknowledge, yes, maybe things would be okay and maybe we would be safe from harm. But then again, maybe we wouldn't.

One day in that same month of August 2013, I decided to go to the grocery store alone. It was a milestone for me because until then, I was too afraid to go anywhere by myself. But Eric and I were in our own place, and I decided I was going to have to figure out how to buy groceries for us even when no one could go with me. I walked around the store, turning my head side to side as I went, trying to be aware of everyone and everything around me. I glanced down at my list, grabbed the milk and the coffee creamer and placed them in the cart. I'm doing it, I thought to myself. And I was.

But then I noticed someone who reminded me of someone else. The zip-up jacket and jeans were perfectly appropriate attire to wear to the grocery store, but they were also the same pieces of clothing someone chose to wear while shooting me. And then I realized how loud everything seemed. The wheels of the poorly maintained shopping carts squeaked at a rhythmic pace and the voices of the shoppers around me suddenly sounded like yelling. All around me it felt as if the aisles were moving in closer together, but no one else seemed to notice. I wanted to scream, but I felt paralyzed. Then, a loud boom. The box of cereal in my hands fell to the floor and I ran out of the store, leaving a cart full of groceries in the cereal aisle. I cried in my car for thirty minutes before I was able to drive myself home. This was my first public panic attack.

I felt embarrassed and sad and angry. I was embarrassed that a whole grocery store just witnessed me running out in a panic. I was sad that I was a twenty-three-year-old woman who couldn't go grocery shopping alone, something I always enjoyed doing. And I was angry this was my life, and I was left to figure out how to make it survivable. Every first time doing anything after the shooting, even things I had done hundreds of times in my life, felt like this. Everything was trial and error to see what I could handle and what was going to be too hard, and I couldn't know which one it would be until I did it. I felt like I was holding my breath all the time.

A lot of the triggers for me were expected: things like loud noises, fireworks, and cars backfiring, or hearing about shootings in the news. Other things, though, surprised me. Any burning smell reminded me of gunpowder and took me right back to the tiny room where I first saw the blood. The sound of ambulance sirens transported me back to the rides from hospital to hospital. The first day when the weather feels like spring still makes all the memories come flooding back. I always have to have my phone with me, even if I'm just running to the bathroom or going into another room. And it's not because I'm addicted to my phone. Rather, it's because the one time I couldn't get to it is the one time I was absolutely desperate for it, trapped in a room with bullet wounds and unable to call for help or to tell my loved ones what was going on.

I still can't sit in a public place with my back to the door. I have to be able to see who is coming in. I have to know what's going on. It's an almost subconscious decision for me, and I think it has become that for people I frequently go out with. Even now, a handful of years later, sitting in church facing the front of the sanctuary still brings me anxiety. I should feel safe in church. I should be able to listen to a sermon or sing worship songs without the fear of being shot there. Except people keep getting shot in churches, so I keep being afraid. Some triggers surprised me though. The most surprising were the Disney World commercials.

When we were planning our honeymoon, we realized that neither one of us had ever visited Disney World, so we decided to go. We bought tickets to swim with dolphins and planned out all the parks we would visit during our week in Orlando. After the shooting, though, it all fell apart. Because of the medications I was on, I couldn't be in the sun for long periods of time. Due to injuries and still needing to wear a sling, roller coasters and other rides were out of the question, not to mention swimming with dolphins. All these things, along with my newly acquired fear of crowds, made Disney World the last place I should be. We made the most of our trip and did a lot of fun things, but it wasn't what we had planned, and it ended up feeling like another thing had been stolen from me. A few weeks after we arrived home, I saw a Disney World commercial on TV and I broke down into tears.

My response took me by surprise. It wasn't a loud bang or an image of a gun or a news story about a shooting. It was simply some children enjoying their first trip to the most magical place on earth and their parents basking in the joy of it all. It just happened to be an experience I was supposed to have that a person with a gun took from me. So I cried. Sometimes I still turn off the TV at the sight of Mickey Mouse ears or the sound of "When You Wish Upon a Star." It's an incredibly tender place in me even now.

The Disney commercial wasn't just about Disney World, of course. It was about all of it. It was the symbol that represented a list of things I wondered if I would ever get to do in my lifetime. It represented the dreams and plans I had for myself that, without warning, someone pressed the pause button on, and I didn't know if they were ever going to move their finger. So I cried about Disney World. And I cried because I wondered if I would ever be able to hold my own babies and take care of them by myself. I cried because I didn't know if I would ever get to work again or ride a bike at the beach or tie my shoes. Disney World felt like the tip of the iceberg.

Having post-traumatic stress disorder has often made me feel helpless. Even after identifying triggers and trying to avoid them at all costs, eventually I came to terms with the fact that I can't avoid them all. I could sit where I wanted in a restaurant and I could make the decision not to go to the movies or to the Fourth of July fireworks show. But even though I knew the sound of a firecracker would terrify me, I couldn't know neighbors would set them off on random nights. And even though I knew the sound of a car backfiring would send me to the ground shaking and ducking for cover, I couldn't stop it from happening in the parking garage of the hospital. I cried silently in the passenger seat of the car the whole way home. It felt like a cruel joke. I could understand what did this to my mind and my body, and yet I had such little control over it happening.

The trauma of surviving the shooting—the physical injuries, the emotional and mental effects—all of it made me feel unsafe in my own body. The flashbacks, anxiety, and nightmares made me distrustful of my own mind. I was living in a new world where everything felt scarier and I didn't know who I could trust. Now it seemed I couldn't even trust myself. Panic attacks can feel differently for everyone, but I think most of us would say we feel like we aren't in control of our body. Our thoughts seem to be running a marathon we don't remember signing up for, and there is a physical reaction that takes over without our consent. It's why so many people go to the hospital thinking they're having a heart attack and are instead sent home with a prescription for antianxiety medicine. Yes, I'm raising my hand to signify I am a member of that category of people. Even closing your eyes to fall asleep feels scary because you are relinquishing any control you might have over your thoughts and your body. You just lose all control, and you have no idea when—or if—you'll get it back.

Someone pointed a gun at me, and in less than a minute, with one bullet, stole so much. It was horrible to lose physical abilities and the feeling of external safety. But for me, losing the ability to feel safe in my own mind—to trust myself, my feelings, my thoughts—may have been the hardest part of all. How could I get through any of this if I couldn't believe myself?

I began seeing a counselor the week after I was shot. I had expressed a supreme disinterest in counseling. I knew deep down I needed to go, of course, but it was too soon. Why the rush? I wasn't ready to talk about anything yet. It was all too fresh and too tender, and I didn't know what I would say. And even if I did want to talk, why would I want to talk to someone I don't even know? As it would turn out, no one around me cared if I didn't want to go to counseling, and I'm really thankful they didn't. My mom asked a family friend for a recommendation, and then just a few days later my mom and Eric put me in the car and drove me across town to meet Martha, my new counselor. I will be forever grateful that I was, for all intents and purposes, kidnapped and taken to counseling. I can't say I widely recommend this method, but for me it proved effective.

Martha wore a long, flowy skirt that looked like something out of a Free People catalog. She was soft spoken and extremely gentle with me as she welcomed me into her office and motioned toward a couch where I could sit. Martha had dark brown curly hair that sat right above her shoulders, and I think I had at least a one-foot height advantage on her. "Would you like some tea?" she asked, as she pointed to her large tea selection and grabbed a mug. I didn't know what I was going to talk about to fill the fifty-minute appointment slot, but I knew I felt at ease with her. I don't remember how the conversation began; all I know is that before too long I was telling her about what happened to me on April 12, 2013.

I spoke about it with her like I spoke with everyone else who wanted to talk to me about it. I told her how scary it was and how much pain I had been in, but interjected phrases about how thankful I was to be alive! And how glad I was that God had saved my life! She was the first person who told me I didn't have to do that. She's the first person who told me I didn't have to qualify my feelings or experiences, and it was okay to just say it was really hard. Full stop.

This took practice. It felt so uncomfortable and foreign to me to say, "It was horrible and I was terrified and it has been really hard" without following it up with a "but I'm thankful to be alive." It made me feel ungrateful and uncomfortable, and I was worried it would make other people uncomfortable too. I spent a lot of time worrying about making people feel uncomfortable. There were so many people who didn't survive things, so I wanted everyone to know I understood that and I knew how fortunate I was to survive. So I told Martha that.

"I really am grateful I survived," I assured her.

"I know," she responded. "But surviving is hard too."

Martha's words to me were like a refreshing drink of cold water after hearing from well-meaning people so many variations of "Thank goodness it was only your hand," and "You're so lucky," or "You must be so thankful, it could have been so much worse." I was trying my best to be positive and optimistic and not let my pain control me. The pain was hardly manageable. The physical therapy was brutal. The nightmares and flashbacks made sleeping impossible. I couldn't bathe myself or dress myself or tie my shoes. I felt alone and isolated all the time, because even though I had an incredible support system around me, no one else was there, no one else lived it.

No one else could really understand what it was like, no matter how hard they tried. And I began to resent people around me for that. It's not because I wanted anyone else to have to experience what I had gone through—I was glad no one I loved was there that day. It's just that I felt desperate for someone, pretty much anyone, to sit with me and know what I was feeling. I didn't even need advice, I just wanted to feel known, and no one around me could do that for me. My physical wounds were so visible, so apparent, and yet every other part of me felt unseen. Some days it felt like everything in my body was screaming, "Why can't you see?"

Then finally, one day while standing in my parents' kitchen, I finally said out loud how I had been feeling for weeks.

"It would have been easier if I had just died." It came out fast and furious, and tears followed closely behind.

I wasn't suicidal. I didn't want to kill myself. I can say in all honesty the thought never crossed my mind. But this? The surviving, the living, and the fact of having to wake up and do it every single day was hard. Some days it felt impossible. I couldn't figure out how the world kept going and seemingly everyone else could go back to their normal lives, but I was stuck here, surviving in the seemingly endless cycle of bandages and pain medication and nightmares. That's how it goes, isn't it? When we are walking a road of grief and trauma, it feels like we should turn on the news to see only stories about ourselves. Somehow, though, all we see is traffic updates for all the normal people on their way to work for their normal days and weather forecasts for the people who don't want to hide under their covers all day. It doesn't make sense to us because it feels like the world has stopped turning on its axis and the walls are closing in on us, and why doesn't everyone else feel it? Even though it can feel like a knife twisting deeper into your deepest wound, there is something comforting about it too. Because the sun still shines when you need warm light to touch your face. And the moon still pulls the ocean tides closer and then further away again; tethering you to the ground your feet are standing on. Things keep going somehow, and the fact of us not knowing how they do it makes us believe maybe we can keep going too, and maybe we don't have to know how yet.

I saw Martha at least once a week for a year. Sometimes I didn't want to go and other times I got there thirty minutes early because I couldn't wait to talk. Whichever way I arrived, when I left I was always thankful I showed up. One day, she asked me how things were going. "Every day there are all these things I wish I could do, or want to do, and I just can't make myself do them. I just lie on the couch all day," I told her. I had been growing frustrated with myself lately because of this, and I was afraid other people were growing frustrated with me because of it too. I tried starting so many projects and nothing stuck. I was letting myself down daily. Getting out of bed was exhausting, and some days it felt like I had to spend the rest of the day recovering from the effort it took. I told her how some days I could, and did, sleep until 4 p.m., especially following tough occupational therapy appointments. And I told her that maybe the toughest part of all of this was that it felt like I could do it because no one was missing me, like my absence from my life didn't matter. She looked at me with such kindness, as she always did, and replied, "That's depression."

Oh. Right. PTSD was covered, and anxiety had been discussed to be sure. But depression? For some reason, it never occurred to me that I was dealing with depression, but of course I was. After this appointment, I went to see my primary care doctor and talked to her about my depression and my anxiety. She was able to coordinate with Martha and together they discussed getting me started on an antidepressant and anti-anxiety medication to help me with the symptoms I was struggling with.

The medication was a game changer for me. It didn't magically solve all of my problems or make my life feel less difficult, but it did help the fog in my mind clear enough that I could begin to discern the lies from the truth. Depression crept into my life and fed me lies. Depression told me that I could hide from my life and no one would miss me. Depression told me that I was the wrong person to be saved from a shooting death. It told me I was a burden to everyone around me, and that everyone's lives would be better off without me and my problems constantly sucking the oxygen out of the room. It assured me things would always be this hard and there was no point in trying to recover or heal because things would never get better. "What's the point?" was the common refrain repeating in my mind. The medicine, the little white pill, helped me start to silence the lies one day at a time.

Martha helped me navigate that first year of grieving and healing. She was with me in the weeks after our wedding when I was overwhelmed trying to figure out how to be a shooting survivor and a new wife at the same time. She comforted me when I felt forgotten and left behind by my friends who were off doing all the things I should have been doing. She was with me during all the court proceedings when I wrote my victim impact statement, watched the surveillance footage of the shooting, and testified in court in front of my shooter. Martha taught me about trauma and my mind and my body so I could be an active participant in my healing. I was able to stop feeling so powerless by what was done to me without my consent and start taking the power back for myself.

The healing and recovery from the emotional trauma was just as hard, maybe harder, than the physical recovery. I actually think it would be better for me to say "healing and recovery *with* the emotional trauma" instead of *from*. That little word *from* makes it seem like I was able to move on and leave it all behind when, really, I needed to figure out how to move on *with* it. Shootings started happening everywhere—churches, malls, bars, restaurants—and it made me scared to go anywhere. I knew I needed to figure out how to live in a world that would always feel dangerous to me.

We adopted a dog from the local animal shelter a little over a year after the shooting. I had pets at my parents' house, but this one would be just ours. Mostly *I* adopted the dog. I went to the shelter to, you know, just look. But when I saw Molly, I knew she was ours, so I told the shelter I would be back for her the next day and then immediately drove to PetSmart to buy a bed and food and treats. I hid everything in our bedroom closet and when Eric got home, I asked him if we could get the dog. He agreed, thankfully, but when he found all the dog supplies hidden in the closet, he asked me if his agreement was just a formality. It was. But getting the dog was Martha's idea, so I had firm ground to stand on, which is how I convinced Eric it was necessary.

I was still having a really hard time getting up in the mornings. Depression, for me, often manifested itself by making me feel like no one needed me or would miss me. I was still being taken care of in so many ways and was feeling like a burden. So Martha suggested a dog. "You need to feel responsible for something. You need to feel needed." It made sense to me and sure enough, it worked. Molly got me up and moving every day, and I finally felt needed. The good news, though, was that she was perfectly content to lie with me on the couch if that's what I needed some days.

Out of nowhere, I found myself imagining the dog dying. I would daydream about finding out she had cancer or her escaping her leash and getting hit by a car. By every standard Molly was perfectly healthy, and yet every time we went to the vet for a routine checkup, I was convinced they were going to tell me she had a terminal illness and our time together would be cut short. Instead of being able to enjoy our time together, I spent my time imagining worst-case scenarios and wondering how I would deal with it. I did it with people too. Some days when Eric would leave for class or work, I felt convinced he would die in a car accident or a shooter would come to his school. One day I couldn't take it anymore and I described to my psychologist what I was feeling. I was seeing someone new at this point and he was helping me understand how the trauma had affected my brain. He gave me a name for what I was feeling: premature grief. He explained that be-cause of what I had been through, it was much harder for me to put off the thoughts of worst-case scenarios than it had been before because I had lived the worst-case scenario. It was no longer effective to tell myself "this bad thing probably won't happen" or "everything will be fine" because the bad thing did happen and everything was not fine.

This concept helped me understand why it felt impossible to get scary thoughts out of my mind. Until April 12, 2013, I was always able to convince myself bad things were not likely to happen to me. I had always believed I would be protected, safe, saved. People who haven't experienced horrific trauma are able to do that, because history tells them they can. After that day, though, convincing myself things would be okay became much harder. I had to create new strategies to help get rid of the dark thoughts whenever they attempted to creep into my mind. I was missing so much of the good parts of my life that were right in front of me because I couldn't stop imagining what might happen. So while it might seem counterproductive, I started letting myself go full throttle on the worst-case scenarios for life. What if someone close to me died? What if this really bad thing happened? What would I do?

That's when it got easier. The good thing about living through the worst-case scenario is that you know you can. For me, letting myself imagine these scenarios in this way brought them out of the darkness and gave me the power back. I couldn't stop them from happening, but I could remind myself that I have come this far, and I can keep going. Sometimes, it would just be easier said than done.

5

LIFE SENTENCE

THE PERSON WHO SHOT ME DIDN'T DIE. He didn't shoot himself. He wasn't shot and killed by police. Neil MacInnis, the shooter, was stopped by an unarmed security guard and taken into police custody. This fact changed everything for me and hung like a weight around my neck for fifteen months, until the verdict and sentence were final. I could, and did, try to run away from it. But knowing he was alive meant knowing I would have to face him, and you can't outrun reality.

The day after the shooting, I woke up to see his face on the front page of the local newspaper. The picture of him was huge, taking up most of the space above the fold. Below him, there were two smaller pictures of me and Kristina, the student who had also been shot. I felt a heavy fear come over my body and the tears came before I could try and stifle them. The last time I saw his face was when he was pointing a shotgun at my face. And now I had it to see it on the front page of the paper, next to mine. It seemed so wrong to have our pictures next to his on this physical object, as if we were all the same.

Eric saw it and took it away as fast as he could, shoving it underneath some bags in the corner of the room. The news was on the TV above my hospital bed. I saw the ticker on the bottom of the screen slowly scrolling the words: "Two women shot on college campus in Virginia." It felt surreal and impossible to comprehend. "Where did they get my picture?" I asked out loud. And we realized they'd taken it from my Facebook profile and cropped Eric out of it. I was angry. I felt completely exposed, as if I had no control over anything happening to me. Being a victim of a crime is to have someone exert total control over you, and then to be revictimized constantly when you realize what little control you have in the aftermath.

Everything started moving so fast on day two. The detectives came to the hospital and talked with my family, and we were quickly on a first-name basis with them. Keith and Randy were so kind to my family and me. They took us into their care and made sure they were available to us whenever we had questions or needed something. Oftentimes they went above and beyond their obligation to us. Court proceedings started that day, April 13, with the arraignment of the shooter. My family went to the courthouse while Eric stayed at the hospital with me. I didn't ask many questions about it.

I did some initial interviews with the detectives, but they were kind and gracious enough to talk to me only when it was absolutely necessary, knowing how hard it was for me early on. One good thing, maybe the only one, about the shooting being caught on security cameras was that it made it really hard to argue with the facts of the day, and it made at least a few things easier for me. The week after the shooting I met my victim's advocate, Carrie, when she came to visit me at home. The job of the victim's advocate is to help offer victims support, help find whatever resources they may need, and to walk with them through the criminal justice system and court proceedings. Until that point most of my knowledge concerning the legal system came from *Law & Order: SVU*. This quickly and not surprisingly proved to be insufficient, so I was very relieved to have Carrie in my corner, especially since I experienced a lack of support and direction from my employer. I expected the school to rally around me, providing support and help, and to care for their students and faculty. Yet, it was near complete radio silence. The extent of their support for me was an Edible Arrangement they had delivered to my house a few days after the shooting, and a call from my boss a few days after that to ask when I would be returning to work. Their support for the rest of the school ended after two days of canceled classes and on-site counseling services. The trauma for those there that day didn't end after two days, as nice as that would have been. I found out later from survivors of different shootings that they were treated the same way by their school or employer. Once you get shot in someone else's building, you tend to stop being a person and instead you become a liability.

After you become a victim of a violent crime, the things you do feel very surreal. One of those things victims have the option to do is register with the victim notification network. When victims do this, they get notified every time their offender is moved to another jail, taken somewhere, etc. For me, this meant any time the shooter got moved to a different jail, or left the jail for any reason, I got a phone call or email alert letting me know. One night in the fall of 2013, I was home alone when I got a call alerting me that my shooter had left the jail and was in an unknown location. I immediately froze. I stood paralyzed in my living room as I tried calling their center to find out what was going on. I even looked online for a news alert about prisoners escaping from the jail where he was being held, which was only a fifteen-minute drive from where I lived. I became convinced he'd escaped from jail, found my address, and was on his way to finish what he had started months earlier. In my downward spiral of fear, I called my dad and asked him to help me find out what was going on. He was able to reach someone at the jail who informed us the message I got was a glitch in the system. My shooter in fact left the jail, but was being taken to a hospital nearby, not an "unknown location." I took myself off the notification system after that. If he ever did escape from jail to try to come kill me, it would just have to be a surprise attack.

Recovery was a cycle. I would make progress with my therapist and start to do better in my day-to-day life. Then I would inevitably face a setback with my hand or get bad news at a doctor's appointment or need for another surgery. Then it was right back to square one. I would start to heal again, but then we would get news from the commonwealth's attorney's office or our detectives, and the emotional toll grew even higher. Again, back to square one. It felt impossible to "move on" with all of it hanging over my head and constantly having to take myself back to that day to talk about it. It often felt like whiplash—like I was being jerked around by something outside of myself and couldn't get my footing to stay still. Oftentimes it just felt like there was no point in trying until it was over. The problem was, we had no idea when it would be over.

One day I was having a particularly hard time accepting some news we had received from the attorney. Eric said simply, "Taylor, if we wait until justice is done on earth to move on, we will never move on." He was right—and it changed everything about how we went through the rest of the legal process. We thought back to episodes of *Dateline* where families lived through years of pain and torment waiting for justice for a crime that had been done to them or to a loved one. We were doing the same thing and experiencing firsthand how hopeless it all felt. Putting our hope in the legal system was like building our house on the sand. The more rain that fell and the harder the winds blew made it weaker and weaker, and it became glaringly obvious that the house couldn't stand for much longer.

We realized that no matter what happened in court, we would never feel like it was enough or that justice had been done. What would justice even look like, practically? What does it mean? Is it a stern punishment that I deem to be acceptable or "enough"? Is it accountability, or does it look more like healing, restoration, and rehabilitation? I didn't know. What I knew was this: I had been shot and it affected my life in countless, irreparable ways. The effects, like they always do with gun violence, rippled out and affected all the people around me. There couldn't be justice for it. It couldn't be made right, not on earth anyway. No jail sentence could turn back time and take the pain away. No punishment could make my hand work again. No scolding by the judge could make me forget the sound of the gunshot or the image of a gun pointed at my head.

If I'm being honest, I didn't even know what I wanted to happen in court or what I thought justice should look like. I still don't. The shooter had been charged with two counts of aggravated malicious wounding and two counts of using a firearm during the commission of a felony. A lot of people, us included, wondered why he wasn't charged with attempted murder instead. It was explained to us that in the state of Virginia, aggravated malicious wounding carried a possibility of a life sentence, while attempted murder only carried a maximum of ten years. So while "attempted murder" may sound more serious to our ears, the court system disagrees. Firearm charges carry mandatory jail time in Virginia, so when it came to sentencing, all we knew is that the sentence could be anywhere from the minimum of six years to the maximum of a life sentence. We were advised that the chances of a life sentence were low, which seemed understandable. At one point the attorney mentioned fourteen years seeming likely. I would be suffering the consequences of his actions for the rest of my life. Fourteen years hardly seemed adequate for him to have to do the same. At the same time, though, I couldn't even say for sure that I wanted him to receive a life sentence, and it meant I would have to come to terms with the fact that this person who tried to kill me and hoped to kill countless victims would someday walk free in the world. That day a verse from the Bible popped into my head. I wrote it in my journal and repeated it to myself at night as I fell asleep: "Do not take revenge, my dear friends, but leave room for God's wrath, for it is written: 'It is mine to avenge; I will repay,' says the Lord" (Romans 12:19).

The first time I went to court was on April 16, 2014, just over a year after the shooting. That day was also the seventh anniversary of the shooting that took place at Virginia Tech in which twenty-seven students and five faculty were murdered in the deadliest school shooting in our nation's history. It was just a few minutes up the road from the courthouse. I graduated from Virginia Tech in 2012, my husband, Eric, in 2009. I wasn't there during the shootings, but Eric was. It was an important and solemn day in our community ever since. I wore Virginia Tech's colors in the form of a maroon and orange ribbon pinned to my blazer to remind me of all the gun violence victims, including those at VT, who never got their day in court. It all felt very weighty.

This was to be a preliminary hearing where evidence would be presented to prove there was enough to convict. The shooter had already entered a guilty plea. This meant, thankfully, we wouldn't have to go through a whole trial. Instead, we would have a preliminary hearing. The sentencing hearing, when the judge would give his sentence, would be later.

Detectives Keith and Randy met us in the parking lot of the courthouse to escort us inside. They led us through the entrance and we stopped at the metal detectors, where we all emptied our pockets and security guards checked the contents of our purses. Cellphones weren't allowed inside and you could always spot someone frantically running to put theirs in their car and trying to get back in time. We were ushered into a room with the other victim and her family where we waited for the hearing to start. They didn't want us to have to come into contact with the shooter, his family, or members of the media. When it got closer to the time for the start of the hearing, we were taken into the courtroom and directed to our seats. The room was large and open, and looked exactly like courtrooms on TV. It was full of very serious looking furniture and devoid of any comfort. I realize a courtroom is a very serious place where very serious things happen, but would it hurt to add a throw pillow or two?

I didn't know what to expect and I was incredibly nervous as we waited for the hearing to begin. I hadn't seen the shooter in person since the day of the shooting, and on this day, we would sit just a few feet away from one another in the courtroom. I wondered how I would feel when I saw him walk in. Would we make eye contact?

Would he be apologetic? Would he be proud? Would I feel scared? Angry? Would my body tense and my mind panic? I had learned enough about PTSD by that point that I couldn't be sure how my body would respond, and I felt scared I wouldn't be able to control it. One of the things I was most nervous about, however, was seeing his family.

I was the victim. Everyone felt bad for me and my family. The public was on my side. We weren't dealing with the anger and vitriol from the community that his family was. I looked at my parents and then looked at his parents and was overwhelmed by the different lives they were now living. One set of parents with a child who had been shot. Another set of parents with a child who had done the shooting. One set of parents that got to keep their child close. Another set of parents who had to speak to their child through a glass window. All of us wondering how we got here and all of us wondering how to get out.

I felt bad for them. I felt such empathy for them that I cried when I thought about them and what they must be going through. Can I tell you the honest truth, though? I didn't want to feel bad for them. I didn't want to worry about how they were feeling. I wanted to be angry. I wanted to be angry with them for somehow letting this happen to me. I only wanted to feel sorry for myself and everyone else who had been victimized by him, not him or his family. But I did feel sorry for them. While this horrible thing brought us all together, I wasn't the one who had to live under the guilt and shame of it. I kept all of this to myself for a long time because I didn't know how to talk about it, or if I should. At my counseling appointment right before the hearing, I told my counselor, Martha, how I was feeling. She encouraged me with a simple truth: for a lot of families who have spent years worrying about their loved one and whether they might hurt themselves or others, knowing they will be in prison is sad, but it can also be comforting. The families know they will be supervised by someone else and won't be able to hurt themselves or others. In my journal that day, I jotted down those thoughts and finished with "I am trying to remember that when I get sad."

to sit in the courtroom or to wait in the lobby. We didn't have to hear anything we didn't want to hear or see anything we didn't want to see. We stayed. I didn't know for sure if I *wanted* to know, but something in me *needed* to know everything about the horror I survived. This needing to know everything thing has kind of been a theme for me. The night the 911 calls were made public, I spent forty-five minutes listening to each one, staring at the computer screen as they played, piecing together the parts of the day I never knew, writing down notes to fill in the gaps in my mind. They were hard and painful to hear, but they helped me remember what I had been through and helped it feel not so far away. That's the thing about trauma. You hope and pray for it to subside, to stop feeling so raw, to just let up its tight grasp on you. Yet, when it does, and the pain is still there, it feels disorienting. Why am I in such pain and having such a hard time when it has been so long? Why does my body still feel tense when I can't remember all the details? So we search for the things connecting us to it, to remind ourselves why it's still hard, why it still hurts, and why it's okay that it does.

During the investigation after the shooting, four homemade videos were found on the shooter's laptop. He recorded them on April 10, 2013, two days before the shooting. As the videos played on a flatscreen TV mounted to the wall at the front of the room, cries could be heard from where his parents sat in the front row. We sat in silence and watched him speak about what he planned to do during the attack. In an ironic twist, he spent a lot of time talking about how he wanted to show people it was too easy for people to get guns, and how schools need better security. "I'm not saying we need cops in schools, but we need to have something where people can't hurt people," he said. "It's just real easy to get guns." The commonwealth's attorney, Mary Pettitt, told the court he had planned to carry out a similar attack at his high school while he was a student there but he was too young to buy a gun. His parents found a story he wrote about his plans and gave it to a mental health professional he was seeing. It took him only forty minutes to buy his gun at a store just up the road from where he would pull the trigger. He anticipated being caught within ten minutes but added, "If I can escape, that would be awesome."

The videos continued to play and every few minutes I would glance over at the shooter to see his reaction. Sometimes he shook his head. Sometimes he smirked and laughed, and I felt sick to my stomach. Other times he watched with a blank stare and no emotion. I had previously become intimately acquainted with that blank stare when he pointed a shotgun at my face. His plan was to come in and shoot the lady at the front desk. It took no time for us all to realize he was talking about me. I clenched my fist and dug my fingernails into the palm of my hand. He planned to lock the doors inside the building and then pull the fire alarm so that everyone would come out into the hallway. He said he would then line us all up and go down the row, shooting one by one. Instead, he attempted to block the front doors to the school with his car, but he didn't pull up far enough and students were able to slide out between the doors. He walked up and down the halls, looking into classrooms, and at one point he even shot out a security camera. He later confessed to police that he pretended to be a victim in order to gain access into a locked classroom yelling, "Help, help. He's gonna get me, let me in." No one listened to him. As more and more details came out, it became glaringly obvious if everything went according to his plan, the devastation would have been unfathomable. Instead, on the day of the shooting he drove to his bank and withdrew three hundred dollars and left it for his manager at the Old Navy store where he worked, saying it was for "anyone who needed it." Then he drove to New River Community College. While he was waiting in the parking lot, he posted on a website called 4chan about what he was getting ready to do.

"Hey /b/ it's time,

My name is Neil Macinnis and I go to new river community college in Christiansburg Virginia. 10 minutes away from Virginia tech. I'm gonna give y'all the details because the news never gets it right.

Stevens 320 shotgun.

Buck shots and slugs

Wanna listen? If tha doesn't work search New river valley public safety.

I'm a bit nervous because I've never really handled a shotgun but a few times with the Christiansburg police. Anyways this is not a highscores game but actually a lesson (that's why I'm at school). Wanna see my eportfolio/what I look like? Make sure there is a slash at end. Also pic related I'm here at school writing this. Wish me luck. An heroing is not necessary unless I get f***** out the a**. It's pretty busy."

Then he walked in, shot me through the door, shot Kristina in the back at point-blank range, and traumatized an entire school of students and faculty who didn't know if they would leave the building alive.

The next hearing, when the judge would hand down the sentence, was scheduled for July. I was thankful to have a few months to recover from this hearing and prepare to testify at the next one. It had been hard to sit and watch those videos at the preliminary hearing. I had trouble sleeping for a few nights as I tried to process everything. I was shot. Someone tried to kill me. I knew that since April 12, 2013. I didn't think knowing anything more about the day could possibly make it feel worse, but I had been wrong. And it turns out, what I heard on that day paled in comparison to what we would be subjected to in July.

Over the next couple of months, I spent time preparing my statement to testify in court. Well, I tried to prepare. I spent most of my time thinking and being nervous and avoiding specific thoughts. I bought a new journal where I could collect all my memories and make notes of things I wanted the judge to know. I would drive myself to the local coffee shop and pull out the journal and wait for the thoughts to come. I think I went to a public place because I thought it would help me keep myself together long enough to write something somewhat comprehensible. I did this a few times before any words came, and I didn't write anything in it until June 15, 2014. On that day, I wrote:

"What do I say? For all intents and purposes, he ruined my life. Do I want him to know that? Do I want him to feel like he wins? No. But I have to show the judge what he did and how he changed my life. I'm having trouble with this.

I want to say that I've thrived, that I've made a good life out of bad situations. That in the face of horrible tragedy, I have become stronger. And I have. But it has felt impossible. It has been so incredibly painful. And even now, I don't feel stronger, or braver, or better. Right now, I don't see that. I don't see it in my future. I know it will happen. But not now. And now, I have to figure out what to say.

It's a moment I have been thinking about since this began. It will follow me for the rest of my life.

And I feel the weight."

This is the tug of war I felt happening inside me. I wanted to stand up and tell the world I was fine—great even! I wanted to show everyone how strong I was, how much I had overcome! Because I didn't want him to think he succeeded in stealing my happiness away from me even when he hadn't succeeded in stealing my life. But at the same time, I knew that what I said in front of that courtroom could have an effect on how the judge sentenced him. So I felt like I had to share the hard details: the feelings of defeat I faced every day, the excruciating pain, and the debilitating depression that kept me in dark and heavy places. Reading back over the journal entry, I can remember the pressure I felt to do and say all the right things. It felt like the weight of the world was on my shoulders. Aside from feeling this unrealistic responsibility for how the shooter would be sentenced, I felt pressure coming from somewhere else too.

I thought of many of the most publicized shootings in the media and how rarely the shooter survived and faced consequences for their crime. I thought of the opportunity I had to face this person in court, tell him how I felt and how what he had done changed my life, and how so many victims of gun violence never get this chance. In all my preparation, in all my journaling, in all my inner tug of war, I carried this weight on my shoulders: the weight of every survivor and every victim who never got this chance. I felt responsible for making sure he got a heavy sentence. I felt like if I said the wrong things, I would let everyone down. It was too much for me to carry. It was too heavy a burden for one person to hold, but it didn't stop me from trying.

We knew the security camera footage would be played at the sentencing, and the attorney and my victim's advocate wanted to give me and my family the opportunity to watch it ahead of time. We took them up on the offer because I wanted us all to be able to see it and respond however we needed to without worrying about the rest of the courtroom or how people were watching us. I tried to make decisions that were good for my whole family, not just me, because they lived a nightmare that day too. As a victim, every move I made in court was being watched and judged by someone, and I didn't want to have to do this for the first time in front of people. I met with the attorney on other occasions to work through my statement and prepare for testifying in court. She asked me questions and I practiced giving my answers so I wouldn't be as nervous on the day of the hearing. This part, I must admit, did feel a little like a *Law & Order* episode.

Despite all of my preparation and agonizing and worrying, I never really felt ready. Turns out the famous quote, often attributed to Corrie ten Boom, about "worrying not emptying tomorrow of its sorrow" is actually true, which is unfortunate because I'm naturally very good at worrying. Even with a prescription sleep medication, I hardly slept on the nights leading up to the hearing. On July 23, 2014, I woke up, nerves still present as I put on a new dress and stood in front of the mirror, trying to see myself the way others would see me.

Eric and I drove the thirty minutes to the courthouse, and with each mile we placed in the rearview mirror, I let go of the weight I had been working so hard to carry around with me. I could no longer bear this self-imposed burden of saying everything perfectly or representing every single victim of gun violence. I couldn't handle the pressure to give an emotionally charged public forgiveness speech. I couldn't control the sentence to be given. When I stood in front of the courtroom that day, I just wanted to be myself. I wanted to say what I felt I needed to say without worrying if I seemed too strong or too broken. I wanted to tell the truth without wondering if the shooter would think he won.

I started to understand the only way he was winning was by me continuing to allow him to occupy this space in my life, making me second-guess myself and believe I didn't know who I was anymore. I was only able to let go of these burdens because God had been right next to me the whole time, assuring me he was strong enough to take them. I knew the only way to get through the day was to let him.

We met the detectives in the parking lot of the courthouse as we had done many times before. As we stood waiting to go in, we saw the armored vehicle carrying the shooter pull into the parking lot. The reality of this day was setting in. We were escorted into the back of the building so we could avoid the media waiting for us in front. In the courtroom I saw familiar faces of friends who had come to support me.

The room was quiet as the security camera footage played on the screen at the front of the room. I watched for a few seconds at a time, turning away when something was coming that I didn't want to see again. I thought this was going to be the hardest part of the hearing. That was before the court-approved psychologist testified about the shooter's mental evaluation. The doctor reported he was still a danger to both himself and others, and that he was "very mentally ill." Through testimony from members of his family, I learned he had previously attempted suicide three times and as a result was placed in a rehabilitation facility and given more mental health treatment. He had been placed on medication but because he was doing better, his doctor took him off of it just four months before he brought a gun to school.

After the doctor testified, Mary Pettitt, the attorney for the state, told the court that while the shooter was incarcerated, he made comments about shooting people, wanting to lie under his victims' bodies and feel their blood on him, and how he felt like a god during his shooting rampage. I had never heard these details before. I felt like I was floating above my own body as I heard that someone sitting in the same room as me—the person who shot me—still dreamed about lying under my dead body. Pettitt stated that the shooter had continually lied to his doctors when he said that he didn't have homicidal thoughts, although the evidence showed he'd had thoughts about shooting people for years. She believed he lied to his doctors in order to move his plan forward as the result of an "I'm smarter than you are kind of attitude." Pettitt finished her statement about his mental health by saying, "Some crimes are so heinous you don't get another chance." She requested that the judge sentence the shooter to the maximum punishment: two life sentences plus eight years for the firearm charges.

Several family members of the shooter were called and testified about his mental health history. The other wounded victim gave her testimony, along with another student who spoke about the effects felt by the students who were not physically injured. The student was in a room where the shooter shot out the glass of the door and tried to gain access. He hadn't been able to return to school since because of his anxiety and panic attacks.

Finally, the attorney called my name and I walked to the front of the courtroom. I sat in the chair and promised to tell the whole truth. Instead of asking me to read a written statement, Pettitt asked me questions so I could tell my story. This relieved the pressure I had felt to have the perfect written statement. She asked about the day of the shooting and what recovery was like, physically, mentally, and emotionally. At the end of my questioning, I told the courtroom, "I thought that April 12 was the worst day of my life, but that was until all these other horrible days. These aren't going away anytime soon. I pay the consequences for his actions every single day, and there are a lot of other people that do too."

Before the judge announced the sentence, the shooter stood to read his statement—an attempt at an apology. He said he "sometimes acts without thinking" and apologized for his actions. He said he understood he was mentally ill and would accept any treatment offered to him. He told us he never stopped thinking about us and praying for us. He told us to "hold on and be strong." I don't remember how I reacted in the moment, but I remember feeling like I was going to be sick. I spent so long waiting to hear an apology. I spent so long wanting to know why he did it. Technically, I got both of these things. And neither of them made even the tiniest difference in the end.

The judge, who had been mostly an observer until this point, began addressing the court. Judge Long began by pointing out the inadequacies of the mental health system in the state of Virginia, which was struggling to treat people as ill as the shooter due to budget cuts. Long said that on April 12, 2013, the shooter was "evil personified" and his actions were "cold and calculated." After apologizing to him for not having a better option, Judge Long sentenced him to sixty-eight years in prison, suspended after he serves thirty-eight. He would then be placed on probation indefinitely and required to pay restitution to the other wounded victims and myself, money we will undoubtedly never see.

In that moment, as the judge read the sentence, it was over. This big thing I had been anticipating for over a year was done. The finality was almost abrupt. People expressed dissatisfaction and anger over the sentence, but I felt numb. I hadn't known what I wanted to happen, and still didn't. I wondered what his family was feeling. Had they expected a sentence this long? We didn't understand, and still don't, why the judge decided to suspend thirty years of the sentence. All we knew was that he could have been sentenced to much less. I felt fortunate I was able to see the person who hurt me face consequences at all, knowing that so many victims of violent crimes never have the opportunity. Fourteen years is what we were once told to expect, so I was trying to feel satisfied by thirty-eight, knowing that no amount of time would ever lessen the pain I experienced. Much like forgiveness, consequences for actions don't erase the actions. Prison sentences aren't a magic trick that make bullet holes disappear.

Anticipating this day and my role in it had long felt like a weight I couldn't figure out how to let go of and a roadblock to the rest of my life. Now it was over and done, yet nothing felt easier. It felt like I had put off a lot of healing and a lot of moving on in hopes that hearings a judge's words would solve a large portion of my problems. It didn't, of course. Now I had to figure out how to do the rest of the healing.

6

STONES TO BREAD

"GOD MUST HAVE BIG PLANS FOR YOU."

I was still lying in a hospital bed the first time someone said this to me. The monitors beeped all around me. The massaging pads wrapped around my legs started to tighten and loosen again, working to prevent blood clots. In this moment, it sure didn't feel like God had big things planned for me. But people were saying it often enough I started believing it, and before I knew, it started making me feel better. If God had big plans for me on the other side of this, then maybe it would all be worth it. If God was going to use me in big ways, then maybe I could survive these long nights of pain and nightmares.

The second day of my hospital stay, the hospital chaplain came to see me. The anesthesiologist from my surgery sent her hoping that I would find speaking with her to be restorative. Everyone else cleared out of the room and she asked if she could sit at the foot of my bed. As she sat down, we started talking about what happened to me and about my relationship with God.

"If God was physically here in this room with us, what would you want to ask him?" she asked me.

I paused for a moment, wanting to be sure of this answer, before I responded.

"I would ask him what he wants me to do now. He saved my life for a reason; he must want me to do something with my life."

Some days, convincing myself of this fact, that God had important plans for me, kept me going. Even when I was angry and depressed and resented the possibility of needing to be shot to be used by God, the familiar thought repeated through my mind: God had plans for me.

As the familiar refrain goes, the days turned into weeks and the weeks into months, and in what came as a shock to me, nothing "big" was happening. I walked the halls of the occupational therapy clinic three times a week, learning how to hold a pencil again or trying to move my pinky finger just a little bit more. I sat on the couch in my therapist's office discussing the same struggles, fears, and memories over and over again, reaching for any sign of healing. How long was this going to take? It felt like I was wasting time. Why wasn't God healing me yet? I wanted to move on to the big stuff.

I am slightly embarrassed to admit this next part. When I thought of the big stuff God planned for me, I imagined national news interviews and sharing my testimony on the stage of women's conferences about God miraculously saving my life, maybe a *Dateline* episode concluding with my incredibly gracious and humble offering of forgiveness toward the shooter. People would be so inspired and would have no choice but to believe in God and devote their lives to him. I sure thought very highly of myself. I was planning big things in my mind. But this is what I saw other survivors of tragedies do for years. Society propped them up as examples of how to survive the unthinkable, how to make the best of awful situations, how to go on living. It felt reasonable for me to assume this is what God wanted from me too.

Almost a year after the shooting, I lay in my bed recovering from my fourth surgery. It was the toughest surgery and hardest recovery since the initial injury, and I was really struggling, both emotionally and physically. My surgeon did a bone graft in hopes of increasing the function of my hand and we were hopeful, but it was becoming increasingly clear it hadn't worked. I was in pain. I was tired. And I was discouraged. I looked around at the symbols of my situation. Half-full cups of water; prescription bottles full of pain medicines, antidepressants, and sleep aids; and bandages covered every surface of my room. I spent my days taking naps and watching movies and trying to relearn who I was. I felt small all the time. I felt forgotten and unimportant. It seemed everyone else in my life was doing their big things: getting married, having babies, going to grad school, making plans, dreaming dreams. And I was still here, lying in this bed, doing nothing, or so it felt. That's when the survivor's guilt started.

I always understood survivor's guilt to be what survivors feel after surviving something others did not. No one told me I could feel survivor's guilt even if no one had died during my shooting. No one told me how it might manifest in my life. I didn't even talk to my counselor about it for a long time because I didn't know that's what it was. I didn't know it was normal. I didn't want to admit I had started believing God saved the wrong person.

I thought survivor's guilt only happened if you survived an event that someone else did not. I didn't know that when I survived my shooting, I would take on the guilt of every other person who didn't survive a shooting. Names and faces of shooting victims I had seen on the news or in books played in my mind like a slide show, and the guilt rose with each one. Why me? Why not them? I usually managed to push the question out of my mind, knowing it was too big for me to answer and that no answer, even if one existed, would feel good enough. Instead, the guilt manifested in my actions. If I could do enough, be enough, accomplish enough then I could prove that my life was a good one to have saved.

THE RIGHT KIND OF SURVIVOR

If you had asked me before I was shot if there was a "right kind of survivor" I would have vehemently told you, "No, of course not!" But, deep down, I probably did have ideas that crept into my subconscious through shows like *Dateline* and *20/20* that showed what "good" survivors did in the aftermath of their trauma. I remember episodes of NBC's *Dateline* where the final moments were dedicated to video clips of the victims publicly forgiving the person that hurt them or their family member. When similar videos were shared on social media, the commentary surrounding them was always, "This is an example of Christ's love. This person is so strong. If they can forgive, we all can forgive!" I remember the anxiety it produced in me as I wondered, *Would I have to do that too? What if I don't want to forgive him in public? Will people judge me if I don't? What if I'm not a good example of Christ's love?*

These moments are private and personal. They come after someone's internal struggle to decide how they want to treat the person who hurt them beyond comprehension. They are not scripted, dramatized moments meant for public consumption. Yet we watch these videos and share them, and maybe without intending to, we hold them up as examples of how victims *should* respond, how victims *should* forgive, how victims *should* live. We create the perfect victim, the good victim, the one people want to follow and look up to. And in doing so, we create an impossible and unnecessary standard for victims to live up to.

No one ever told me what kind of victim or survivor I should be, not explicitly anyway. I discovered the desired traits simply from the things said to me in casual conversation.

"At least it was only your hand."

"This will make you stronger."

"You will overcome this."

"God saved you for a reason!"

"God has great plans for you!"

With every comment such as these spoken to me, I learned who people wanted me to be. They wanted me to be optimistic, positive, and happy. It became clear people often felt uncomfortable talking to me about what happened. They wanted to be kind and supportive by asking me about it or asking me how I was doing, but they didn't really know what to say. I knew if I was honest and said I wasn't doing so well, people would be uncomfortable letting it hang in the air like the heavy summer heat without offering a shallow platitude. The phrases, "I'm sure you'll come out stronger," "Well, if anyone can handle it you can," and their cousin "Everything happens for a reason" rarely help anyone other than the person offering them. They are an easy, low-risk way to avoid having to sit with the idea that sometimes we can't handle things, and sometimes awful things happen for no reason at all.

For a while, I carried the burden. *They feel more awkward than I do,* I would remind myself and even say to others when they asked if it was hard to talk about it with people. I took on the responsibility of reassuring people I was fine and okay and great—so they wouldn't feel bad for bringing it up or making me think about it.

I couldn't do it. I couldn't live up to some standard of how shooting victims were supposed to act. And I didn't really want to. I didn't know everything about how to grieve and mourn and heal, but I knew enough, and had learned enough from my counselor, that these were odd societal standards. Those were not the way.

If God had big plans for me, I was absolutely not crushing it. I was failing miserably. Some days I slept until 4 p.m. and went to bed again at 10 p.m. It's hard to accomplish world-changing goals in six hours of waking time, after all. *Maybe if someone else had survived instead of me, they would be using their time better,* I thought. Maybe they wouldn't still be lying in their bed in the middle of the afternoon or too depressed to get up and do the laundry. Maybe they would have been better at surviving than I was. I was wasting time with all this recovering and healing and thinking. Time to get moving.

I sat up in my bed and grabbed my computer. I perused Amazon for what felt like hours and added no fewer than ten books to my cart: books about healing, God's love in the midst of suffering, goal setting, etc. Oh and journals! And notebooks. Can't forget those journals and notebooks. I was about to kick this recovery into high gear via an abundance of self-help and Christian nonfiction literature.

The books and the journals arrived a couple of days later, and I was determined to read them all. I made a nice little stack on my nightstand. I opened the journals and began writing. I wrote out the entire story of what happened the day of the shooting and everything since. I wrote my hopes for healing and for all those big things I was going to do too. I started writing on my blog again, sharing bits and pieces of my recovery, what I was learning, and trying to share faith-based encouragement for my readers.

On good days I was eager to share and to write. On the bad days, though, I wondered why I was even bothering. The bad news I got from the doctor didn't seem to translate well to an encouraging blog post. I didn't want people to feel sorry for me; I wanted them to think I was strong and resilient. But I didn't feel that way—I felt like a fraud. So then I laid down the journal on the nightstand where it stayed for months, and I let the blog sit without update because writing it all down and sending it out into the world made it too real and too hard, and I didn't want to do it anymore.

The books collected dust on the nightstand and finally I moved them to the floor, where they sat in little piles along the bedroom wall. I didn't understand that sometimes one of the biggest effects of depression is having a ton of things you really and sincerely want to do, and just never being able to find the motivation to do them.

I was living with an overwhelming weight on my shoulders and it was getting too heavy for me to carry. Every day, I went through my list of things to do: stretch my hand, change my bandages, do my physical therapy, go to the doctor, go to counseling, fill out medical expense reports—and it all felt so invaluable and inconsequential. That didn't even include all the regular life stuff: dishes, laundry, cleaning, getting groceries, and paying bills. None of it seemed to mean anything. None of it was making a difference in the world. Beyond that? I had no dreams for my life anymore. I had no vision. Everything I ever wanted to do felt impossible. When I did think of things I would like to do, I was scared to admit it or commit to them because I couldn't trust myself to follow through. I tried to commit to things and make plans with people. But when time came to follow through on those things and plans, I might be too depressed or in too much pain that day. It became obvious to me, and it felt like everyone else was thinking it too—God saved the wrong person.

What do you do?

There's this question we ask each other sometimes, usually when we are meeting someone new for the first time. It's only four words. Four short words. I never knew how much power they held until the day I no longer had an answer to the question they asked.

What do you do?

I always had an answer to this question. In college: I'm a student. I work at the Boys and Girls Club. I work at the pregnancy center. After college? I'm a social worker for the city. I'm a program specialist at the college. All of these answers, I gave with confidence. I was proud of what I did. And then one day, I didn't have an answer.

In the early months after the shooting, I would simply say I worked at the college. I quickly realized that if I didn't want to answer any more questions, I couldn't say that anymore. Local people would put two and two together and see the sling around my arm and assume I was one of the women who was shot. It wasn't true, anyway. I wasn't working there. I wasn't working anywhere. Workers' compensation was covering my medical bills and paying me a small weekly wage to make up two-thirds of my salary. And, also, I didn't want to think about the college ever again. I was never going back to that job, and I couldn't pretend like I was. More than once, I got frustrated trying to come up with a pretty answer and before I knew it the words, "Well, I got shot at work, so right now I am mostly busy dealing with that" came flying out of my mouth. Sometimes I would say I was between things, other times I would pretend I didn't even hear the question. Thankfully, in the months after the shooting, I wasn't meeting new people very often so it only came up every now and again. Then, we moved to a new state.

In August of 2014, Eric and I packed up our townhouse in my hometown of Salem, Virginia, and moved to Johnson City, Tennessee, where he was going to attend pharmacy school. The move itself was bittersweet for me. I was sad to move away from our families and where we had lived our entire lives, but at the same time, I was ready to leave a few things behind for a fresh start. More than once I had been recognized at the grocery store for being "the girl from the news." Sometimes Eric and I would be out running errands and would see a group of people looking at us and whispering to each other, only for me later to be told they were friends of the shooter or his family. There were places in town I avoided, ones that were too hard to drive by and too painful to be near. Too many things reminded me of something bad. The already-small town of 22,000 people had gotten smaller and smaller. No matter where we went, it seemed we were always avoiding something, whether consciously or unconsciously. I was tired of it. It's hard to heal fully when things won't stop pulling at your scabs.

When we arrived in Johnson City, it quickly felt like home. I was eager to make friends and build a community. I was excited to start a new chapter of my life. It just never occurred to me how hard it might be. I thought I wanted to meet people that didn't know who I was or what happened to me. I thought I wanted to remain anonymous and just start over. But as we started to meet people, I began to realize I couldn't, or didn't want to, build friendships with people without them knowing about the event that shaped who I was. It felt shallow. To be with people who knew me but didn't know about the shooting made me feel even lonelier. It was still a huge part of my life and was still shaping who I was. If they didn't know about the shooting, they didn't really know me.

As an introvert through and through, small talk already gave me anxiety. If bringing index cards with lists of conversation topics were more acceptable in society, I would do it every time. Now, though, the dreaded question was added to the things I feared when I knew I was going to meet people.

What do you do?

One day in the car with Eric, we were on our way to meet some of his new classmates for dinner. He asked if I was excited to meet people. I was quiet for a moment and then replied, "They're going to ask me what I do." Being asked this question started feeling like someone was interrogating me instead of trying to casually get to know me. It felt like an evaluation of my worth as a human being and not a simple interest in my vocation or how I spent my time. I felt inferior to almost every person I talked to, all because I didn't have a "job." My adult life thus far had been spent focusing on the goal: graduating college and getting a job, finding a title, a purpose. I followed the plan. I did what I was supposed to do. Then without my consent, the rules of the game changed and suddenly none of that mattered. That's when I realized, for years, without even realizing it; my identity had been completely tied up in what I did.

The question repeated itself over and over in my head, as if I was asking it of myself: *What do you do, Taylor? What are you doing?* I thought if I could find one answer, one simple but perfect answer, I could tuck away in my back pocket to use anytime I was asked, then the anxiety would go away. Maybe I could think of something to say about myself to make me proud, and maybe if I said that thing enough then I would start to believe it too. I ran through the typical answers and nothing felt good enough or worthy enough. I was spending my days working harder than I ever worked in my life. I was giving all my energy, physical and mental, to regaining the use of my hand. I was going to counseling and trying to heal and become whole from the inside out. None of the answers I could think of for that dreaded question encapsulated what I was really doing. Nothing could show the full picture of what my life was like. At the same time that I was dealing with shooting survivor stuff, I was also trying to figure out newlywed and human being stuff. None of those things took a back seat just because I got shot; they all just got more complicated.

One day as I sat overwhelmed by the weight of my life and the shame I heaped on myself for not being enough or doing enough,

God kindly sent me a reprieve in the form of a gentle nudge. Maybe none of the answers I could come up with felt good enough because no answer would be good enough. I was trying to put all of my identity, everything I believed about myself and who I was, into a one-line sentence that could be spoken in casual conversation while standing around a backyard barbecue or during the quick greeting time at church. I sure was putting a lot of pressure on a few words to do for me what only God could do for me.

The lies I believed about my worth and where it came from began to quickly unravel. I had realized there was no way I would be able to move forward in healing if I continued to be held hostage by the belief that my identity was based on what job title I held or what I decided to do with my life as a shooting survivor.

The truth of the gospel began to reveal itself to me in a way I never experienced before. I had learned as a young child in church that I didn't have to earn my salvation and I didn't have to work to be loved by God. I didn't have to prove to him I was worth the death of Jesus Christ. The gifts of God's salvation and love were just that—gifts. Gifts I didn't have to earn and couldn't earn no matter how hard I tried. And yet, when I needed these foundational truths about God to be big and true in my life, I found glaring cracks in my understanding of them.

Ephesians 2:8-9 says, "For it is by grace you have been saved, through faith—and this is not from yourselves, it is the gift of God—not by works, so that no one can boast."

It's all right there. We are saved through faith. It's a gift. We can't earn it. Suddenly it felt like I had been reading those verses my entire life while imagining God winking at me—"Yes, of course you are saved through faith,"—wink wink. It's like when your parents compliment your B-riddled report card and tell you they are proud, but you know deep down they did, in fact, expect a little bit more. It felt too good to be true. And I realized as much as I believed it to be the truth, I also believed I should try to earn it, just a little bit! Just in case! And the little bit of earning I was trying to do, the little bit of doubt and unbelief in my heart, was wrecking my life and my faith.

There's a reason God reminds us that we can't earn any of it. There's a reason he tries to help us understand the importance of this truth. Because any attempts at earning his love or proving our worth to him, or to anyone else for that matter, will always come up short and unfulfilling. It only causes us to strive harder, and we end up spinning our wheels in a field of mud. I was learning this the hard way.

The new physical needs of my body were exposing what was already inside my heart. So much of what I thought I knew about the world and about God shattered right along with my hand when that bullet hit me. My constant striving for approval revealed a heart and mind that never truly rested in the promise that God loved me no matter what I did, because I never had to. I had never been limited like I was after the shooting. I could always work at it, without ever really realizing what I was doing. I'm not saying I didn't truly love the Lord. I believe I was serving God and loving him the best I knew how. I had a really comfortable life for the most part. I never had so little that it felt like God was all I had, and I was learning now what it looked like to sit in a valley of death and look to the Lord as my sole source of comfort and hope.

In the summer of 2015, I began meeting with a pastor, Rick, once a week for some pastoral counseling. I was seeing a psychiatrist for my intensive therapy needs, but felt a strong desire to have someone speak into my spiritual life. I still believed in God and loved him deeply, but I was having trouble feeling him and finding him in my everyday life. I felt far away from so much of what I knew, and there were a lot of days when that included God as well.

I had known Rick for a few years after attending his church in college. He knew my husband's family well and had checked in with us often after the shooting. The first time I met with him in the summer of 2015, I knew God would use him to speak into my life. I told him the story of what happened and what life had been like in the years since the shooting. "What are you struggling with?" he asked me. "What feels hard? What feels impossible?"

"I don't know what I'm supposed to be doing. There has to be a grand plan for my life. God has to have something he wants me to do. And I just feel stuck," I told him plainly. I told him about all the things I wanted to do or felt like I should be doing. I went through the list of everything I had tried. He looked at me and said, with only kindness in his voice, "You're in the wilderness and you're trying to turn stones into bread."

At first I didn't understand what he meant, and then he recounted the story from Matthew 4. Jesus had been led out into the wilderness by the Spirit to be tempted by Satan. He fasted for forty days and forty nights, and Satan came to him saying, "If you are the Son of God, tell these stones to become bread." Jesus was away from his home, his people, and the provisions civilization afforded. I'm sure he was hungry and exhausted and bread probably sounded pretty good because bread always sounds good. Satan was in front of him tempting him to turn the stones around him into the provision he was desperate for, in order to prove who he was, and how powerful he was.

I was trying to do the same. I was wandering around in my own wilderness, feeling isolated and alone, waiting for God to meet me and show me what to do and where to go. I was looking at all the stones around me, desperately searching for a way to turn them into what I felt like I needed. I was in a season of waiting, a holding pattern. Now when I look back on that time, it's obvious that it was meant to be a time of healing and restoration. God was giving me the gift of time; time to be still and to feel his love. In the aftermath, though, I was so busy striving and attempting to manufacture purpose that I couldn't see all God was asking of me was to simply *be*. Rick told me that. He told me all God wanted from me was to live a life pleasing to the Lord, to delight in him, to be his. He reminded me God loves me as I am now, not who I could be if I worked hard enough. He reminded me that I didn't have to validate myself to anyone. I didn't have to use worldly measurements to assess my achievements and my value. God didn't save my life expecting me to prove anything to him or anyone else. I had nothing to prove.

I'm going to be honest; I didn't walk away from those counseling sessions and immediately feel the weight lift off of my shoulders. I still hated being asked, "What do you do?" and I still spent a lot of time feeling guilty for not doing "enough." Like a lot of things God teaches us, this wasn't a one-time deal or a magic fix. It was a seed planted in my life that I had to let grow. I had to cover and protect the truth of having nothing to prove, even when everything in me was pulling me back into believing the lies that nothing I was doing would ever equal what I had been given. I had to, and still have to, continually remind myself: my worth is in Christ Jesus alone, and that nothing I do or don't do will ever take away from that.

These realizations also led me down a path of discovering what I believed about other people. If I was internally tying my value to what I did, there was a good chance I was evaluating other people by the same standard, even subconsciously. Maybe it looked like passing by a person who was homeless and having a passing thought of wondering what they did to end up there, or meeting a stay-at-home mom and wondering, just for a second, what else she could be doing if she wasn't just a mom. So much of how the world works forces us into believing that our worth as people is connected in large part to our job title, our productivity, or however we find ourselves answering the question of what we do. If the measurement of who we are is how important we are in the world, it will be nearly impossible to remember all of us have inherent worth simply because we are made in the image of Christ. Even when you know it and believe it to be true, when someone is standing in front of you asking, "So, what do you do?" and expecting an answer, it's hard to remember that what God thinks of you matters so much more than what they think of you.

Overcoming these societal pressures that I felt to be, say, and do all the right things was incredibly difficult. I kept hoping someone would make an announcement to the world over some sort of global PA system, letting everyone know that, "Taylor Schumann is enough! She was shot and she is doing her best! Don't worry about what she does;

she's doing so much stuff! I promise!" Alas, that was not a thing that happened. Instead, I realized something terrible: I was going to have to believe I was enough because of Christ. I had to believe God loved me and sustained my life. I had to believe on my own, not because of something anyone else said to me. I did not have to earn God's love or approval, nor the approval of humanity. The global announcement would have been easier, I think. It's easy to say these things to others; it's harder to believe them about yourself.

For a long time, when I remembered the exchange with the hospital chaplain, the one where she asked me what I would want to ask God, I always seemed to block out the part after I told her what I wanted to ask him: What does he want me to do now? I blocked out how she responded to me. She nodded and took in what I had said, and then replied, "I think he wants you to rest in him. He loves you very much."

I wish I could go back to that moment so I could let those words sink in a little deeper and let the truth of them take hold of my heart. I wish I wouldn't have spent such a long time trying so hard to prove my worth to myself, the world, and God. I feel overwhelming sadness when I think back to that time. I was hurting and suffering tremendous grief. I felt alone and left behind. In the midst of all of that, instead of allowing myself to be loved and comforted by the God who sees, the God who hears, the God who heals, I spent all my time and energy trying so hard to make sure everyone thought I was good enough to have lived.

I knew I couldn't keep going the way I had been, and I didn't want to. I had a lot of life left to live and I didn't want to spend it trying to prove to the world that I mattered, and that my life was worth saving, and that I was good enough. I just wanted to move forward and live my life confidently, knowing that because of Jesus, I was already exactly who I needed to be. For two years I felt I was wasting time by not recovering fast enough, or not doing enough, or not getting over my trauma fast enough. In reality, I was only wasting time believing those lies about myself and letting them steal my joy and my belief that even in my weakness, God could show himself as mighty in me.

I began telling people the truth.

One day, I went out to lunch with a friend and some people she wanted to introduce me to. We sat down at the table and began the familiar introductions. They each introduced themselves to me, offering their occupations and job titles. Then it was my turn.

"What do you do?" one woman asked me.

I paused and took a breath, "I'm not doing anything right now. Just staying home and settling in!"

"Oh, that's great!" they responded.

The feeling of uneasiness and awkwardness I was so afraid of slowly dissipated when I realized this group of women didn't care if I had a job or not, they just wanted to get to know me. I didn't have to prove anything. I didn't have to justify my answer with a full autobiography of my life or a laundry list of all the things I was busy doing and handling. I could just be honest. That didn't mean it was always easy to do. Sometimes I wanted to keep talking, to qualify, to justify, to make people understand. Over time, though, it became easier to let it be, and there was freedom in allowing God to lift the pressures I was living under. There was freedom in believing everything his Word said was true.

No more striving. No more doubting. No more believing I was insignificant if I couldn't do enough or be enough. No more believing it about other people either. It was time to finally allow God to take hold of my heart and my mind, and let him show me the abundant life he planned for me; the one I didn't have to do a thing to earn.

7

A HEART FOR JUSTICE

AFTER THE SHOOTING I received a lot of interview requests. I watched these types of aftermath interviews with other victims of shootings before I became one myself, and I anticipated a lot of questions about guns. I didn't want to talk about guns. I didn't want to be used to "further an agenda" (something I heard muttered about these particular interviews—to be honest, I'd probably said it myself), and I didn't want to be put into a position where I was forced to talk about things I wasn't ready to talk about. When I would communicate this to reporters, many of them never contacted me again.

I am from an area of the country, southwestern Virginia, where owning a gun is common. People there aren't necessarily obsessed with guns, but owning them is normal, even expected. My dad owns guns and is, by my standards, an extremely responsible gun owner. It was the quintessential "God, guns, and freedom" type of culture, and I fit right in until I didn't. I had always been staunchly pro-Second Amendment, always asserting guns were not the problem—the problem was an abundance of evil in the world and a severe lack of available mental healthcare. And yet there I found myself, pro-gun opinions and all, a victim of gun violence.

I wrestled to understand my feelings in the wake of the shooting. All of my former arguments for gun ownership now felt hollow. No good guy with a gun had protected me. No one pulled out their concealed weapon to take down the shooter in an act of heroism. In fact, the man who stopped the shooter didn't have a gun at all. At the same time, I countered, playing out all sides of the argument in my head, the shooter bought the gun legally. What laws could've stopped him? I lived in this tension of feeling negatively toward both pro-gun rhetoric and people who wanted me to be anti-gun. I didn't know where I fit in.

I considered staying silent on the issue forever. That seemed like the easy thing to do, and it worked for a while. But something inside me knew that silence wasn't the answer. Being a shooting survivor means being retraumatized every time another shooting occurs. Many of the people around me were able to move on from the immediate aftermath and trauma of the shooting. They were able to forget—but I didn't have that option. As a result, I felt forgotten, and I didn't want anyone else to have to feel that way. If I stayed silent, despite not feeling ready to wade into the public discourse around gun violence, was I contributing to the suffering of others?

Every time a shooting made its way into the news, I was forced to analyze all of these conflicting emotions. I read the names of the victims and their ages and what they liked to do. I memorized their faces and I read about their injuries. I prayed for them by name and begged God to take away their pain and heal their wounds. I used my own memories to imagine what it was like for them as they wondered whether they would live or die. I found myself reading everything I could about the different shooters, their histories, and how they acquired their weapons. I read about the damage to the body caused by weapons such as the AR-15 and accessories such as bump stocks that allow guns to be fired in rapid succession, causing as much carnage as possible. I read about people who, by all accounts, shouldn't have been allowed to purchase guns, but who were allowed to buy them anyway—due to one oversight or another. All of it wreaked havoc in my life. I was plagued by nightmares and was anxious simply sitting inside my house. Every time I heard the sound of an ambulance or police sirens, I was certain it was another shooting. I knew I couldn't keep this up for the rest of my life, but I couldn't bear to forget these people and what happened to them. I knew what that felt like, and it felt like my responsibility to remember them, their names, their pain, their stories. If no one else did, I would.

Every mass shooting that dominated the news cycle was inevitably followed by offerings of "thoughts and prayers" from one side and promises to do something about gun violence by the other. Thoughts and prayers was where I had always lived: feeling terrible pain for those affected by gun violence, but only going as far as praying for them and wondering what could be done to stop this terrible evil. I usually arrived at the conclusion that there wasn't anything we could do. How else could you move on after hearing the terrible news of twenty children and six of their teachers being murdered in their elementary school? How could you not collapse under the weight of it unless you convinced yourself it was beyond your power to stop it?

I understand why people resort to thoughts and prayers; it's self-preservation. And it is effective for everyone but the victims. In the months after my own experience, this response began to feel increasingly insufficient. As I watched more lives taken and more lives ruined by gun violence, I found little solace in people offering to think and pray. Instead, I was feeling pulled apart at the seams and broken open.

It wasn't only the tragedies pulling me apart and breaking me open. God was doing it too—in what I now know was a loving and kind act offered to me. Suddenly, the God I read about in the Bible— the one who said he was near to the brokenhearted, that the poor are blessed, that we are to welcome the immigrant—was revealing himself to me in a different way. No longer could I read those words and simply see them as things Jesus said or Jesus cared about. I now understood that if Jesus cared about those things, I was to care about them too. And not in the donating-money-to-charity kind of way, though donating money is important. I was to care about these people because they are my fellow image bearers of God, made in his likeness just as I was. And because I am called to care about their humanity and their eternity, I am also called to care about the issues affecting their physical bodies, not just their spiritual lives. I could not separate these things any longer. So I found myself enveloped in other issues of social justice.

The election primary cycle preceding the 2016 election had forced me to consider where I stood on issues such as poverty, racial injustice, clean water in Flint, Michigan, immigration reform, refugee acceptance, and disability justice. I found myself slowly speaking out on all these issues, making a comment during a conversation or sharing an article on social media. I had often been outspoken about politics and in sharing my opinions, so in some ways this felt normal. Yet after a few months, when I looked back, I could see the gradual change I had experienced. I found myself shifting from complacency and denial—whether subconscious or not—to awareness and advocacy, one issue at a time. I was uncomfortable with the way Christian Republicans were speaking about police brutality and Black Lives Matter. I was grieved by the rhetoric they were using about immigrants and refugees. Thanks to friends I made on Twitter who spoke out on issues of disability, along with my newly disabled body, I was seeing up close and personal the lack of care and concern for disabled people. My heart was being turned toward people who were marginalized by society. I was always an extremely empathetic person, always acutely aware of the needs of those around me. But this was different. God was using my experience as a shooting survivor to bring me closer to people who I otherwise wouldn't have had much in common with, or even thought of at all.

I lived my entire life as a Christian and only at age twenty-six did I find myself reevaluating where I stood on issues of social justice. It became clear to me that I had only ever filtered what I thought about things such as poverty and immigration, and even guns, through the

lens of my identity as a Republican rather than my identity as a follower of Jesus. This isn't uncommon. I would venture to say that many
of us experienced this path. I always believed Jesus would've been a
Republican, had he been forced into the two-party democratic system
we have in America, based solely on the issue of abortion. Republicans are the pro-life party, so Jesus would've been a Republican, I
had concluded at an early age. But now, as my eyes began to open to
different forms of suffering around me, my conclusions began to
waver. Not providing healthcare to people didn't seem pro-life to me.
Wanting to end the refugee program in America and locking our
doors to people who were fleeing violence and terror didn't seem pro-
life to me. Not seeing the clear evidence of police brutality or systemic
racism against Black people didn't seem pro-life to me. The lack of
clean water in Flint, Michigan, leading to horrific and permanent
health issues did not seem pro-life to me. The lack of care and concern
for disabled humans did not seem pro-life to me. And, for the first time,
the unwavering allegiance to guns and the right to own guns over
potentially saving lives was glaringly not pro-life to me.

I didn't flip a switch and all of the sudden become a gun reform
activist. The transition happened slowly and naturally for me. Years
of internalizing the pain and suffering of the survivors' community
and hours of poring over gun violence statistics culminated in a base
of knowledge that pushed me into working on gun reform. I began to
speak out about issues of gun violence, first on my Twitter account.
This was my way of testing the waters, seeing how it felt to say things
to other people that had been floating around in my head. I was
nervous for people in my life to find out I had changed my mind, and
sending one-hundred-forty-character tweets here and there seemed
like a harmless way to see how my opinions would be received.

For the most part, I received positive feedback, and I began to form
relationships with other gun control and social justice activists online.
Then, after one mass shooting, one of my tweets about gun reform
landed on the front page of the BBC. The response was immediate

and vitriolic, and the harassment forced me to make my account private for the first time—although not the last. Pro-gun activists and a legitimate member of the Nazi Party targeted me. I knew how passionate people were about guns and the Second Amendment, and I knew how nasty people could be online. Yet when I found myself the personal recipient of the hate, I was still shocked. The fact that people can be so mean and hateful to people they don't even know still baffles me. Even though so much of it was coming from strangers and faceless Twitter accounts, it still hurt. It was the first time I was confronted with the idea that my personal pain and story wouldn't be enough to convince people. And even though I knew these were probably empty threats, I still often felt afraid for my personal safety. If this was just the beginning, I wasn't sure how I would keep going, or even if I should.

Closer to home, things became more difficult as well. Many of my family members and friends found out about my tweet and began asking me about my feelings regarding guns and how they had shifted. I started having more in-person conversations with people. A lot of these conversations were really uncomfortable, but as I pushed through the discomfort, my passion and fervor for gun reform only grew. Not everyone in my family supported my stances, or even understood how I arrived at them, but I found that it didn't matter. They still loved me and I them, and I knew I would be in this for the long haul.

I became diligent about educating myself about gun laws and statistics. I wanted to know what I was talking about. I wanted to be able to answer questions when people asked me about my opinions about guns. I didn't want to rely solely on my experience as a victim, so I started talking to other victims of gun violence and other activists. Over time, I began to feel more comfortable speaking out in support of new gun laws and against the pro-gun rhetoric used by the Republican Party and the National Rifle Association (NRA). I was slowly finding myself in this new role of fighting for gun reform and I was navigating the emotions of it all too. I was allowing myself to step into it slowly, figuring it out as I went.

Then the next mass shooting happened.

PULSE

On the morning of Sunday, June 12, 2016, I woke up to news of another mass shooting this one in Orlando, Florida, at a nightclub. The numbers of casualties increased as I watched the news. Every time I checked, the number got higher: twenty-five, thirty, thirty-eight, forty-two.

I could barely contain my emotions as my husband and I headed to church that morning. Honestly, I didn't want to go, but I figured it would be comforting to be with others. I fully expected the pastor to bring up the shooting and offer corporate prayers for those affected. I expected other worshipers to be talking about it, to be mourning together. Certainly, I thought, we are going to acknowledge the hurting and suffering of that community. Certainly the pastor will notice me in the congregation, see the connection, and realize this is important. I waited throughout the whole service—and not one word was uttered about it. No acknowledgment, no prayer, nothing.

I was devastated. How could the church have failed to mention this horrific act of violence that had claimed the lives of so many? And yet even in my grief, I realized that I had attended lots of church services following mass shootings during the years before this and never expected those events to be brought up in church. Until my own experience with a mass shooting, I don't think I'd ever even thought about the possibility before. It's almost as if deep down I innately understood no one in church was going to use their platform to talk about gun violence. That day, I realized how sad that was. A man with a gun had murdered forty-nine people and injured fifty-three. It was the deadliest mass shooting in US history at that point, and it was met with silence by my church, and largely the church as a whole. This was no longer going to work for me. I was tired of the silence from the church. I was tired of my own silence too.

I was overwhelmed with grief, crying off and on throughout the day. I always felt this way after another shooting took place. Each one took me right back to April 12, 2013, right back to the tiny room I was trapped in, right back to the suffocating feeling of not knowing if I would live or die. I knew all of the things the Pulse victims were about to walk into. Yes, they were "survivors," but they were victims too—they would not be spared suffering. I knew that even though it felt like it at the time, the day of the shooting probably wouldn't be their toughest day. The toughest days were ahead, when they would be sobered by the reality of all of this pain and trauma being the new normal, for a while at least, and not just the past. I was devastated at the thought of all these people joining the unfortunate club of those whose lives were changed by a person with a gun. I had all the same flashbacks and feelings I always did: sadness, anger, and fear. If you held up one of those feelings charts kids have in their elementary school classrooms, I probably would have waved in a general direction of all of the feelings. That day, though, it was more than that. The tweets from politicians offering thoughts and prayers, the Facebook posts from friends and acquaintances offering the same . . . finally, it just wasn't enough for me.

How, I wondered, could all these people not see what guns were doing to our fellow human beings? How could people not care more than this? Why were people so loyal to guns in this way when they were literally tearing people apart? I posed a question on Twitter: "If you are a gun owner, and giving up your guns would mean no more mass shootings, would you do it?" There were a few yes responses compared to the many no votes, just as I had anticipated.

I shed many tears in the days following the Pulse shooting. In the three years between my shooting and the one at Pulse, my most common emotion after shootings had been sadness. I always felt so deeply sad. I was dealing with my own trauma, too, and sometimes that was the only emotion my brain and my heart had room for. The day following Pulse, though, I finally felt the anger. It was like the inside of my body was burning and I couldn't stop it. The tension crept up my shoulders and into my neck, and it felt like if I didn't figure out what to do about it that it was going to overtake me completely.

Pulse marked a turning point, when I went from occasionally speaking out on social media to full-fledged gun reform activist in every area of my life. I began making it a point to use my social media platforms to start educating people on the realities of gun violence. I began offering a daily update on the total number of people that had been killed with a gun so far that year. I started pointing out bad gun laws that were making America more dangerous and attempting to educate people on laws that could potentially make a difference. I frequently sent out updates when new bills were going through Congress and gave information on how to contact representatives in government. I joined my local Moms Demand Action for Gun Sense in America chapter and began volunteering. I started using my writing platform, writing various articles and blog posts in attempts to communicate the painful realities of gun violence in America and urge people to consider a different perspective.

Part of me still feels ashamed that it took so long to get to that place. I knew what gun violence could do to people. I lived it. I knew what people went through and were going through every day, and it still took me years to change my mind. It took me years to arrive at a place where I finally felt confident enough to speak out. Looking back though, I had important inner work to do before I could begin to do any of this. I had to learn how to come back to my life after tremendous trauma. I had to begin to heal and get to know myself again. Ultimately, I think I had to see for myself the impact that the lack of action has on victims and their families. And for me it took a little while to really feel those effects—to really feel abandoned by my fellow believers.

To be honest, I don't love admitting that. Admitting that it took the trauma of being a survivor to push me into action makes me afraid other people need to see it up close and personally in order to come to the same conclusions. I think that's how it works for a lot of people, and that's a problem. Because that's not how things should be. That's not how loving our neighbors and fighting injustices should work. We are called to fight injustice because it grieves God's heart when any part of our community suffers—whether we experience it personally or not.

Scripture tells us all we need to know about how to love and support our neighbors. "Therefore encourage one another and build each other up, just as in fact you are doing," we read in 1 Thessalonians 5:11. Or consider 1 Corinthians 10:24, "No one should seek their own good, but the good of others." Isaiah 1:17 instructs us, "Learn to do right; seek justice. Defend the oppressed. Take up the cause of the fatherless; plead the case of the widow." Finally, Jesus tells us in Mark 12:31, "'Love your neighbor as yourself.' There is no commandment greater than these." In Romans 12:15 we are told to "mourn with those who mourn."

We are told these things because we belong to each other. We are created as different parts, but all of the same body. In 1 Corinthians 12:24-26 Paul says, "But God has put the body together, giving greater honor to the parts that lacked it, so that there should be no division in the body, but that its parts should have equal concern for each other. If one part suffers, every part suffers with it; if one part is honored, every part rejoices with it." We cannot be separated from one another. We cannot separate rejoicing and we cannot separate mourning.

When I was shot, I often heard, "At least it was only your hand!" It's true. I was wounded; "only" my hand was wounded. It took the brunt of the trauma. Yet, my entire body suffered. I couldn't pretend my hand didn't exist, and I couldn't ignore the pain emanating from that part of my body because it's all part of me. When one part of the body of Christ suffers, we all should feel that suffering. When one part of the body of Christ experiences the trauma of gun violence, we should come closer—bearing the burden of it and recognizing that until that part of our body is whole, none of us will be whole.

I confess to you, reader, I am not a theologian. But it sure seems like God is trying to tell us something, don't you think? Throughout Scripture we are consistently told to love our neighbor, encourage them, and build them up. We are told to carry their burdens, defend them, take up their cause, and plead their case. We are even told to only seek the good of others. And above it all, we are to love them as we love ourselves. If something is our neighbor's burden, it is our burden too. Gun violence is your neighbor's problem, so it is your problem too.

I'm thankful that God opened my eyes to this at age twenty-six. I'm thankful to have the perspective I have now. This is the reason I believe so strongly in sharing our stories and putting faces to issues and experiences because it helps make them real to other people who have not had the same ones. If I don't tell my story, how will people know what it was like or why things need to be different?

This perspective is why I thought, for sure, my story would help all the people out there who fought against gun control to change their minds. It's also why it was a tough pill (like one of those horse-sized ones) to swallow when I discovered it wouldn't be as simple as I thought.

It's personal.

I should have known it wasn't going to be easy to change hearts and minds when it came to guns. After all, not only had I grown up familiar with gun culture but also I knew full well the devotion and dedication people have to it. It took me a long time to come around, and I was actually shot with a gun. Still, there was this tiny part of me that just assumed when people heard my story of pain and trauma, they would suddenly realize how terribly wrong they had been about guns. They would be so overcome with empathy for me they would instantly change their minds, right? *Maybe they just don't understand how bad gun violence really is, maybe they just don't see what it's doing to real people,* I told myself.

I regret to inform you, that of course, it wasn't that easy. I regret to inform you that it turns out a lot of people do know and do understand, and even the intimacy of looking into the eyes of a real-life human victim oftentimes isn't enough.

This, for me, is the hardest part about being a victim of gun violence who does advocacy work. I am not a bystander; I am in it. It is personal.

It's not an idea, theory, or statistic—it's my life. When people don't agree with me about guns, it often feels like they not only disagree with my opinions, but they disagree with me as a person—with my experience. Victims of gun violence who are desperate for change are forced to hold up their personal suffering like some sort of protest sign and say, "Look at my pain. Look at my experience. Look at what I've suffered—don't you want to help me? Don't you want to stop this?" And people shrug their shoulders and they say "No" or "That's not the right way to do it" without offering a better one. They are able to turn and look away and not think another second about it. The realization of my pain not being enough for some people is one that chips away little pieces of my heart every time. I don't know if this part will get any easier because right now it mostly feels like someone is kicking me in the lungs.

I say I wish it got easier to bear because that would be, well, easier. But the truth is that pain is part of what keeps us all going when it feels impossible and the efforts seem futile. The pain is what hangs around in the back of my mind, reminding me I shouldn't have had to go through this, and that I don't want anyone else to have to either. The pain is what pushes me to fight and to speak out and to work as hard as I can to reduce gun violence rates as much as possible. The hurt I feel is what drives me to keep going to try to keep anyone else from having to feel it too. The panicked feeling I get when I envision someday having to send my son into a school is what spurs me on to make schools safer for him and every other child in America. I wish I could do the work without all of these heavy things, but I truly think they are all necessary. I believe God makes beauty from ashes, so I've come to believe maybe the ashes are critical in the making of the beauty.

It's hard to change your mind about something, isn't it? To realize you might be wrong about something you've believed for years of your life is a disorienting experience. We find so much of our identity in our belief systems and our opinions; when one of the threads gets pulled, it begins to feel like the whole thing might unravel with it.

That's how I felt. I still feel that way sometimes. Especially when I'm talking to people I knew when I was younger who remember me a certain way with certain beliefs. I've been asked a few times why I changed everything I believe in. What a casual and very easy breezy question to be asked. The truth is, though, I didn't change everything I believe in. I think I just decided what I believe in should look a different way.

At its core, the issue of gun violence is so much more than an argument over whether or not we should have stricter gun laws. When I think about ending gun violence, I think about children being able to go to school to learn math instead of learning how to hide. I think about babies in their car seats who will live through the drive home without a bullet flying into their car. I think about neighborhoods and cities not being torn apart by gunfire whizzing across the streets and through windows. I think about teenagers who can't see a way out of their sorrow having access to mental healthcare instead of their parents' gun. When I think about ending gun violence, I think about women in abusive relationships that would have another day to get out before their partner used a gun to murder them. I think about a world where fewer people die at the hands of police officers because the fear of guns being in the hand of everyone on the street is a distant memory. I imagine Americans going to the movies and concerts and church without glancing toward the exit signs to make an escape plan. I think about bodies remaining whole, with no gunshot wounds destroying bone and tissue. I imagine myself picking up my son without struggling because both of my hands are perfect, neither one familiar with the devastation of a bullet.

Are you picturing it with me? Don't these images look a bit more like the abundant life Jesus speaks about than the ones we see right now?

What I know of Jesus is that he calls us to life and life abundant, and yet what we seem to have created, often invoking his name in our handiwork, is more like death and death abundant. This realization is ultimately what did it for me, what changed me. In his book *Beating*

Guns, author Shane Claiborne writes, "Some will say all we can do is pray. That is a lie." It is a lie because every day we are given a choice. In a choice between life and guns, I'm going to choose life. I'm going to choose even the hope for life over the current reality of lives ravaged by guns and bodies and minds torn apart by bullets. Every day we are given a choice, and I'm going to choose life. I'm hoping you will too.

PART 2

OUR SOCIETAL
CHALLENGE

8

DOMESTIC VIOLENCE, FAMILY FIRE, AND FIREARM SUICIDE

EVERY NUMBER IS A PERSON

Sometimes I hate talking about gun violence statistics. It's easy to hear numbers and percentages and forget each number represents a real person. We get number fatigue. Maybe it's a defense mechanism on our part. It's hard to fathom these numbers sometimes, and it's sad and scary to picture a face with each one. I would like to ask you, though, as we begin this chapter, to do just that. I'm going to be giving you a lot of numbers. It's the only way to talk about gun violence. But I'd like to ask you to never forget that every number represents a person, someone just like you and me. If gun violence isn't already personal to you, then make it personal. Picture the faces of someone you love when you read the numbers. This conversation means nothing if a number is just a number—it has to be personal. It's going to be uncomfortable and hard—but important things often are.

Every day in the United States, more than one hundred people are shot and killed and two hundred people survive gunshot injuries.

That's over three hundred lives every day irrevocably changed because of a gun.[1] Of course, it doesn't stop there. They've got parents, grandparents, aunts and uncles, cousins, and children. They've got friends and coworkers and neighbors. Now all of their lives are changed too. Maybe there were witnesses to the shooting or bystanders who ran for their lives who are now living with the trauma of what they saw. Then there are the first responders who are called to administer first aid to the victims and have a front-row seat to the injuries. And we can't forget the emergency room doctors and nurses, the trauma surgeons and operating room staff who are responsible for attempting to save the lives and limbs of their patients, left forever with the images of the wreckage left by bullets. And we must remember the ones responsible for telling the patient's loved ones they'll never be coming home or their bodies will never be the same again.

The person who did the shooting has a ripple too. They have families and friends, and their lives are now changed forever, possibly for generations to come. They will have their own grief process to walk through. Before we know it, thousands of lives are forever altered in a span of twenty-four hours, only to repeat the next day, and the day after that.

I lay it out this way for a reason. When I say, "One hundred people are shot and killed every day in the United States, and two hundred ten are injured and survive," you will probably remember those numbers. While those numbers are helpful in examining the rates of gun violence, they aren't the whole picture of how gun violence affects our communities. If we want to gain a full picture of what gun violence is doing to our country, we have to do our best to examine every aspect and every ripple, and we have to remember it is largely unquantifiable. The numbers are where it starts but far from where it ends.

When we think of gun violence, it can be easy to only think of Columbine, Sandy Hook, Virginia Tech, Las Vegas, and Parkland. These tragedies and others like them make up the large majority of the types of gun violence we see in the news. The events permeate our culture and stay with us forever. Yet they are not representative of the

types of gun violence impacting us every single day. I wonder sometimes if that's why people don't understand what a large crisis gun
violence actually is. If they don't see it in the news, they feel like it isn't
happening. If they do know it's happening, it's easier to ignore it if the
news alerts aren't popping up on their screens.

Every day, neighborhoods and communities are devastated by
gun violence. Firearm suicides, domestic violence incidents, and unintentional shootings by children are the types of gun violence that
ravage communities and often go unnoticed and unacknowledged.
If we want to reduce rates of gun violence in America, we have to
pull back the curtain on how every single category is affecting this
country and its people.

In these chapters, I'm going to outline various types of gun violence,
how they affect communities, and the ways we can work to reduce
them. While I wish this could be an exhaustive resource of gun violence and that I could include every single statistic, that's not the goal.
This is a starting point for you, meant to be a big picture, zoomed-out
view of the issue that will equip you so that if you want, you can dig
further into the information on your own.

THE GUNS IN OUR HOMES ARE KILLING US

On March 23, 2013, Hollie Jo Ayers dropped off her two-year-old son
for a supervised visit with her ex-husband in Petersburg, Pennsylvania.
At their meeting, her husband shot her in the legs and her face. She
survived, but he murdered their son before fatally shooting himself.
Prior to the shooting, she took out a restraining order against him,
which meant he shouldn't have been able to possess a firearm. However,
due to laws in Pennsylvania, he was not required to surrender any
firearms he already owned.[2]

Every month in the United States fifty-two women, on average, are
shot to death by an intimate partner, and many more are shot and
survive their injuries.[3] If you are a woman in America, you are twenty-
one times more likely to be shot and killed than women in any other

high-income country.[4] And if you are a woman living in violence and a gun comes into the hands of the abuser? You are five times more likely to die at their hands.[5] Beyond the yearly statistic, a staggering one million women alive today reported being shot or shot at by an intimate partner.[6]

The use of guns by domestic abusers doesn't always end in death or even physical injury. About 4.5 million women in the United States today reported being threatened with a gun by an intimate partner.[7] Guns are frequently used by abusers to control their partners and as a weapon in the act of psychological terrorism. Victims watch as their partners clean their guns at the kitchen table, reminding them that they have no control over their lives; one wrong thing, one mess up, and they'll be shot. A lot of abusers even use the possibility of using a gun as a threat. Dr. Tami Sullivan, the director of Family-Violence Research at Yale University told *The Trace* in 2018, "The fear of a firearm threat—just the fear of the threat—is significantly associated with PTSD."[8]

The connection between shootings and domestic abusers is un-deniable. When a shooting makes the national news, I wait to hear about their history of violence against women. Even boys at just seventeen or eighteen years of age who commit acts of gun violence at school have a history of abusing girlfriends or other women in their lives. It is now a familiar refrain, and research backs it up. Research conducted by Everytown for Gun Safety, America's largest gun violence prevention organization, concluded that in 54 percent of mass shootings between January 2009 and December 2017, the perpetrator shot an intimate partner or family member.[9] The analysis also shows shooters often had histories of stalking or harassment.

The thing about guns and domestic violence is that guns in the hands of abusers often end up harming far more people than just those in their homes. They kill children, law enforcement officers, first responders, and even themselves. A study published in 2013 analyzed the deaths of law enforcement officers in the line of duty and showed that 95 percent of deaths in response to domestic disturbances between

1996 and 2010 were from a firearm.[10] For law enforcement, domestic disturbance calls are the deadliest assignments they take. For children under age thirteen who die of gun homicide, almost one-third are connected to intimate-partner violence or family violence. In an analysis of data done by Everytown, they found that 80 percent of child victims of mass shootings died in incidents connected to domestic violence or family violence.[11] The research also provides evidence to show that children who witness the death of their parent this way often suffer from PTSD, behavioral problems, and suicidal thoughts. This damage inflicted on children can follow them their entire lives, affecting school performance and the trajectory of their lives.

As I write this section about guns and domestic violence, I truly feel overwhelmed by all the statistics and numbers I am throwing at you. It feels too big to fit into a section in this book. It feels like I have notes written on index cards (which I do), and they are covering the floor of my home (which, at times, they are) and I have to figure out a path through to get where I need to go. I am trying to choose the statistics to accurately portray the gravity of this issue because I don't want you to miss it. But, honestly, they all feel like that. Because people who begin their use of firearms to inflict violence on their intimate partners often end up using the guns on children, law enforcement officers, first responders, in mass shootings, or even on themselves. It feels never-ending.

Hope isn't lost, though. Through a variety of methods, we have a path forward to help drastically reduce incidents of firearm assaults in domestic violence situations.

CLOSE THE BOYFRIEND LOOPHOLE

One of the most important things that can be done to help victims of domestic violence is to close what is widely known as "The Boyfriend Loophole." Currently, federal law prohibits people from possessing or purchasing a gun if they have been convicted of domestic violence and/or are under a restraining order, but only if the abuser has been married to, lives with, or has a child with the victim. It doesn't cover abusive dating partners.[12] This is a shortcoming of a law that feels increasingly more outdated as family structures have become more diverse and varied. The number of homicides committed by dating partners has been increasing since 1980, and now women are more likely to be murdered by a dating partner than a spouse.[13] This is why even though federal law does prohibit convicted domestic abusers from buying and owning guns, so many are able to do it anyway. If a dating partner is convicted of assault on their partner, it is often a charge of "simple assault," and in most states someone convicted of simple assault is still allowed to purchase a weapon. So, if a potential purchaser of a gun is a dating partner who doesn't have children with the victim, doesn't live with them, and has never been married, the NICS (National Instant Criminal Background Check System) will clear them to purchase a gun.

We need to change the law to reflect the reality of who is committing the violence. Dating partners are killing women because current law gives allowances for them to do so. We must close the boyfriend loophole to make sure people convicted of a violent misdemeanor against former or current dating partners, living partners, and family members are prohibited from buying and possessing firearms and ammunition.

CLOSE THE STALKING LOOPHOLE

Another gap in the current federal law is a loophole known as "The Stalking Loophole." As it stands, federal law does not prohibit people convicted of misdemeanor stalking crimes from having guns.[14] Twenty states and Washington, DC, have passed laws prohibiting all convicted stalkers from possessing firearms.[15] Twenty states and DC have adopted laws prohibiting abusive dating partners who have been convicted of domestic violence crimes from possessing firearms,[16] and twenty-one states and DC prohibit dating partners under domestic violence restraining orders from having firearms.[17] One study of female murder victims in ten cities in the United States found that 76 percent of those murdered and 85 percent of those who survived an attempted murder by a current or former intimate partner experienced stalking during the year prior to the murder. Stalking is one of the strongest predictors of future violence.[18]

In states like these where firearm prohibition laws have been broadened to include abusive dating partners, research shows a 16 percent decrease in intimate-partner firearm homicide rates.[19] The same study also found the same laws to be associated with a 13 percent decrease in intimate-partner homicide rates overall.[20]

States that have reduced their rates of intimate-partner firearm deaths have shown us what works. We need federal legislation to close the stalking loophole and prohibit anyone convicted of misdemeanor stalking crimes from purchasing or possessing firearms and ammunition.

CLOSE THE CHARLESTON LOOPHOLE

This loophole got its name because it's how the shooter who murdered nine people at the Emanuel AME Church in Charleston, South Carolina, in 2015 was able to purchase his gun. Current federal law requires that all licensed gun dealers run background checks on every gun buyer. However, due to a provision added to the 1993 Brady Bill at the urging of the National Rifle Association, the law allows for sales to proceed if the background check hasn't been returned after three business days. So even if the dealer doesn't receive confirmation the buyer is legally allowed to have a gun, by default they are allowed to sell the gun to the prospective buyer.

FBI data shows that from 2005 to 2016, 6,700 firearms were sold to individuals with prohibitive domestic violence records because the background checks were not returned until after three business days.[21] This resulted in the cases being transferred to the Bureau of Alcohol, Tobacco, Firearms, and Explosives for them to retrieve the purchased firearms. During the same time period, 20,000 background checks involving people with domestic violence records and protection orders didn't come back within three business days, but those dealers chose not to transfer the firearm.[22]

We need federal legislation that closes this loophole nationwide. If the background check system has this much trouble completing the background checks in the allotted time, then the law needs to change to reflect reality.

Notification to local authorities should be required when a domestic abuser or convicted stalker tries to buy a gun and fails a background check. As it stands, federal law does not require the federal authorities to notify state and local authorities if someone who is prohibited from buying a gun tries to buy one and subsequently fails a background check. Many gun rights activists will say it's a right-to-privacy issue, but it isn't. It is breaking the law. It is a criminal act to attempt to buy a gun when you are legally not allowed to buy one. Laws need to be passed at the federal level to require the businesses running background checks to notify local law enforcement when someone fails a background check. Nine states currently have these laws on the books. Additionally, resources need to be dedicated to investigating and prosecuting abusers who falsely state they aren't prohibited from possessing firearms when they try to buy guns. This could further protect victims by identifying abusers and stalkers who may then attempt to buy a gun through illegal avenues. Victims of abuse also deserve to be notified if their abuser attempts to buy a gun so they can be connected with resources for protection.

We need legislation requiring all states to have mandated reporting to local authorities when a domestic abuser who is prohibited from buying a firearm fails a background check. Protocols must be in place along with resources allocated to further investigate each instance of failed background checks. Victims should also be able to choose to be notified if their abuser attempts to purchase a firearm.

States should require abusers to turn in their guns once they are prohibited from possessing them. Only twenty states and DC require abusers under domestic violence restraining orders to turn in their guns, and only sixteen states and DC require abusers convicted of domestic violence misdemeanors to do so. Only fifteen states[23] require all individuals convicted of domestic violence crimes to turn in their guns.[24] Even fewer states actually require proof that the abuser has relinquished their weapons. One 2009 study found that cities with relinquishment laws saw a 25 percent decrease in domestic gun homicides compared to cities without them.[25] In some states that have relinquishment laws, judges simply do not order abusers to turn in their weapons. Everytown for Gun Safety analyzed Rhode Island's relinquishment policy and found that between 2012 and 2014, judges ordered only 5 percent of abusers with domestic violence histories to turn in their guns. Even in the cases where a judge knew the abuser had access to a gun or had threatened to use one, the order to surrender the guns was only issued for 13 percent of cases.[26]

Part of the problem with relinquishment laws seems to be that police departments and local authorities either aren't familiar with them or don't have the resources to enforce them. In some cases, there simply isn't a protocol for the seizure of the weapons or for what to do with the weapons once they have been seized by law enforcement. Many police departments do not have the space to store them and don't want to be responsible for them. There are solutions to these problems, though. In California, a system was instituted where the convicted abuser calls and leaves a voicemail identifying all of their guns. The gun owners then choose to either sell the guns, store them with a licensed gun dealer, or turn them over to law enforcement.

Every state needs to pass relinquishment laws and require proof that the convicted person has relinquished all firearms and ammunition in their possession. State governments must help their localities develop protocols and provide the resources to enforce them.

REQUIRE UNIVERSAL BACKGROUND CHECKS

Second Amendment activists argue that universal background checks won't help because criminals don't obey laws. However, it's simply untrue that these laws wouldn't help prevent convicted criminals from purchasing guns. Since the FBI created the National Instant Criminal Background Check System (NICS) in 1998, 400,000 gun sales to domestic abusers have been blocked. Every year one in nine failed background checks is a domestic abuser.[27] We have the proof right there that background checks work to protect victims of domestic abuse, which is why we need to expand background checks in all states to be required for private gun sales and sales at gun shows.

Every state needs to pass universal background check laws to ensure we are preventing as many domestic abusers as possible from obtaining weapons.

IMPROVE DOMESTIC VIOLENCE RECORDS IN THE BACKGROUND CHECK SYSTEM

The background check system is only as good as the records being fed into it. A report issued in 2016 by the United States Government Accountability Office indicated that many court records for abusers are missing from the background check system, and others aren't flagged correctly. According to the report, the FBI completed 90 percent of denials involving misdemeanor crime of domestic violence convictions within seven business days.[28] This was a longer time period than any other prohibiting category. When states submit records to the NICS, they aren't required to flag records prohibiting a person from obtaining guns, causing delays in the background check process. Arrest records are often not updated to show whether the arrest was followed by a conviction, creating a need for further investigation. And as we learned before, if the investigation takes longer than three business days, the gun sale can proceed.

If the current background check system is unable to fulfill the requests for background checks within three days to comply with federal law, then either the system needs to be overhauled, or the law needs to be changed. Until then, law enforcement should be required to flag records that would prohibit the person from purchasing a gun. This would speed up the current system tremendously and make it more effective at the same time.

◉ ◎ ◉

When it comes to gun violence, we often have the tendency to throw up our hands and say, "We don't know what to do! We don't know what works!" And sometimes it's true. Sometimes it feels too big and too overwhelming to see the solution. This, though, isn't that. When it comes to intimate-partner and domestic gun violence, we have the research. We have the statistics that show what works. At this point, not acting on what we know is willful complicity. With every day we allow women to be shot and murdered by an intimate partner, we are sending a clear message to women that we do not care enough to do anything, that we don't care enough about their pain and their trauma to save women like them. We are saying, "We care more about the right to access a firearm than your right to your life and your safety." We are saying, "We don't think domestic and intimate-partner violence are violent enough to warrant infringing on the rights of others." We are saying these things; we just aren't using words.

FAMILY FIRE

In March of 2018 in Aberdeen, Mississippi, a nine-year-old boy fatally shot his thirteen-year-old sister in the back of the head after she refused to give him the video game controller. The boy had gone over to his mother's nightstand and got the gun. Thinking it was a toy, he had walked up behind his sister and shot her. The mother was home at the time of the shooting. Mississippi has no laws requiring safe storage of a firearm, and they don't require a gun safety device to be provided with each purchase of a handgun which is at odds with federal laws. The police sheriff blamed violent video games.

By the end of today, eight children will be injured or killed as a result of this type of gun violence,[29] often referred to as *family fire*, the term used to describe shootings involving unsecured firearms in the home. It will repeat again tomorrow, and the next day after that.

In the United States today

- 4.6 million kids live in a home where a gun is loaded and unlocked.[30]

- Every year, 350 children under the age of eighteen unintentionally shoot themselves or someone else, and nearly 77 percent of these shootings happen inside of a home.[31]

- Six hundred and thirty-seven children die by gun suicide every year; with 80 percent of them using a gun they got at their home, a relative's home, or from a friend.[32]

- In acts of gun violence on school grounds, almost 80 percent of shooters aged eighteen and under got their guns from their home or from the home of someone they know.[33]

These types of shootings are often reported in the news using the term "accidental shooting," but the truth is these shootings aren't accidents. Unlocked and unsecured weapons inside of our homes are killing our children, and they are all preventable.

A severe lack of safe-storage laws and requirements for gun owners puts millions of kids at risk. Research from the Center for Injury Research and Policy found that even though most parents assume their kids don't know where their guns are kept, 75 percent of kids knew exactly where to find the guns.[34]

SAFE-STORAGE LAWS

Federal law requires gun dealers to provide a gun safety device or secure gun storage with every handgun sale, however there is no federal law requiring gun owners to actually use the device or adhere to any other type of safe storage requirement. As usual, laws vary at the state level. Six states, along with Washington, DC,[35] have laws requiring the owners of firearms to secure them.[36] San Francisco and

New York City have local ordinances that mandate gun owners must secure their guns when they are not in their possession.

Fourteen states have passed what are called Child Access Prevention (CAP) Laws,[37] and those CAP laws can be different in each state.[38] The weakest CAP laws prohibit adults from providing guns to minors, and the strongest CAP laws impose criminal liability on adults who allow minors unsupervised access to firearms. Even in the states that allow for liability of adults, the standards vary widely. Even the definition of *minor* varies from state to state with definitions ranging from under fourteen to under eighteen. One thing we do know is that states with CAP laws saw an 11 percent decrease in firearm suicide rates among teenagers ages fourteen to seventeen.[39] It's not just the firearm owners and their households who are safer when their weapons are properly secured; all of us are safer. A study published in 2005 showed "households that locked both firearms and ammunition were associated with a 78 percent lower risk of self-inflicted firearm injuries and 85 percent lower risk of unintentional firearm injuries among children, compared to those that locked neither."[40]

Often when safe-storage laws are mentioned, people push back by saying the whole point of having a gun in the home is for self-defense and that it must be readily accessible if it's going to be of use. At face value, this seems like a valid pushback and it might deter someone from thinking safe-storage laws are doable. However, this is based on a common misunderstanding about safe storage. In reality, there are many options to securely store your firearm that allow for access to the gun in a matter of seconds, while still keeping others safe.

Safe storage of firearms should be the foundation of being a responsible gun owner. Gun owners should understand the damage firearms could inflict when in the wrong hands or the hands of our littlest family members. This is a great starting point where both sides of the gun reform debate can come together to find a path forward. Leaving a deadly firearm in a place where anyone can find and use it is not an action of a responsible gun owner.

Home invasion statistics can be difficult to track, because agencies often use different terms for them in their reporting. However, according to the FBI's Supplementary Homicide Reports, "430 burglary-related homicides occurred between 2003 and 2007 on average annually."[41] This number equals less than 1 percent of all homicides during that period. And between 2003 and 2007, "approximately 2.1 million household burglaries were reported to the FBI each year on average. Household burglaries ending in homicide made up 0.004 percent of all burglaries during that period."[42]

Research consistently shows that having access to a firearm doubles your risk of homicide and triples your risk of suicide. Beyond that, it is estimated anywhere from 200,000 to 500,000 guns are stolen each year.[43] Being irresponsible with guns in our homes will translate to others being irresponsible with guns on our streets. People often use the argument that "criminals will always find ways to get guns" to argue against meaningful gun reform. It turns out that the statement is often true, and it is often those who claim to be responsible gun owners who allow it to happen.

When it comes to family fire shootings, we treat them as if they are some horrible, unavoidable tragedy where no one is at fault. We treat the parents involved as if they are innocent victims of a freak accident. Instead of simply admitting that the gun and the irresponsible be-havior of the gun owner are at least part of the problem, we look all around, searching desperately for anything and everything else to blame. Meanwhile, a child lays dead in the ground because the person who is supposed to keep them safe made a gun accessible to them, and because a country where they should be given the right to life con-tinues to operate as if the right to bear arms is more important. Even in the case in Mississippi, a thirteen-year-old girl died because a mother left a loaded firearm unattended on her nightstand, and we still blamed video games.[44] Blaming video games makes it easier to convince ourselves it isn't our fault and ultimately makes it easier to continue to deny the need for better gun laws and policies.

These deaths are not accidental, and they are not unavoidable. We know that without safe-storage laws children will have unsupervised access to guns. We know that without the same laws, no one can be held liable for the deaths or injuries of eight children a day. And we know that when a gun is present, no matter the situation, death is always a possibility. We have chosen these deaths. We have collectively decided the deaths of these children is the price we are willing to pay to let gun owners do as they please with their weapons. The evidence is there; we simply have to choose to believe it.

FIREARM SUICIDE

Often when I recite the statistics about yearly gun violence deaths in the United States, I am met with the same question: "Well, how many of those are suicides?" The question always made me feel uncomfortable but I could never quite put my finger on why. When I first started advocating for gun reform and educating people about gun violence, I would simply answer the question: "About 23,000."[45] I would think, *This is a huge number! People have to care about this!* But somehow, for many people, the opposite was true. This number, roughly two-thirds of yearly gun deaths, for some reason gave people permission to care less about gun violence, as if these deaths aren't really deaths or as if these people matter any less than a person who is shot and killed by someone else. "Well, those shouldn't be included," they would say. "They chose that for themselves. They made the choice." For some people, thinking of someone doing this to themselves takes away the sting. Without the idea of an immediate threat to others or a dangerous person with a gun, people felt freed from a responsibility to care. We are conditioned to think of the person as the danger, instead of viewing the gun as inherently dangerous. Therefore, firearm suicide simply doesn't seem as bad, urgent, or devastating as something like a mass shooting.

In general, we don't really understand suicide and we don't really talk about it. Still today, there is shame, embarrassment, and a stigma attached to the discussion. Even attributing suicide to mental illness comes with a stigma because we don't really know how to talk about it. We have a pattern and a history of ignoring things that are difficult to understand and discuss. Instead of confronting them head-on, we hide them away, allowing them to embed themselves deeply into the fibers of our society and spread until the problem is too big to ignore. By then, though, we have no idea how to talk about it. All of this has allowed us to ignore firearm suicide and to treat it as if it isn't really a form—the largest form—of gun violence.

I'll be the first to admit this used to be me. I would've heard the number of the firearm suicides and immediately written off the issue of gun violence as not being as bad, or accusing advocates for gun reform of inflating the numbers by including the people who died by firearm suicide. I didn't understand suicide in general, and I surely didn't understand how the presence and availability of guns increases the risks—not only for those who are already considering suicide, but also for everyone in the home. I think in order to gain widespread support for measures to help end gun violence, we have to gain widespread understanding of suicide and how firearms impact it. Without it, we will always be able to explain away the numbers, instead of truly feeling their impact.

Each year in the United States, 23,000 lives are lost to firearm suicide.[46]

This is sixty-three people every single day.

This is 1,100 children and teenagers every year.[47]

This is two-thirds of all gun violence deaths and makes up one-half of all suicides.

The firearm suicide rate in the United States is currently ten times higher than that of other high-income nations and sadly, the numbers of firearm suicide in the United States is only increasing. The rates of firearm suicides have gone up by 19 percent over the past decade. For children and teens, the increase is even higher, areas with an increase of 65 percent over the last ten years. White Americans make up 86 percent of firearm suicide victims—the highest rate by race.

Rural areas of the country have far higher rates of firearm suicide than urban areas, with the most rural 2.5 times higher than the most urban areas.[48] No demographic or location in the United States is immune to the risks of firearm suicide.

GUNS MAKE SUICIDE FATAL

Why are guns the problem? This is the question I am asked most often when it comes to firearm suicide. Why go after guns? Why not advocate for better mental health services? Well, we can do both. But we still have to talk about the guns.

There is a widespread misconception when it comes to suicide, one I have believed myself, that for people who struggle with suicidal ideation, death by suicide is inevitable regardless of means. Although I didn't know it by name, I believed in something called *means substitution*, which is the idea of people finding another way to attempt suicide even if they can't gain access to a gun.[49] However, the truth is most people who attempt suicide don't die unless they use a gun. Only 5 percent of all suicide attempts not using guns end in death.[50] Yet 85 percent of suicide attempts using guns end in death.[51] Guns make suicide fatal. Beyond that, most people who survive a suicide attempt do not go on to die by suicide.[52] According to the *New England Journal of Medicine* 70 percent of suicide attempts occur within an hour of the person's decision to do so, and 24 percent of those occur within five minutes of the decision.[53]

Not everyone who attempts suicide has a long history of mental health struggles. For some, their lives can change in an instant, prompting such intense levels of suffering that suicide feels like the only option. In a moment of crisis, filled with crushing despair and the belief that the only way to end the pain is to end your life, the presence of a gun makes that moment, that one short moment . . . deadly. For a teenager going through a devastating relationship breakup or experiencing horrific bullying, access to a gun makes their pain fatal. For a man experiencing sudden job loss and feeling the pressures of supporting his family, access to a gun makes his feelings of hopelessness fatal. Research shows that access to a firearm, whether through personal or household gun ownership, increases a person's risk of suicide by three times.[54] This number even takes into account other factors such as poverty, unemployment, mental illness, and substance abuse. This truth applies to every single person living in the same vicinity as the gun, not just the owner of the weapon.

There are countless factors contributing to suicide attempts. We can talk about systemic injustice. We can talk about job loss and debt. We can talk about addiction and alcoholism. We can talk about depression and various forms of mental illness. We can discuss lack of mental health services and the prohibitive costs of the services available. We can talk about the stigmas, which make it more difficult to seek help. But the numbers and the facts prove it: if we don't talk about the accessibility and presence of guns in connection with suicide, the rest will be meaningless.

WHAT CAN WE DO?

According to Liza Gold, a clinical professor of psychiatry at the Georgetown University School of Medicine and editor of the book *Gun Violence and Mental Illness*, for every step between a suicidal person and a gun, you decrease suicide, injury, and homicide rates.[55] If you keep a gun in your house unloaded, your risk of suicide decreases. If you keep a gun in your house locked and unloaded, your risk decreases even more. If you keep a gun in your home locked and unloaded, and keep the ammunition locked somewhere else, your risk decreases even more than that. By prolonging the time it takes for someone to attempt suicide, the longer they have to decide not to. Once the gun is in the household, it's harder to prolong that period of time. So along with laws requiring safe storage, it's important to examine ways to keep guns out of the house altogether or remove them temporarily to keep people safe.

PERMIT-TO-PURCHASE LAWS

Permit-to-purchase (PTP) laws require every potential purchaser of a gun to obtain a license, or permit, to buy a gun. Currently, just nine states[56] and Washington, DC, have a licensing requirement for firearm purchases.[57] The evidence for the effectiveness of these laws speaks for itself. A study done by the Center for Gun Policy and Research at Johns Hopkins Bloomberg School of Public Health found that after Connecticut enacted its licensing law in 1995, the state experienced a 15 percent reduction in firearm suicide rates.[58] After Missouri repealed its PTP law in 2007, the rates of firearm suicide increased by 16 percent over the following five years. The firearm suicide rate has increased more rapidly in Missouri than in the rest of the United States.[59] These numbers show that having to obtain a license before purchasing a gun can delay an impulsive action, giving the person more time to change their mind or giving someone else a chance to intervene before it's too late.

Permit-to-purchase laws are also shown to make the current background check system more effective. There is evidence that when states combine mandatory licensing or permitting of handgun purchases with comprehensive background checks, lives are saved by lower rates of both firearm homicide and suicide.[60]

PTP laws can also decrease the likelihood of straw purchases, which is when someone buys a gun for someone else, most often a prohibited buyer. Requiring gun buyers to come face-to-face with law enforcement in order to obtain a firearm license can deter people from breaking the law. A straw purchase is how the shooters at Columbine High School in 1999 obtained some of their guns. Reducing straw purchases can help reduce the number of guns that end up circulating illegally and then get into the hands of people who aren't legally allowed to have them.

RED FLAG LAWS

Red Flag Laws (RFL), also known in some states as Extreme Risk Protection Laws, allow loved ones and/or law enforcement to intervene to prevent a person from accessing firearms, whether by preventing them from purchasing new guns or by temporarily removing guns already in their possession. In many instances of gun violence, there were clear warning signs beforehand that the shooter could be a serious threat to themselves or others. By implementing these Red Flag Laws, family members and law enforcement have the option to petition the court for a protective order, called an Extreme Risk Protection Order (ERPO), to temporarily remove guns from someone they believe poses a threat to themselves or others. Once an order is filed, the recipient will receive a notice, and a hearing is held. Due process is followed and if the court finds this person is a danger to themselves or others, then they will be temporarily prohibited from buying or possessing guns. If the person already owns guns, then law enforcement or another authorized party will hold those guns for the duration of the order. Most states allow courts to issue orders that last up to one year; some states, including Illinois and Vermont, allow the orders to last up to six months. In extreme cases, courts also have the option of granting an ex parte order, which is given immediately and without notice to the recipient. These last for a shorter period of time and are an emergency measure used to stop the threat of imminent violence.

Extreme Risk Laws help to fill a gap in the current federal law. Under the current law, a person is only prohibited from having guns if they fall into certain categories: those who have been convicted of certain crimes, found mentally ill by a court or committed to a psychiatric facility, or are subject to a final domestic violence restraining order. People who do not fit into any of those categories but who are displaying warning signs that they are considering suicide or committing a violent act are still legally allowed to buy guns.

Extreme Risk Laws have gained visibility in recent years, however. The first one was actually passed in Connecticut in 1999 after a mass shooting at the state lottery headquarters that left four people dead. Indiana passed a similar law in 2005 after a man killed his mother and a police officer, and wounded four other officers. In the months leading up to that shooting, authorities had seized eight firearms and hundreds of rounds of ammunition, but the state law required they be returned to him. After Indiana passed its Extreme Risk Law in 2005, the suicide rate decreased by 7.5 percent. A study found that for every ten gun removals, one suicide was prevented.[61]

These laws came back into the public view after a shooter in Parkland, Florida, killed seventeen and injured an additional seventeen. The shooter in Parkland was reported multiple times by teachers, students, and his mother after displaying threatening behavior, and he was known to possess firearms. Since then, fourteen states, including Florida, along with Washington, DC,[62] have passed Extreme Risk Laws, bringing the total number of states with a version of this law to nineteen.[63] An analysis of these laws by Everytown found at least 7,119 order petitions were filed between January 2018 and August 2019, and the number is increasing over time.[64]

In February 2020, the Associated Press reported that the Red Flag Laws have been used in Florida 3,500 times since their passing.[65] One of the most interesting aspects of this reporting is that in small communities in Florida, police officers say they rarely need to invoke the law. Instead, the deputies know the community members and are able to intercede quickly if someone is threatening violence against themselves or others. They seek out potential Red Flag cases and ask them to surrender their weapons to a relative who can keep them until they receive mental health treatment. Major Randy Crews in Florida's Baker County told the Associated Press this method has worked well for them and "hasn't backfired," but if someone didn't cooperate, they wouldn't hesitate to use the law. This story shows there can be other ways to intervene in a potential gun violence situation, and Red Flag Laws only strengthen the options.

MANDATORY WAITING PERIODS

A mandatory waiting period may help prevent firearm suicides by requiring a certain number of days between the purchase of a firearm and when the person can actually take possession of it. We have some evidence to show that this would be effective.[66]

SAFE STORAGE

Safe storage isn't just effective for preventing accidental shootings involving children; it can also help prevent firearm suicide. This is especially true for children and teenagers. In over 80 percent of child firearm suicides, the gun belonged to a family member. A study published in the *Journal of the American Medical Association* found that households that safely stored firearms and ammunition were associated with a 78 percent lower risk of firearm suicide than households that didn't.[67] In the states that require safe storage or have Child Access Prevention Laws, there has been an 11 percent decrease in firearm suicide rates in teenagers ages fourteen to seventeen.[68] A study published in 2019 found that if just half of the households with unlocked guns chose to safely store and lock away their guns, 251 firearm suicides involving youths in a single year could have been prevented.[69]

Every year in the United States, around 154,000 Americans die from lung cancer.[70] Eighty to 90 percent of them are linked to cigarette smoking.[71] You know what we do since we know about the risks of smoking? We tell people about the risks. We tell them their risk of getting lung cancer is up to thirty times higher than people who don't smoke. We tell them to stop smoking. But if they don't, and they get lung cancer, we still help them and treat their cancer. When they die, we say they died of lung cancer. Lung cancer is lung cancer whether the person smoked or not. Gun violence is gun violence whether the person hurts themselves or someone else.

Reader, we are not hopeless. Our hands are not tied. We are not unable to do anything about the people who are dying by firearm suicide all around us. But in order to move forward, we're going to have to decide to believe the numbers, trust the evidence, and name the problem. Many things contribute to suicide attempts. But guns make it fatal.

In May of 2018, a high school student in Florida was stalking his girlfriend after she broke up with him. He posted photos of an AR-15 online and threatened to kill himself. Two resource officers filed a petition and all firearms were removed from his home, and no one was harmed.[72] Based on what we know about domestic violence related shootings involving teenage boys, the use of a Red Flag Law in this situation may have prevented a homicide, suicide, or mass shooting. Red Flag Laws are just another tool we can use to save lives and reduce gun violence, from both firearm suicide and homicide—and the good news? They work.

9

SCHOOL AND MASS SHOOTINGS

GUN VIOLENCE IN SCHOOLS

I was eight years old when twelve students and one teacher were killed at Columbine High School on April 20, 1999. My mom picked up my sister and me early from school and when I asked why, she said, "I just wanted you to be with me." I didn't really understand her need until I became a parent myself.

On the way home we listened to the local Christian radio station. When they began talking about the shooting, Mom turned the volume way down and I strained to hear what they were talking about. I remember sitting in the car, quietly listening as my world changed around me. I don't really remember what they said; I just know it was the moment when I realized that getting shot at school was a possibility. That possibility began to weave its way through my life with lockdown drills and learning how to find the best hiding place in every room of our school. My parents shielded us the best they could from the realities of school shootings, and my teachers as-sured us that lockdowns were just drills we had to do, like tornado drills. But once you learn that sometimes kids go to school and never come home again, it's hard to forget.

There were school shootings before the one in Littleton, Colorado. In 1997, a student killed three people and wounded five others at a high school in Paducah, Kentucky. In 1998, five died and ten were wounded at a middle school in Jonesboro, Arkansas. Columbine, however, changed things. It was the first large-scale school shooting where students had cellphones, which offered a more personal look into the tragedy. Even now, images of students walking out of the building, hugging and crying, are flashing in my mind. So much of the tragedy occurred onscreen and in real time. As the day wore on, the number of casualties kept rising, the media kept reporting, and we kept watching. We didn't know what else to do. The events at Columbine changed everything.

The federal government doesn't track school shootings, so data is collected by independent organizations who piece together the numbers from news articles, law enforcement reports, databases, and direct calls to police departments and schools. It's also hard to give accurate numbers as I write this book since they change so often. As of October 2020, 147 people, including children and school staff, have been killed with a gun on school grounds, and 310 have been injured since the attack on Columbine. The *Washington Post* found that, since Columbine, 240,000 children at 249 schools have been exposed to gun violence at school. These numbers don't even include gun incidents on college campuses.[1]

The organization Everytown for Gun Safety tracks every time a firearm is discharged inside or into a school building or on school grounds, including college campuses. Their database includes only incidents in which the gun brought onto campus was discharged. They began tracking incidents at the beginning of 2013 and found that from 2013 to 2019, there have been 549 incidents of gunfire on school grounds causing 129 deaths and 270 injuries.[2]

THE COST OF LOCKDOWNS

"Lockdown, lockdown, lock the door.

Shut the lights off, say no more.

Go behind the desk and hide.

Wait until it's safe inside.

Lockdown, lockdown, it's all done.

Now it's time to have some fun!"[3]

—Lyrics sung to the tune of "Twinkle, Twinkle, Little Star," seen
on a poster at Arthur D. Healy School in Somerville, Massachusetts

I remember the first time we had a lockdown, or active-shooter drill, at school. I was in the fifth grade. They sent home information sheets to all the parents and explained to us that we were just practicing staying safe in case a bad person came to the school wanting to hurt us. When the drill started, it was one student's job to turn off all the lights, and another's to lock the door. We all gathered along the wall beside the door and huddled together on the floor, staying as quiet as possible. I remember someone asking what would happen if we were in the bathroom during a lockdown. We were told to lock the door, stay put, and hide there. I went to the bathroom sparingly. I didn't want to be alone. The teachers always stressed that this was just a drill, and nothing bad was going to happen to us. But it was hard to believe them when we all knew that bad things happened at other schools. When the drills were over, we turned the lights on and were expected to go back to business, pretending like nothing was wrong, as if we weren't just taught how to survive a school shooting.

After I was shot, I was in favor of anything to help prepare students and school staff to respond to a shooting at school. This included active-shooter drills and training on how to treat gunshot wounds. When I was sitting in that room, hiding from a shooter, trying to stop my own bleeding, I felt so unprepared and so unqualified to be dealing with it. I didn't want that for anyone else, and I felt that if school shootings were just going to keep happening, then people should be prepared. I boldly proclaimed in Facebook posts that people needed to stop pretending it couldn't happen at their school and start being prepared. I really believed it, and I don't blame myself for feeling this way. I just never considered the effects these drills were having on kids, even though I can remember how they affected me. I never considered how they were affecting teachers and school staff, who were doing their best to shepherd the kids in their care through a very scary event. And I didn't know a thing about the $2.7 billion school security industry behind the training for school security drills and products such as bulletproof whiteboards, bulletproof backpacks, clear backpacks, and facial recognition software.[4]

Lockdown drills increased after Columbine, and by the 2015 to 2016 school year, 95 percent of schools had lockdown drills, up from 40 percent during the 2005 to 2006 school year. Forty-two states currently require schools to participate in these drills; eight of them designate the requirement as active-shooter drills.[5] The training program many schools use, called ALICE (Alert, Lockdown, Inform, Counter, Evacuate), offers what is called an "options-based" training, essentially presenting different options from which the schools can choose to respond to shooters. They often teach a "run, hide, fight" approach. This means the details of how the drills are to be conducted are often vague and left up to the interpretation of whoever is in charge. There is very little oversight in how students and staff are treated during the drills.

During an active-shooter training exercise at an elementary school in Indiana, law enforcement officers forced teachers to line up and then shot them with air soft rifles. According to one of the teachers, the officers told them, "This is what happens if you just cower and do nothing."[6] Schools in multiple states, including Pennsylvania and Ohio, have allowed the police to fire shotgun blanks during active-shooter drills to expose students to the sound of real gunfire. A school in Muncie, Indiana, played 911 recordings of a teacher pleading for her students to hide during the Columbine shooting.[7] Some schools don't warn students they are just drills, instead allowing them to think there is really an active shooter inside their school. This has prompted some students to send final goodbye text messages to their loved ones, only to find out later that it was just a drill.

In recent years, parents and mental health professionals alike have become increasingly concerned about how these active-shooter drills are affecting students and teachers. One mother in Tucson, Arizona, told NBC News that her son started biting his nails and "refused to go anywhere alone, even to his room or a bathroom at home."[8] One school psychologist, Joy Levinson, said she had patients who soiled themselves at school because the drills made them afraid to go to the bathroom alone.

In Dave Chappelle's Netflix comedy special *Sticks and Stones*, he tells a story about an active-shooter drill at his son's school. It's a poignant commentary on the reality of these drills. He says, "When you're doing these drills, well, aren't you training the shooter too?" It's one of those jokes that feels painful to laugh at, but if you don't, you'll cry. It's also a joke based in truth. Research about how these drills have affected our kids hasn't kept up with how fast the drills have changed, and there is little research that shows the drills are even effective at all. But what we do know about school shooters tells us the student in-volved drills may be counterproductive. A study of mass shooters from 1966 to 2019 found nearly all of the mass school shooters were students who exhibited warning signs before the incident.[9] Not only are kids being traumatized during the active-shooter drills, but po-tential shooters are being trained right alongside of them in the exact protocols and procedures to avoid if and when they decide to bring a gun to school.

What can we do differently? In February 2020, active-shooter drills came to the forefront of the news when a leading gun-control advocacy group and the nation's two largest teacher unions published a policy paper. This paper called on schools to halt extreme active-shooter drills, like the ones that happen without warning and include simulated gunfire and fake wounds.[10] The groups presented recommendations for schools that are backed by research from child psychologists and criminal justice experts, and data from law enforcement. They suggest trauma-informed training for school staff in responding to an active-shooter situation. They don't recommend training for students. If the school does include students in the drills, then students and parents should be informed prior to the event, and drills should not include any simulations that mimic an actual shooting. These organizations also recommend the drill content be age and developmentally appropriate, and created by a team that includes school administrators, teachers, mental health professionals, and law enforcement.

We have a substantial lack of research to prove active-shooter drills for students do anything beyond traumatizing kids and informing potential shooters of protocols. Additionally, for-profit companies such as ALICE charge school district thousands of dollars to provide the training.[11] All the funds going into this type of training could be better spent investing into measures proven to be effective: threat assessment programs, mental health professionals, physical security upgrades, and working to improve the school climate.

In April 2019, a gunman opened fire on the campus of University of North Carolina at Charlotte. A campus-wide message was sent out saying, "Shots reported near Kennedy. Run, hide, fight. Secure yourself immediately." A twenty-one-year-old student named Riley Howell charged at the gunman, who shot him two times and then fired again. The third bullet went into Howell's brain and he died of his injuries. Just over a week later, another shooter opened fire at STEM School Highlands Ranch in Colorado. An eighteen-year-old student named Kendrick Castillo was killed after charging the gunman, attempting to stop his rampage. Castillo would have graduated just two weeks later. We see similar stories about teachers and staff as well. In 2018 a teacher named Jason Seaman tackled a gunman to the floor, allowing his students to hide in the back of the classroom.

The media and people close to the events called the students "heroes," and fellow students reported that they "refused to be victims." By all accounts, these people were heroes, and their actions surely kept other students and staff from being killed or injured. And yet, they lost their lives because they live in a country where, instead of adults taking responsibility for the gun violence epidemic in the United States and working to change gun laws, we teach students they have to be heroes and lose their lives in the process. I can think of no other symptom of our sickness as horrific as this one.

MASS SHOOTINGS

On the night of October 1, 2017, a gunman opened fire on the crowd of people attending the Route 91 Harvest Musical Festival on the strip in Las Vegas, Nevada. Shooting from the thirty-second floor of his hotel room, he fired more than 1,000 rounds of ammunition in just ten minutes. He killed fifty-eight people and wounded 413. This shooting in Las Vegas is the deadliest mass shooting in the history of the United States.[12]

These are the types of mass shootings that most often make the news. They make us pause for a second before entering a movie theater or a concert or even church. They make us scan crowds for anyone who looks out of place. And they are the ones we so often clearly remember seeing on the news for the first time. I still remember where I was and what I was doing when I heard reports of the active shooter in Las Vegas—maybe you do too. The reality, however, is most mass shootings don't make the news the way the shooting in Las Vegas did.

It can be hard to understand what the term *mass shooting* really means. A *mass shooting* is most widely defined as a shooting that kills at least four people, not including the shooter.[13] However, definitions vary widely across organizations, which results in different numbers too. This makes it difficult to find accurate statistics on mass shootings in the United States. Historically we have used two factors in defining mass shootings: how many people were injured or killed, and the type of violence or motivation of that violence. For example, the Gun Violence Archive (GVA) organization, which updates its numbers every single day, doesn't remove any type of shooting from its counting of mass shootings. They include both domestic violence and gang related violence in their tallies, as long as they meet the number requirement of four victims shot and injured or killed. This leads to a much larger count than other organizations. The FBI now uses a different term and definition altogether, referring to these incidents as *active-shooter incidents* and defining an *active shooter* as "one or more individuals actively engaged in killing or attempting to kill people in a populated area."[14] They also exclude gang and drug related violence. In 2019, the FBI reported twenty-nine total incidents as active-shooter incidents,[15] while the GVA reported 417 mass shootings.[16] Obviously, these are widely different numbers.

So which numbers do we use? In my opinion, both are necessary and important numbers to gain a full picture of gun violence. I think that until there is a more widely accepted definition, we should use both numbers and provide a context for both.

Using the narrower definition the FBI utilizes in their numbers is a more appropriate use for the way the general public understands the term *mass shooting*. When we think of a mass shooting, we tend to think of Las Vegas, Virginia Tech, Sandy Hook, or Pulse. For most of us, our minds immediately assume it means an active-shooter situation in a public place. We don't usually equate the same term to a drug deal gone wrong in a private home or a domestic violence–related shooting spree at someone's backyard barbecue. While *mass shooting* may unequivocally mean any shooting where four or more are shot and killed, not including the shooter, it's important to recognize how the public actually understands and uses the term and acts accordingly. At the same time, using the broader definition the GVA uses is just as important because it takes into account the gunshot injuries as well, a number that often doesn't receive much public acknowledgment. I don't know about you, but I want to know how many times in the

United States at least four people are shot in a single gun violence incident. In December 2019, researchers from the Johns Hopkins Center for Gun Policy and Research published a paper in *Injury Epidemiology* recommending a federal definition of *mass shooting* to help improve public awareness and understanding, as well as research credibility.[17]

Everytown uses a definition I think is most helpful for the purposes of understanding the occurrences of mass shootings. For their research purposes, they define a *mass shooting* as any incident in which four or more people are shot and killed, excluding the shooter.[18] Their definition includes any occurrence of this type of shooting, including those in public or private spaces, having one or multiple shooters, and as a result of many different motives. This helps us to understand better how to prevent these types of shootings in the future.

Because of the horrific circumstances of these shootings, the way they affect entire communities, and the extensive media coverage, it may seem like the majority of gun deaths come from mass shootings. However, more than 99 percent of gun deaths in the United States are from other types of gun violence and not mass shootings. In November 2019, Everytown released an analysis titled "10 Years of Mass Shootings in the United States," which included data from 2009 to 2018. During those ten years:

- One hundred and ninety-four mass shootings killed 1,121 people and wounded 836.

- Among the deaths were 309 children and teens and nineteen law enforcement officers.

- Among the injured were 194 children and teens and twenty-three law enforcement officers.

- Sixty-one percent of the shootings occurred in homes.

- Twenty-nine percent occurred in public places.

- Ten percent were a combination of both.

- During this ten-year period, one in three mass shooters were legally prohibited from possessing firearms at the time of the shooting.

- In the mass shootings where the shooter was prohibited from having a gun, 318 people were killed and eighty-seven were injured.[19]

One thing the research has shown repeatedly is the strong connection between mass shootings and domestic violence. We see it in the news over and over; the shooter had a history of family or intimate-partner violence, especially toward women. In 61 percent of the mass shootings between 2009 and 2018, the shooter had a known history of domestic violence. Everytown found in at least 54 percent of mass shootings, the shooter shot a current or former intimate partner or family member during the attack. Domestic violence–related mass shootings account for almost half of all mass shooting deaths and one in ten injuries. Among children who die in mass shootings, 72 percent of them died in one connected to domestic violence.[20]

The analysis by Everytown also found in 54 percent of mass shootings, the shooter exhibited at least one warning sign beforehand.[21] It could be anything from threatening violence to violating a protection order. In the aftermath of public mass shootings we often feel powerless, hearing familiar refrains about how nothing could have prevented these senseless tragedies. However, the fact that so many shooters display warning signs ahead of time proves there is often time to intervene and stop these attacks from happening. We just have to figure out how to do it, and we have to decide it's worth trying.

THE GUNS

After mass shootings, we hear a lot about assault-style weapons and high-capacity magazines, and rightfully so. These are used far more often in public mass shootings than in other types of shootings. The five deadliest shootings in the last ten years (Newtown, Orlando, Parkland, Sutherland Springs, and Las Vegas) all involved the use of assault-style weapons and high-capacity magazines. While handguns are used more often in mass shootings than assault-style weapons, when assault-style weapons were used the shootings left six times as many people shot and are responsible for 32 percent of mass-shooting deaths and 82 percent of mass-shooting injuries.[22]

What can we do? When it comes to reducing mass shootings in America, many of the recommendations are the same as they are for other types of gun violence: universal background checks, closing the loopholes that allow dangerous people to legally purchase weapons, extreme risk laws, and permit-to-purchase laws. A study published in *Criminology & Public Policy* in February 2020 by researchers at the Johns Hopkins Bloomberg School of Public Health analyzed fatal mass shootings and the association between the rates of these shootings and the existence of different firearm laws in forty-five states between 1984 and 2017. Their research found firearm purchaser licensing laws, or permit-to-purchase laws, "that require an in-person application or fingerprinting are associated with an estimated 56 percent fewer fatal mass shootings in states that have them."[23]

Limiting assault-style weapons and high-capacity magazines. In addition to the laws already mentioned, an increasing amount of research supports limiting access to assault-style weapons and high-capacity magazines as a way to reduce mass shootings. The research done by Johns Hopkins also found evidence of laws banning high-capacity magazines, or magazines that hold more than ten rounds of ammunition, were associated with "significant reductions in the rate of fatal mass shootings with four or more fatalities and the number killed in those shootings."[24] Dr. Michael Siegel, a researcher at Boston University, stated, "Whether a state has a large-capacity ammunition magazine ban is the single best predictor of the mass shooting rates in that state."[25]

The federal assault weapons ban. From 1994 to 2004, a federal assault weapons ban, officially called the Public Safety and Recreational Firearms Use Protection Act, was part of the Violent Crime Control and Law Enforcement Act of 1994 signed into law by President Bill Clinton. This law was issued "to prohibit the manu-facture, transfer, or possession of a semiautomatic assault weapon."[26]

The bill banned over a dozen specific guns and certain features on them. It also banned the transfer or possession of large-capacity ammunition devices that carried more than ten bullets. One of the biggest shortcomings of the bill, however, was that it only applied to items manufactured after the bill became law. This essentially provided a loophole for all the weapons and magazines created before the bill was signed. It also allowed the sale or transfer between private parties for these items even after it was signed into law.

When the assault weapons ban took effect, it was signed into law with a ten-year sunset provision, meaning that unless Congress chose to renew it, it would expire after ten years. The law expired in 2004.

While opinions differ about how effective the ban actually was, as time has elapsed, the data researchers have been able to gather has provided evidence that continues to clarify the ways in which the ban did help. A 2018 study in the *Journal of Trauma and Acute Care Surgery* found "mass shooting fatalities were 70 percent less likely to occur from 1994 to 2004, when the federal prohibition on assault weapons and high-capacity magazines was in effect, than during the twelve years studied before and after the prohibition."[27] The researchers also concluded that if there had been an assault weapons ban during the period of time studied when it wasn't in effect, 314 of 448 mass shooting deaths might have been prevented.[28]

Research done at Stanford University found mass shootings decreased during the time the ban was in effect, but in the fifteen years since the ban ended, the trend of these shootings has sharply increased, following a pattern similar to the growth in ownership of assault-style weapons and high-capacity magazines. In their research they defined a *mass shooting* as being an incident in which the gunman killed at least six people. The researchers found that in the ten years after the ban expired, there was a 347 percent increase in gun massacres. Comparatively, the rates of other crimes trended downward. As the number of mass shootings fell during the ban, so did the number of fatalities per shooting event.[29]

It's not that hard to see how and why the assault weapons ban worked. When high-capacity magazines and the guns that use them aren't available for purchase for ten years, it has an effect on gun violence and the resultant deaths. If a person decides to commit a mass shooting but can't access their weapon of choice, even if they follow through with their plans, fewer people will die. Letting the ban expire was devastating for Americans.

According to the National Shooting Sports Foundation, two-thirds of the 8.5 million AR- or AK-assault-style rifles that came onto the market between 1990 and 2012 became available after 2004. It is estimated there are now between fifteen and twenty million assault weapons in the hands of Americans.[30]

Even though there isn't a federal assault weapons ban in place, seven states and Washington, DC,[31] currently have a variation of the ban in place. Two more states, Minnesota and Virginia, regulate these weapons but do not ban them. Some states prohibit specific weapons while other states classify disqualifying features of guns. The District of Columbia even allows its chief of police to designate a specific firearm as an assault weapon if they determine it would pose a similar danger as other assault weapons. Each of these states may also have different policies regarding how they deal with the pre-ban weapons already owned. DC doesn't allow the possession of these weapons at all, while states such as California and Connecticut allow them but require registration for them. New Jersey only allows them for legitimate target-shooting purposes. Their law required over sixty models of assault weapons to be rendered inoperable (destroyed), surrendered to law enforcement, or be transferred out of state.[32]

Taxing assault-style weapons and ammunition. One way activists and experts have offered to reduce the number of assault-style weapons in circulation would be to introduce a heavy tax on them. A proposal by Saul Cornell, a historian at Fordham University, offers tax breaks for gun owners who own gun safes. He wrote, "Taxation offers a more flexible set of tools to achieve a goal all Americans seek: lowering the costs of gun violence to Americans."[33]

Extreme Risk Protection Orders. While Extreme Risk Protection Orders are known to be extremely effective primarily in preventing firearm suicide, a new study done in California outlined twenty-one cases in which a Gun Violence Restraining Order (GVRO, which is their name for an Extreme Risk Order) was used to prevent mass shootings.[34]

In one case, an employee at a car dealership threatened to shoot his supervisor and other employees if he was fired. A manager reported this to the police and a GVRO was obtained the next day. Police seized five firearms from his home, and no one was hurt.

In another case, the California Department of Justice received a report about a twenty-one-year-old who had just been fired and was threatening to shoot coworkers. During their investigation, they found out he had recently purchased a shotgun and the ten-day waiting period was about to run out—just two days later. He was served with a Gun Violence Restraining Order the next day, and the retailer was notified not to transfer the weapon. Law enforcement found 400 rounds of ammunition in his home. This case specifically shows how two different measures, a waiting period and a red flag law, can work together to save lives.[35]

Safe storage laws. Evidence shows that in most school shootings, the gun was obtained from family, relatives, or friends. In their research on school shootings, Everytown was able to identify the gun source in 45 percent of school shootings that involved shooters younger than 18 years old, and they found that "74% obtained the gun(s) from their home or the homes of relatives or friends." A study done by the US Secret Service found that in half of the school shootings between 2008 and 2017, the firearm was easily accessible or not stored securely. Other similar studies show the findings are consistent. Across the board, 73 to 80 percent of school shooters under age eighteen get their guns in the same way: from their homes or the

homes of someone they know. This evidence suggests that laws requiring firearms to be secured safely could have a powerful impact on
reducing school shootings and their deadliness.[36]

CONCLUSION

A new ban on assault-style weapons and high-capacity magazines
could be effective at preventing gun violence today, but only if its
deficiencies are dealt with. And only if it is paired with other prevention measures we know to be effective. Barring a nationwide mandated buy-back program and weapon confiscation, which is unlikely
to happen in the United States, a ban like the 1994 bill will not be effective. The United States has been flooded with weapons and the
accessories to magnify their danger. In that regard, the damage is
done. What we have to do now is acknowledge the obvious: the ban
was effective. Once we do that, we can take what we know worked and
figure out how to use it going forward. A new assault weapons ban
with laws such as permit-to-purchase, universal background checks,
and a tax on these weapons and ammunition could create an incredibly effective way to curb gun violence across the country.

Both mass shootings and school shootings cause far-reaching devastation for both survivors and communities where they live. Although
we shouldn't need scientific studies to be convinced, the studies of
survivors from mass shootings consistently show the damaged mental
health of direct survivors and community members alike. Even people
who only watch coverage on the news in the safety of their living rooms
are known to suffer from increased fear of crime or uncertainty as they
walk around their local grocery store or go see the newest movie. And
it's affecting not only our mental health, but also our local economies
and our healthcare systems. Mass shootings, for years, have wreaked
havoc on our physical and mental health and have caused our children
to grow up in a world where getting shot at school cannot be considered an irrational fear.

We don't have to live like this—having our communities ravaged by gun violence. This can be one of those times where we can actually make the world better for our children, when we can leave things better than what we had. But we're going to have to decide: Do we care more about people's lives, or a distorted interpretation of the right to bear arms? I know which side I want to be on.

In the wake of the shooting at Parkland, a group of survivors started a gun violence prevention organization known as March for Our Lives. They organized the largest single-day protest against gun violence in history and have helped more than 850,000 people register to vote. After the March for Our Lives event in 2018, a record number of forty-six candidates backed by the NRA lost their election bids.[37] There is a movement to end gun violence, and there is hope that we can get it done in this lifetime.

10

THE COSTS OF GUN VIOLENCE IN OUR COMMUNITIES

IF YOU ARE A TAXPAYER, you have been personally affected by gun violence. When we talk about gun violence, we usually do it in terms of the human impact, and rightfully so. The human cost is always the most important issue. However, this means people are often in the dark about the financial cost of gun violence. According to the Giffords Law Center to Prevent Gun Violence, gun violence costs the American economy $229 billion every year.[1] The financial costs are measured by different categories, including healthcare, criminal justice expenses, law enforcement costs, costs to employers, and lost income. This number also reflects the costs of pain and suffering experienced by the victims. However, this number will always be underestimated as there is no possible way to accurately measure lost business opportunities, lowered property values, and lost jobs.

After I was shot, I was left with not only my injuries, but also without the ability to work and with a lifetime of medical needs. After a three month long battle with my employer and their insurance company, I finally got approved for worker's compensation. They paid my medical bills, including counseling and therapy appointments, and my lost wages at a rate of 66 percent, or two-thirds of my salary. It's hard to accurately measure the financial impact this had, and continues to have, on my family and me. And yet, as someone who was wounded at work and was approved for worker's compensation, I will always be one of the fortunate ones, and that will never be lost on me.

If you've never personally been affected by gun violence, it's easy to think the ripples of it haven't affected your life, but it's simply not true. Much of the financial burden of gun violence rests on the shoulders of taxpayers. Law enforcement expenses and criminal justice system costs are almost fully funded by taxpayers. And because approximately 85 percent of gunshot victims are uninsured or on publicly funded insurance, a majority of the healthcare costs for gun violence victims are funded by taxes as well.[2]

Florida has some of the country's weakest gun laws and some of the worst mass shooting tragedies, including the shooting in Parkland that killed seventeen and injured seventeen, and the shooting at Pulse nightclub in Orlando that killed fifty and injured forty-nine. There are more than 6,000 shootings in Florida every year, costing the state over $5 billion.[3] When adding in the estimated costs of pain and suffering, that number rises to over $14.1 billion. The annual cost of gun violence for Florida taxpayers is approximately $950 million. In Pennsylvania, the yearly directly measurable cost of gun violence is over $3 billion, with the estimated annual cost to the taxpayers over $590 million. The state has the thirty-first highest gun death rate in the country.[4]

Are these numbers still feeling too far away? Think of it this way: gun violence costs each American, including you, roughly $700 every year.[5]

The costs of gun violence go beyond this, though, and pervade multiple areas of local economies and the community residents' quality of life. Think about it with me. If an area experiences a surge in the rates of gun violence, how does that affect local businesses? Home values? Quality of life for residents and children? It's not just about the people who get shot and the people who do the shooting, it's about everyone—even the people who live daily with the effects of this crisis without even realizing it. An analysis by researchers at The Urban Institute found sharp increases in gun violence can "significantly reduce the growth of new retail and service businesses and slow home value appreciation." Higher gun violence rates can also be associated with fewer retail and service businesses, fewer new jobs, lower credit scores, and lower homeownership rates. In Minneapolis, each gun homicide in a census neighborhood in a year was related to eighty fewer jobs the next year. In Washington, DC, every instance of ten gunshots in a census tract in a year was related to one business closing.[6]

Business owners in high gun violence areas have to spend a significant amount of money on top of their regular business expenses just to deal with the threat of gun violence. They install bulletproof windows, plexiglass, bars over their windows, and security systems. They hire extra security staff. They reduce their hours to avoid more dangerous times, resulting in reduced income. Even during operating hours, they lock their doors to filter and screen people who want to come inside. For communities that experience a high rate of gun violence, the possibility of being directly affected by it feels imminent. This one fact informs numerous decisions they make on a daily basis. It becomes the way they live their lives. The way gun violence affects local economies and slows an area's population growth helps perpetuate a cycle where gun violence continues to ravage communities that are already at risk.

Instead of identifying gun violence as a cause of economic distress for various communities, we often simply label them "bad neighborhoods" or "the bad side of town." In Roanoke, Virginia, a city right outside of where I grew up, we knew all the "bad areas." We knew the places where we shouldn't even drive down the road. After college, I worked there as a social worker and was often scared to go out on calls because I knew I was going to a place where there was often violence, including gun violence. Driving down the road, my eyes would catch sight of a convenience store with bars on the windows or a retail shop with a gate across the front door, and I would think to myself, "No wonder no one wants to live here." I was ignorant to the systemic injustices affecting these neighborhoods and to the ways we write them off as hopeless or lost causes. I had no framework to understand the cycle of economic depression, due in part to gun violence, affecting certain areas of Roanoke. It's almost a chicken and egg situation. Is the gun violence worse in these areas because they are "bad" areas? Or are they "bad" areas because we've allowed gun violence to consume them, and therefore suppress any chance of economic resilience?

It's time for a widespread acknowledgment of the economic impacts of gun violence. Gun violence isn't just killing people, it's killing communities. It isn't just costing people their lives, their body parts, or their mental health. It's costing them their hopes, their sense of security, and their opportunity to build meaningful lives for themselves and their families. By reducing gun violence, we won't only save lives and prevent the suffering of thousands of people, but also we can help communities rebuild and thrive. We can stop a cycle that continues to oppress our neighbors. I don't know about you, but that seems pretty pro-life to me.

POLICE-INVOLVED GUN VIOLENCE

On July 6, 2016, police officer Jeronimo Yanez pulled over a thirty-two-year-old Black man named Philando Castile for a broken brake light. His partner and her four-year-old daughter were also in the car. After the officer asked for his license and proof of insurance, Castile said to him, "Sir, I have to tell you, I have a firearm on me." The officer told him not to reach for it. Castile repeatedly told him, "I'm not pulling it out" and tried to tell him he was getting his wallet. Before he could, though, the officer pulled out his own gun and fired seven shots into the car. Castile was dead within minutes, the untouched firearm still in his pocket. One year later, Officer Yanez was found not guilty of second-degree manslaughter after his lawyers argued that the presence of a gun, even untouched, even in the possession of someone with a legal permit to have it, was enough to justify the killing of an innocent Black man, pulled over for nothing more than a broken brake light.

In March of 2018, police officers in Sacramento, California, confronted Stephon Clark as he stood in his grandmother's backyard. One officer began shouting "Gun! Gun!" and the officers fired twenty rounds, hitting the twenty-two-year-old Black man eight times, mostly in the back. The officers believed that Clark was holding a gun—but it was a cellphone. Because the officers claimed they believed Clark was pointing a gun at them, they were not charged with any crimes. Clark's family filed a lawsuit against the city, and a year after his death the city awarded the family $2.4 million. The family said most of the money has been placed in a trust for Clark's two young sons.

The shooting deaths of these Black men by police officers are just two examples of stories we seem to hear about with increasing frequency. While these stories are almost polar opposites in circumstance —one man with a legally owned and legally carried gun, and the other unarmed—they both offer important insight into how guns in America affect policing and police violence.

There are a lot of guns in America. According to a report from the Small Arms Survey in 2018, American civilians own approximately 393,000,000 guns. That is about 46 percent of all the guns in the entire world, and it is certainly more guns than we have people.[7] It's . . . a lot of guns.

You may be wondering why I'm starting a section about police-involved gun violence with statistics about how many guns are in the United States. It's because it's impossible to understand or evaluate policing in the United States without taking into account the expansive number of firearms in circulation among civilians. These two things are forever linked and forever locked in a vicious cycle.

Here are a few things we know about police-involved shootings. According to a database created by the *Washington Post*, about 1,000 civilians are shot and killed by law enforcement each year.[8] We know unarmed Black civilians are five times more likely to be shot and killed by police than White civilians, and shootings by police happen more frequently in states with high rates of gun ownership.[9] We also know there are more police killings in states with more permissive gun laws.[10] Moreover, police officers are killed with a firearm in the line of duty more often in states with high rates of gun ownership.[11]

Research shows police shootings are linked to many causes, including personal biases, structural racism, and departmental policies. Researchers at the University of Colorado and California State University reviewed ten years' worth of evidence about police officers and implicit bias. Their analysis indicated that implicit bias among many officers cause them to be more likely to shoot Black suspects than White ones, and experimental research supports these conclusions.[12] In one study done on implicit bias that used video game simulations, officers were quicker to shoot Black suspects than White ones.[13] Another study, published in 2014 in the *Journal of Personality and Social Psychology*, found officers commonly dehumanized Black people and "those who did were most likely to be the one who had a record of using force on Black children in custody."[14]

The United States has far more police shootings than any other comparable developed nation. A damning analysis published by *The Guardian* in 2015 stated, "US police kill more in days than other countries do in years."[15] According to an analysis done by the Prison Policy Initiative, US police kill civilians at more than sixteen times the rate of police in countries where police officers work unarmed.[16] We don't have more overall crime than other developed countries, what we have is more deadly crime, caused largely in part due to gun violence. When a gun is involved, the ceiling for how badly something can go is much higher. Frank Edwards, a sociologist at Rutgers, calls this the "ceiling effect." If a gun is present, death is always a possibility.[17]

There are many things that can be done to reduce the rates of police shootings, such as implicit bias training, de-escalation training, community policing, and more accountability for officers. However, these things can only help so much when police officers know that anyone they come into contact with might have a gun on them. Whether it's a call about a domestic violence incident, a noise complaint, or a simple traffic stop, the risk of encountering an armed person is always present for police officers. And they're right to fear this. Police officers don't just *perceive* many people to have guns—many people actually *do* have guns. And it's deadly not only for civilians, but for the officers too.

A study published in 2015 by the *American Journal of Public Health* found that "every 10 percent increase in firearm ownerships correlated with 10 additional officers killed in homicides" over the fifteen-year study period.[18] Guns lead to deaths of civilians, deaths of police officers, and deaths of civilians by police officers. In every encounter with a civilian, an officer may fear the presence of a gun. This fear changes their behavior, just like it would for any one of us—leading them to be more guarded, more fearful, and more defensive. If an officer is already anticipating the need to use their weapon, the decision to use it may be made easier. Officers are trained to believe hesitation is fatal and to shoot even before a threat is fully realized. This is why even the possibility of a threat of a gun is enough for them to shoot, and so they do.

I'm writing this chapter as, across our nation, people in every state are protesting police brutality and systemic racism after the tragic deaths of George Floyd, Breonna Taylor, and Rayshard Brooks. One thing activist groups and protestors have asked for is the *demilitarization* of the police in the United States. For a lot of people, this is the first time they're hearing this term. So what does it mean?

The militarization of police has become common across the country. It essentially refers to the use of military equipment and tactics by state and local law enforcement. This involves the use of things such as automatic weapons, heavily armored military vehicles, flash bang grenades, and tear gas, which is typically equipment only allowed to be used by the nation's military. Police departments across the country gained access to this type of equipment after the Department of Defense created a controversial program known as 1033. This program came into existence in 1997 under the Clinton administration in order to help communities across the United States in the War on Drugs. Program 1033 gives surplus military equipment to police departments for only the cost of shipping.[19] The use of this equipment and aggressive tactics by law enforcement has created a big problem: an unequal power dynamic and an eroding trust in police across the country.

The military and police have different purposes. The military's foundational function is to fight foreign enemies and keep them at bay, often requiring the use of specialized weapons and artillery. The police, however, are meant to be peace officers who protect communities and honor civil liberties. An overly militarized police force detracts from this purpose by using often unnecessarily aggressive tactics and over-enforcement, both more prevalent in communities of color and poor neighborhoods.[20] It also encourages the use of force instead of collaborative problem solving. It's hard to develop meaningful relationships between police officers and the people they are to protect and serve when the police departments can turn into a military force at any moment. We saw much of this during Black Lives Matter protests during the summer of 2020 in places such as Portland, Seattle, Denver, and Chicago.[21]

Demilitarizing the police is not a wild idea. Other countries have demilitarized their police with great success. But police in the United States have a problem that is unique among police departments across industrialized countries: guns.

Many countries, including Iceland, Ireland, New Zealand, and the United Kingdom, don't even arm the majority of their police officers. In those countries, only specially trained officers are allowed to use guns when they have to respond to situations in which a suspect is armed. Conversely, in the United States, almost every police officer carries a weapon and is trained that they should use it if they deem it necessary. Officers in countries where they aren't permitted to carry guns go through extensive training in policing. In Norway, for example, policing is an elite occupation and only 14 percent of applicants are accepted to police schools. They are required to complete a three year bachelor's degree, spending one year studying society and ethics, another year shadowing officers, and a final year completing a thesis. Compare this to the United States where, on average, police spend twenty-one weeks in training.[22]

The use of guns by police isn't the only thing making these countries different. Policing in other countries is often based entirely on gaining the respect of the people they serve and only using excessive force in limited circumstances. They also work closely with social workers, psychiatric specialists, and medical professionals who go on calls with police officers when dealing with someone who is exhibiting signs of mental illness. In the United States, police are often expected to handle these individuals on their own with limited or no training. An analysis done by the *Washington Post* found that 25 percent of people shot by police officers in a six month period during 2015 were experiencing severe mental health issues.[23]

Limiting the amount of guns in the hands of civilians would not only reduce fatal police shootings, but would save police officers as well. In 2019, firearms killed forty-four of the forty-eight officers killed in the line of duty by a suspect.[24] In 2019, the United Kingdom, which has some of the strongest gun laws in the world, had no officers killed by gunfire.[25] In the United Kingdom, gun ownership is considered a privilege, not a right, and firearms make up only 0.2 percent of all recorded crime.[26]

This all sounds pretty great, don't you think? A police force trained in ways to defuse situations without the use of guns, people struggling with mental health being helped by people trained to help them, better relationships between police officers and civilians? Fewer civilian deaths by police, fewer police deaths by civilians? Please, sign me up! Sign us all up! I have good news for you: this is possible. I also have bad news for you: we have to deal with the guns first.

Without greatly reducing the prevalence of guns, demilitarizing the police will not work, and if anything, would cause more damage to an already broken system. As with all the aspects of gun violence, fatal police shooting deaths are rooted in many causes. Police officers face dangerous situations daily, just like police officers in other countries do. But like all of these things, it is often the guns that make them deadly. With nearly all police officers armed, and the largest gun ownership rate in the world, it's like the United States is locked in a standoff most of us didn't sign up for. Until we deal with the number of guns in America, any effort to improve policing practices will feel like putting out a forest fire with a garden hose. All the data we have shows that the prevalence of guns and weak gun laws contribute, without a doubt, to the rates of fatal police shootings and shooting deaths of police officers. If we reduce the possibility an officer may encounter a gun, we can change policing altogether.

Maybe you're reading this chapter and feel uncomfortable with the data because you support police officers and aren't sure what to make of police brutality in general. Maybe, like me, you're friends with one, or you're married to one, or have one in your family. This may seem counterintuitive, but if you are pro-police officer, you should also be pro-gun reform. And if you are reading this and fully support demilitarizing the police but haven't taken up the cause of gun reform . . . it's time to take that step.

More guns kill more civilians. More guns kill more police officers. More guns mean more police officers kill more people. There are no winners in this scenario. And yet we let this pattern continue to wreak destruction on our society and our people all in the name of a right, or a tradition, or because it's the way things have always been. History continues to show us just because we've always done something a certain way doesn't mean we should keep doing it. It means we learn from it and figure out a better way forward.

In this case, it may mean confronting the idea that guns really do inflict damage on every area of our lives, including the groups and people we claim to care the most about. If we want to be a society that truly cares about our neighbors, supporting the people who serve us, and making the world better, we have to consider the possibility of changing our minds on guns.

Gun violence in the most vulnerable communities. During Father's Day weekend of 2020, 104 people were shot across the city of Chicago. Fourteen people died from their injuries, and five of them were minors. One boy, a three-year-old, was shot and killed while riding in the car with his dad. It was the deadliest weekend for gun violence in the city up to that point in 2020.[27] During the same weekend in Philadelphia, thirty-two were people injured by gun violence, and six people died.[28]

The gun violence crisis in the United States reaches every corner of the country, affecting each and every citizen. However, no one is more affected by gun violence than those in underserved, urban communities. In these areas, including Chicago, the homicide rate often reaches ten times the national average.[29] Black men in America are at the greatest risk of being affected by gun violence. In America, Black men are sixteen times more likely to be shot than White men.[30]

One of the most tragic parts of urban gun violence may be the ways it impacts children. In one study published in the _Journal of Adolescent Health_, 42 percent of urban youth reported having seen someone shot or knifed, and 22 percent reported having seen someone killed.[31] Black children and teens are fourteen times more likely than White children and teens to die by gun violence.[32] Children who experience gun violence, whether directly witnessing a violent incident or hearing gunshots as they lie in their beds or sit in their classrooms, are at risk for depression, anxiety, PTSD, poor school performance, engaging in criminal activity, and abuse of drugs and alcohol.[33]

A childhood experience of gun violence, or even the constant threat of it, affects them for the rest of their lives. Disturbingly, research even shows that youth who are exposed to gun violence are more likely to resort to violence themselves.[34] For children in these communities, gun violence isn't just something they worry about happening to them at school, like it is for many other children; it is simply a part of their everyday lives. Life for these children is growing up under the truth that playing outside isn't an option, and if they go to the local play-ground they may never come home. Teenagers in these communities sometimes obtain guns for self-defense, knowing the threat of gun violence is real for them and their family members, which only con-tributes to the cycle of violence. Gun violence steals the childhoods of thousands of children across our country.

I used to think if people didn't want to live in a dangerous city then they should just move. I interpreted staying in an unsafe neighborhood as being part of the problem. This was another sign of my privilege. I didn't have to consider how expensive it is to move, and how impos-sible it can be to do so without a support system. I didn't know how hard it is to find affordable housing when you have no, or very little, money. And it didn't seem to occur to me that people shouldn't be forced to leave their homes and the cities they call their own because we as a society have turned away. Gun violence isn't the only cycle occurring in these communities. Poverty, lack of resources and educa-tional opportunities, and more—all of these things are systemic issues influencing a community's resilience.

High rates of illegal activities, such as drug dealing and other gang activity, often contribute to the violence. Another factor is retaliation. Often retaliation shootings for other acts of violence play a significant part in community gun violence. These shootings target the perpe-trator but often also target innocent family members and friends, and other members in the community, who have nothing to do with either act. This is how isolated incidents of gun violence begin to spread throughout neighborhoods, inflicting suffering on a large scale. For many, retaliatory shootings stem from lack of trust in law enforcement and high levels of unsolved homicides, which leave people feeling that the only option is to handle it themselves. Law enforcement officers themselves have recently been sounding the alarm that they need more resources to be able to investigate nonfatal shootings. In some big cities, nonfatal shootings are often not even assigned to an investi-gator.[35] Law enforcement officers say leaving these shootings unsolved can lead to escalation including retaliation and homicides. "No justice, no peace" rings true in these cities.

Urban gun violence keeps communities that already struggling locked in a cycle of poverty, poor health, homelessness, poor education, and more. In his book *Bleeding Out*, criminologist Thomas Abt calls it "the linchpin of concentrated urban poverty." He says, "Until we pull this pin, poverty in our cities will remain as persistent as ever. A neighborhood that is not safe will never prosper."[36] Higher rates of gun violence are often associated with poor economic growth and deteriorating home values.

Next to gun suicides, urban gun violence is the second biggest category of gun deaths, making up a majority of gun homicides.[37] And urban gun violence, like firearm suicide, is largely ignored. We know about the gun violence happening in these communities, yet for some reason we seem to go on without acknowledging the suffering, relegating these communities to continued violence just because that's the way it is. Media portrayals of urban violence may be partly to blame. Gun violence in underserved and low-income areas is often depicted in TV shows and movies; but it isn't portrayed as something that needs to be fixed or even addressed. Rather, it is presented as an accepted way of life by the people who live there. It may make for interesting plot lines and must-see TV, but the people who experience the pain and pay the price of this violence don't want to see it. For them, it is not an interesting or perennial plot line—it's their lives. They want better. And we should want better for them.

Interestingly enough, though, urban gun violence just happens to be the category of gun violence we know the most about, which in turn, may make it the most addressable. Due to the episodic nature of mass shootings, they are traditionally difficult to study, which in turn makes them much harder to predict and address. Urban gun violence, however, is totally different. For urban communities, gun violence is a chronic condition they deal with on a daily basis. While devastating, it is easier to research and analyze. Which begs the question, does that make it easier to address? Many experts, including Abt, say yes. He points out that even in urban communities, the gun violence is heavily concentrated. Twenty percent of all firearm homicides occur in the twenty-five largest cities in the United States.[38] In 2015, more than one-fourth of gun homicides happened in 1,200 of the neighborhoods that house just 1.5 percent of the US population.[39] This fact alone offers helpful insight into possible solutions by showing that maybe we don't have to focus on a huge area of a large population. Instead, we can focus our efforts in the areas and populations who are most at risk for the cycle of violence.

What can we do? Urban gun violence in itself is a unique problem. Both the causes and aftermath are different for urban areas than for rural ones, which means they require unique solutions. A study published in the *Journal of Rural Health* found that universal background checks led to a 13 percent reduction in urban-based fatal homicide rates.[40] Laws prohibiting people with violent misdemeanor convictions from purchasing guns yielded a 30 percent lower fatality rate in rural areas. Requiring permits to buy and carry guns led to 21 and 20 percent reductions in both urban and rural areas, respectively. Cities with high rates of gun violence need more than just laws to reduce gun violence rates and support the people in their communities who are affected by it. Thankfully, we have some examples to look to that may help forge a path forward for cities and neighborhoods across the country.

In 2012, Oakland, California, adopted what is now known as the Oakland Ceasefire, also called "focused deterrence."[41] Oakland had historically struggled with high rates of crime and gun violence. In the early 2000s, however, it reached a breaking point. After an 81 percent increase in homicides between 1999 and 2003, city leaders and community members knew something had to be done. After many attempts at programs and solutions, the city adopted the Ceasefire program in 2012. The first step was to identify the groups of people most at risk of committing acts of gun violence. Incredibly,

400 people, 0.1 percent of the city's population, were found to be the highest risk.

The city started hosting call-ins as interventions with that group and connected them with social services, faith leaders, community activists, healthcare professionals, and police officers. Local officials followed up with people afterward as needed. This was meant to send a message to these people that they had a way out, they had other options, and they had help if they wanted it. Officials were also clear that if they chose to continue on their path and commit violence, there would be consequences. After five years of the Ceasefire program, Oakland's homicide rate fell by almost 50 percent between 2012 and 2017. Meanwhile homicides increased in other major cities such as Baltimore, Chicago, and St. Louis. The solved rate of homicides in the city went from 29 percent in 2011 to over 70 percent in 2017.[42]

More research supports focused deterrence as an effective way to help communities and curb violence rates, with multiple reviews of the research showing it reduced "gang violence, street crime driven by drugs markets, and repeat individuals offending."[43] Other places have tried a similar approach. The difference here, however, seems to be the integration of law enforcement and other service professionals. Using law enforcement alone has proven to be ineffective because it gives the impression that their only goal is to serve warrants and make arrests. Offering social services with enforcement tells the community members that the city cares about their lives and what happens to them.

Along with focused deterrence, other programs such as Chicago's Becoming a Man offer teens cognitive behavioral therapy and recreational activities as an intervention before teens choose the path of violence.[44] There is less evidence for the effectiveness of these programs, but all signs point to them being important tools for helping young people and reducing the possibilities of violence. The best part about options like Becoming a Man and focused deterrence? We don't have to sit around on our hands waiting for gun laws to get passed; we just have to get everyone on the same page and committed to the program. That in itself is a hurdle, though. Making sure law enforcement, city officials, faith leaders, and social services are all on the same page about how to reduce violence is no small order, especially when there is often rampant distrust of the police. It would also require help from the media, advocates, politicians, and community leaders to maintain focus on this type of gun violence, reminding people what is at stake.

CONCLUSION

This section on urban violence has felt especially weighty for me, as we are living in a time of calls for police reform, racial justice, and an end to systemic racism. The thing about urban gun violence, which affects so many of our most vulnerable neighbors, is that it doesn't happen in a vacuum, and the concentration of violence isn't an accident. Through past segregation, housing discrimination, and redlining, White people created areas where they could force "undesirable" (majority Black) residents to live, removing themselves from any perceived danger of the people they oppressed. They viewed these people as less-than, second-class citizens, and began a cycle of systemic and structural racism that is still moving just as fast as it ever was. This isn't just anecdotal; we know this to be true. When White people zoned the city of Philadelphia in 1937, they used a hierarchical system, color coding areas and designating areas as "red zones" for people they deemed to be "low grade" and "undesirable." Researchers conducted an analysis of the concentration of firearm assaults and violent crimes in 2013 and 2014 in Philadelphia, comparing them to the zoning maps from 1937. Their analysis found, not surprisingly, firearm injuries are the highest in historically red-zoned areas of Philadelphia.[45]

During the summer of 2020, the phrase "Defund the Police" became a common refrain at Black Lives Matter protests and online. It isn't a new idea, but one that has gained more visibility in recent months. It also gained a good bit of misunderstanding and misinterpretation. I admit I had absolutely no idea what it meant the first few times I heard it, and I consequently wrote it off as a horrible idea and an impossibility. What would we do without police? Then, when I actually learned what it meant, it opened my eyes to how defunding the police could impact the rates of gun violence in a positive way.

Defunding the police doesn't mean abolishing the police. It doesn't even mean totally defunding them altogether. According to the ACLU, defunding the police means to "cut the astronomical amount of money that our governments spend on law enforcement and give that money to more helpful services like job training, counseling, and violence-prevention programs."[46] As Chrissy T. Lopez wrote for the *Washington Post*, "Defunding the police means shrinking the scope of police responsibilities and shifting most of what government does to keep us safe to entities that are better equipped to meet that need. It means investing more in mental-health care and housing, and expanding the use of community mediation and violence interruption programs."[47]

Over the years, often due to budget cuts in other areas, police have been expected to perform duties for which they were never trained or should have never been expected to do. Shifting resources and funding away from police departments and instead toward job training, educational opportunities, healthcare, and mental health services could pave the way for people in underserved communities to overcome the cycles of poverty and, perhaps as a result—gun violence. At the same time, it would give police officers the ability to focus on their primary job: ensuring a safe community for the people they are meant to serve.

I believe it is fair to say that White supremacy, racism, and hatred led to the rates of firearm violence we see in these urban communities today. The White people in power, the ones who made these past decisions, may not have been able to predict just how horrific the rates of violence would become, but they also simply didn't care. They decided Black people were dangerous and violent, and built neighborhoods around that premise. This has led to mass incarceration of Black people, generational poverty, and contentious relationships between the police officers and the communities in these areas. And at the center of so many of these things lies an epidemic of gun violence, which we've largely chosen to ignore. We may not have created these systems ourselves, but we can, and should, do everything in our power to dismantle them.

If we truly want to live in a country where all people are created equal, and if we want to take care of the most vulnerable among us, we have to confront the long history of systemic and structural racism in this country. We have to confront the high rates of urban gun violence. And as it turns out, those two things often happen to be one and the same, and we can't do one without the other.

11

COMMON ARGUMENTS
AGAINST GUN REFORM

WHEN IT COMES TO TALKING about gun violence and gun reform, a few talking points often come up over and over again. Whether you feel intimated by these types of conversations because you feel like you don't have answers for questions you'll get asked, or you are wondering about them yourself, these thirteen common myths and talking points are a great place to start and will provide an opportunity to help you get comfortable and build a foundation of knowledge about gun violence and reform.

"CRIMINALS DON'T FOLLOW THE LAW."

It isn't that criminals don't follow laws, it's that weak laws don't deter them. If a person wants to buy a gun but isn't legally allowed to do so in his state, he can go to a nearby state with weaker gun laws. He can find a seller that doesn't require a background check, like from a private sale or even a gun show. He can even have someone else buy the gun for him (known as a *straw purchase*). In March 2010, a California man named John Patrick Bedell attempted to purchase a firearm at a gun store but his background check was denied due to a history of mental illness. So, he just went next door to Nevada, where the gun laws are weaker, and he was able to purchase a gun at a gun show with no background required. He then shot two police officers in front of the Pentagon.[1] We know we have loopholes in the current laws being exploited by criminals to purchase guns. It is disingenuous to be aware of the weaknesses in the laws and then say there is nothing we can do.

"WE CAN'T STOP CRIMINALS FROM BUYING GUNS OFF THE STREET."

Getting guns off the street and out of the hands of criminals is a tall order for sure. The Bureau of Justice Statistics found that 80 percent of criminals say they obtained their guns from a friend or street sources.[2] The number of guns isn't the only problem; it's the flow of them into the illegal market. What this tells us is that the best way to keep illegal guns off the street is by creating regulations for transactions and the supply of guns. By lowering the supply and increasing the cost of guns on the black market, we can make transactions harder and more expensive to complete, deterring criminals. Most guns in circulation illegally get there after having been stolen.[3] Yet, because of ATF regulations, we have no effective way of monitoring and tracing gun thefts.

"IF I HAVE TO LOCK UP MY GUN, I WON'T BE ABLE TO USE IT TO DEFEND MYSELF QUICKLY."

This is a common misconception about safe storage equipment. The reality is that there are plenty of options that can be opened within seconds, some simply with the swipe of a finger or with your fingerprint. There are even many affordable options for quick access. With the availability of these types of firearm storage, there is simply no excuse to be reckless with a gun in the home. Defensive gun use in America is actually so infrequent that it is difficult to measure and analyze. However, a study done by the National Crime Victimization Survey found that "victims of crimes used guns defensively in less that 1 percent of attempted or completed crimes."[4] In fact, the same study showed when another type of weapon is used in self-defense, such as a baseball bat or a knife, property was stolen from them in 34.9 percent of cases, compared to incidents in which guns were used where property was stolen in 38.5 percent of cases.[5] Even the NRA has admitted that the odds of needing to use a gun to protect ourselves are less than a magician randomly laying out two decks of cards in the same order.[6] When we look at the data, the odds of a gun injuring someone in the home are greater than it being successfully used for self-defense.[7]

"WOMEN WOULDN'T BE VICTIMS IF THEY HAD A GUN."

This is a commonly used argument. However the truth is that a woman's chances of being killed by her abuser increases more than five times if he has access to a gun—that includes her gun.[8] One analysis showed women who own guns are more likely to become homicide victims than men who own guns.[9] Just because a woman has a gun doesn't mean her male partner or spouse won't be able to overpower her, take the gun, and use it against her, which is how these situations often end. A woman's greatest risk isn't a stranger she meets on the street; it's the man inside her home. Firearms are often called the great equalizer between the sexes; however, everything we know about gun ownership says the presence of a firearm simply makes the gap in equality wider and more lethal. The NRA consistently argues that more guns would make women safer. However, the evidence we have today shows the opposite to be true. Moreover, the NRA works to defeat legislation that we know works, such as requiring people under restraining orders to surrender their firearms. If the NRA's goal is to make women safer, it would support reforms. Instead, its resistance to reasonable laws shows the real goal is to sell more guns, not make women safer.

"WE DON'T NEED MORE GUN LAWS; WE JUST NEED TO ENFORCE THE ONES WE HAVE."

This would be true if the laws we had were good and effective laws. However, there are obvious flaws and loopholes in many of the laws currently on the books. We know that many dangerous people are able to obtain their guns legally because of weak laws and because of sellers who are willing to break rules to sell the guns. Beyond that, between 1994 to 2015, background checks have stopped the sales of more than three million guns, showing that even prohibited people do attempt to buy guns legally.[10] Imagine how many more could be stopped if we simply closed the loopholes that allow these people to slide through without suspicion?

"KEEPING A GUN AT HOME MAKES YOU SAFER."

For every time a gun is used in self-defense in a home, there are seven assaults or murders, eleven suicide attempts, and four accidents involving guns.[11] It is estimated that 4.6 million children in the United States live in a home with an unlocked and loaded firearm.[12] In one experiment a third of boys ages eight to twelve who found a handgun pulled the trigger.[13] One study found that a gun in the home was six times more likely to be used to intimidate a family member than to be used in a defensive manner.[14] In general, research shows having a gun in the home makes you much more likely to be killed by a friend or family member.[15]

"KEEPING A GUN FOR SELF-DEFENSE MAKES YOU SAFER."

On September 21, 2014, Eusebio Christian woke up in the middle of the night after hearing a strange noise. He went to his kitchen with his gun and began to fire shots. All his shots missed except one, which struck his wife in the face. These stories aren't uncommon, but they are all a result of the myth that we unequivocally need guns for self-defense. It is normal to be afraid of threats; the problem is we are afraid of the wrong ones. People are taught to be more afraid of an intruder entering their house with a gun than they are to be afraid of the gun in their home, when the truth is the odds of an intruder entering your home are extremely low. This may be the most important and widespread myth about gun ownership. The argument of needing guns for self-defense is the foundation for nearly all resistance to gun reform laws. There is no doubt that people have used guns in acts of self-defense and have protected themselves and people they love. However, by all research available, this is the exception, not the rule. One study in Philadelphia found if someone carrying a gun was assaulted, he was 4.5 times more likely to be shot and 4.2 times more likely to be killed.[16] The National Crime Victimization Survey found "more than 9 times as many people are victimized by guns than protected by them."[17] Carrying guns is also associated with greater escalation of arguments instead of ending them. Even in instances where guns were reportedly used for self-defense, studies show that in more than half of them, the gun was used illegally—meaning the gun was used to harm someone else or intimidate them rather than for actual self-defense.[18] Gun Violence Archive analyzed police reports from the year 2014 and found there were only 1,600 verified uses of guns in acts of self-defense.[19] Yet lawmakers and lobbyists insist on structuring our gun laws on the need for self-defense. The truth is the good guy with the gun stopping a bad guy with a gun is mostly a myth. Usually the good guy with the gun just ends up being harmed with it.

"IF MORE PEOPLE WERE ARMED, OUR COUNTRY WOULD BE SAFER."

More guns do not make us safer. If more guns made us safer, the United States would be the safest country on earth. Instead, the opposite is true. Within the United States, states with higher rates of gun ownerships see more firearm injuries and homicides than states with lower rates. Compared with other countries, the difference is even greater. The US gun homicide rate is twenty-five times higher than that of other high-income countries.[20] We have been living in an experiment, trying to force this myth to be true. We tried it, and it didn't work. Research shows that more guns have not made us safer. It's time to try something else.

"THERE IS NO SUCH THING AS AN ASSAULT WEAPON."

Pro-gun people often say anti-gun activists made up the term *assault weapons* and that there is no such thing. They tend to use the term *modern sporting rifle* in its place. However, this isn't true. Gun manufacturers, wholesalers, and dealers used the term *assault weapons* to help buyers identify these firearms. The term was used on the covers of magazines such as *Guns & Ammo* and *Gun Digest*, even one literally called *The Gun Digest Book of Assault Weapons*, where it was used alongside photos of AK-47s and AR-15s. It was only after the shooting at Sandy Hook School, where the shooter used semiautomatic rifles, that the gun industry began rebranding *assault weapons* as *modern sporting rifles*. Technically speaking, an *assault rifle* is a rapid-fire gun that uses magazines to fire bullets. They are designed for military use and allow the shooter to make a choice between semiautomatic firing, which involves pulling the trigger for each shot, and fully automatic firing, which allows the trigger to be held down for continuous firing. An *assault weapon* technically has no definition but is used to refer to semiautomatic weapons such as an AR-15 rifle. The *AR* in AR-15 is the abbreviation for Armalite Rifle, which was the company that first developed the weapon. The reason weapons like the AR-15 can fire so many shots is that they can use high-capacity magazines, allowing the shooter to fire dozens of rounds within a short period of time. The term *assault weapons* isn't used officially as a classification for firearms. Still, it has a storied history to describe weapons and market them to people looking for guns that look like military-style weapons. Pro-gun people may suggest that using the term takes away your credibility, when it really just shows that they don't want to take responsibility for the marketing that was used by gun enthusiasts to get assault-style weapons into the world. It is disingenuous for them to act as though the term doesn't exist. If they do, just show them the cover of *The Gun Digest Book of Assault Weapons*, fifth edition.

"GUNS DON'T KILL PEOPLE; PEOPLE KILL PEOPLE."

It is true that guns can't grow legs and get up and kill people on their own. It is also true that people who have access to guns kill more people, and they do it with the guns they have access to. So, it's reasonable and correct to say that it's the guns that make people deadly. Nearly every statistic about gun ownership rates and firearm deaths and injuries supports this conclusion. States with higher gun ownership rates have higher gun murder rates; in some states the rate is almost 114 percent higher.[21] In states requiring safe storage of firearms or banning certain types of firearms under an assault weapons ban, gun deaths are lower.[22] Refusing to believe the data about gun ownership and gun deaths is a refusal to see the truth. Guns do not make us safer, and they do get people killed.

"CHICAGO HAS THE TOUGHEST GUN LAWS AND THE MOST GUN CRIME. CHICAGO IS PROOF LAWS DON'T WORK."

This is a common argument and one of the greatest myths used in the gun debate. Illinois does, in fact, have tougher gun laws than many other states, and the city of Chicago has tough gun laws as well. But it is not true that it has the toughest gun laws in the country. For example, Chicago doesn't have safe storage laws. So why is there so much gun crime there if they have such tough laws? There are a couple of reasons. The reality is this: state lines and city limits don't stop guns, and Chicago is close to Wisconsin and Indiana, two states with very weak gun laws. We can't evaluate the gun violence in Chicago, or other cities like it, without taking into account the gun laws in surrounding areas. These states allow guns to flow into Chicago. In fact, a study from 2015 showed that more than 60 percent of guns used in gang-related crimes and 31.6 percent of guns used in non-gang-related crime in the city were bought in other states. Indiana supplied almost one-third of them.[23] If anything, Chicago is an example of how patchwork gun laws, as in trying to enact different laws in different states and cities, is simply not an effective way to reduce gun violence.

Additionally, research shows states with strong gun laws bordered by other states with strong gun laws see fewer firearm fatalities.[24]

"LAWS WILL NEVER STOP ALL GUN VIOLENCE, SO WHAT'S THE POINT?"

For some reason, we have a much higher standard for how effective we think gun laws should be compared to other laws. When speed limits were first created, I don't think we said, "Wow, no one will speed!" Instead we thought this would help reduce instances of car accidents, injury, and death. When laws were created requiring people to wear seat belts, the same was true. Laws are not written under the notion that every person will obey them. They are written for the purpose of reducing dangerous situations and creating a pathway to prosecute people who don't obey them, in hopes of furthering compliance by fear of consequences. We don't expect every person to obey every speed limit. In fact, I was driving thirty-eight in a thirty-five miles-per-hour zone just this morning. Yet there is this notion that for gun laws to be worth our time and effort, they must be 100 percent effective. We have never expected any other public safety initiative to be 100 percent effective, so why are we using that standard for guns? If that is the standard we wish to set, then we should expect to just get rid of laws altogether. And doesn't that sound a bit ridiculous?

"GUN LAWS INFRINGE ON DUE PROCESS."

This is an argument especially common when it comes to Extreme Risk Protection Orders (ERPO). However, it is simply inaccurate. Every state and locality that has passed ERPO laws also outlines an extensive policy to ensure the right to due process. All it takes is a quick internet search or call to your local government offices to find out how they protect due process. Though, it is likely people who are concerned about due process infringements will not trust any government entity that says otherwise. In those situations I like to ask, "Who will you trust?" At some point, to be an involved and productive member of society, you simply have to trust the people who are leading you.

12

SO YOU WANT TO TALK ABOUT GUN VIOLENCE

A FEW YEARS AGO, I found myself talking online to a friend from high school about gun reform. I was only beginning to step into having these conversations with people I knew in real life. I was the kind of nervous that makes you feel like your stomach is taking over your entire body. I knew that this person—I will call him Kyle—owned guns and was very pro-gun. I mentioned to him that I had recently learned many of the gun laws on the books had glaring loopholes that allowed people to get guns who really shouldn't have them. I was typing fast and digging my thumbnail into the tip of my pointer finger, a nervous habit, in between exchanging messages.

I knew I wouldn't be able to answer every specific question, and I was terrified of being asked one I didn't know how to answer and looking like I didn't know what I was talking about. At the same time, I was intimidated because Kyle is a notoriously good arguer. Sure enough, he asked me a question right away that I didn't know how to answer. I decided to reply honestly. I commented back saying, "I don't know the answer to that, but I'll find out." I hoped for a cordial break in the conversation. Instead, he responded by telling me I was just using my victimhood to manipulate people into being anti-gun. This was the first time I had been told something like this, but not the last. I was so hurt and angry I responded with admittedly unkind words and then later deleted the post from my Facebook timeline.

Deep down in my soul, I hoped I could change a mind that day, and not being able to do so had discouraged me. It did something else as well. It taught me some important truths about having these conversations. Talking with Kyle that day, I knew I would not be able to change his mind. He had deeply held beliefs, and throughout our conversation, it was obvious in hindsight he did not want to talk *with* me as much as he wanted to talk *at* me. I was spending time and energy on a person who had not wanted to engage in the conversation for the same purpose that I did. It also taught me some people would always be bent on misunderstanding me and my motives.

The most important thing the conversation with Kyle taught me, though, was that an awkward and poorly conducted conversation about gun reform was not the end of the world. The worst that happened was some hurt feelings and anger on my part, and some aggressiveness on his. It lit a fire in me to have more of these conversations, knowing after each one I would learn even more.

Talking about guns, like talking about anything controversial, can be difficult and intimidating. Even when you feel really strongly about your position and can back it up with all sorts of statistics and data, it is still hard. Sometimes, it doesn't feel worth the effort. Sometimes it simply feels like too big of a bridge to gap. I get it. It may surprise you to discover I actually don't love talking about gun reform with people! It makes me feel a bit sweaty and nervous, and I can have a full conversation in my head, acting as both myself and the other person, and end up utterly intimidated by an imaginary discussion. This all comes with the territory. What I'm saying is that if you're waiting to have hard conversations until you don't feel anxious anymore, you'll probably never have them. I think it's good to feel nervous; it means you deeply care about what you're talking about enough to have a physical response to it. If you didn't care, you wouldn't feel nervous. I'm not an expert and I don't know everything, but I have learned some things over the years about how to have these conversations, knowing which ones are worth my time, and how to create and honor boundaries around them for myself.

Get comfortable saying, "I don't know." This is where we start. Most often when I ask people what keeps them from engaging in conversations about gun reform, they say they don't know enough. I'm going to let you in on a secret—most of us don't know enough. I have had a lot of really good, productive conversations with people about gun reform, but none of them went that way because I had all the answers. If you feel intimated by not having all the answers, chances are, the person you're talking to feels the same way. They want accessibility. They want to talk to someone who doesn't make them feel embarrassed for not knowing something. If someone feels intimated by your knowledge, they'll be more defensive and less likely to engage with you. In my experience, a posture of humility is an asset, not a liability. I frequently say, "I don't have all the answers, but what I do know is. . . ." and start there. If you care about reducing gun violence rates and saving lives, that is enough to enter the conversation.

The goal is not for someone to change their mind by the end of your conversation. This part can feel the most frustrating. It's always tempting to enter into these conversations with hope that the person will say, "Wow, you've convinced me! I've totally changed my mind!" I'm not saying this never happens, but it has never happened to me. If that is the goal, we will always be disappointed and find ourselves discouraged. The likelihood you will change someone's mind about long-held opinions on guns by the end of a ten-minute conversation is low. So it's a good thing that isn't the end goal. The goal is always to plant new seeds of knowledge and offer new ways of thinking. You may not be with that person the next time news of a mass shooting happens, but hopefully they'll remember the conversation they had with you, and they will filter the current news through a lens you helped create. Think about something you changed your mind on. How long did it take? Was it because of one conversation? Or was it because your eyes were opened to something and it made you keep paying attention? For me it has always been the latter. When I first started talking about gun reform, I had a friend, Keegan Divant, who is a gun owner, who would throw every common argument my way about why gun laws don't work and how guns make us safer. Now, years later, he fully believes in gun reform and is outspoken about his change of heart. It took years, though, not minutes, for him to change his mind. Here's his story in his own words:

> One of the most exciting things about Scout camp is being able to try things that are truly extraordinary. From wilderness survival to swimming, every merit badge has its own sense of adventure. But there's one merit badge that seems to stand out above the rest—the rifle merit badge.
>
> When I went to the rifle range for my first lesson, I could barely contain myself. I didn't grow up around guns, so this was going to be my first time actually firing the real thing. I was in for a shock, as we didn't get to shoot on that first day. Why? Before anything else, we had an extensive course on gun safety.
>
> You may be familiar with some of the basics, like never point a gun at anyone and always treat it as if it's loaded, even when it's not. It's seemingly simple on the surface, and something that could be covered in fifteen minutes. However, that's not how the instructor saw it. We took a deep dive into every rule around safety.
>
> Almost every rule begins with "never." While that makes the rule clear cut, our instructor gave us examples of how to make sure we always follow them. He also gave advice on how to tell our friends that there's no way we're touching a gun without an adult. Which, by the way, is to just say your dad will be furious when he finds out. These lessons were so engrained in me that it's second nature. When I'm handed a gun, I still make sure it's unloaded, even after I've watched someone else check it.

I have to admit when I heard what had happened to Taylor, my first thought was, "I wish there had been a good guy with a gun there." For a while, this actually galvanized my belief that people should carry to protect themselves or others. I wanted to be that good guy with a gun.

I no longer think that. What I noticed was that there wasn't that emphasis on safety anymore. I know too many people who don't have respect for how dangerous guns are. They talk about how they keep it loaded by the bed in a drawer, ready to go if someone breaks in. Once, I was at a small get together when the homeowner noticed someone's five-year-old going up the stairs. He quickly ran to stop the child because there was a loaded gun sitting out in the bedroom.

That was the end of my belief in "good guys with guns." I no longer trust that others understand the responsibility of owning a gun and the gravity of carrying one. Many of them have the same logic I once had: "If only I had been there with my gun." But they overlook that it's infinitely better to keep guns out of the wrong hands to begin with.

It still seems a little weird that my beliefs were changed in part by the pro-gun crowd. But it has also changed my thought process. Now, instead of wishing that I had been there to protect Taylor, I wish the shooter had never had that gun.

Make yourself someone who people can talk with and possibly change their mind. Changing our minds about things, especially deeply held personal and societal beliefs, is really hard. We live in a society that encourages firm and solidified opinions and values. We tend to set our opinions in stone and place them on our shelves as symbols of who we are. The problem with this is that stones can easily become idols. We attack people who change their minds, calling them a "flip flopper" and "inconsistent." Instead, we should honor and respect people who look at information and are willing to learn and say, "Maybe I was wrong about this" instead of doubling down on an opinion simply because it's the one they've always held. Sometimes when we are in the process of changing our minds, we feel like we don't know ourselves anymore, and we feel a bit out of control because our beliefs become such a part of us. My husband often says we should be able to remember the last time we changed our minds about something. I think he's right. Changing our minds, or at least being open to new ways of thinking, shows that we are paying attention. It shows that we care enough about something to listen and reflect. When we have conversations about gun reform, it's important to be a safe person who allows people to ask questions and work through new information. Better yet? Tell them about how you changed your mind about something big. Remind them that you don't think you're perfect or better than them, but you've been on a journey just like they are.

Consider what makes them who they are. If you're speaking with a person you know pretty well, consider all the things that might contribute to their opinions about guns. Where did they grow up? Does their family own guns? Do they hunt? Do they have personal ties to gun violence, assault, or the military? All of these things influence what someone believes about guns and should influence how you talk to them about it. If you don't know the person well, ask them about it: Did you grow up with guns? What influenced your opinions about guns? Asking these questions is meeting them where they are to gain understanding about why they feel a certain way and what matters to them. This is how we make it a conversation and not a lecture. Doing this lets people know you want to talk with them, not at them. Don't we all want that?

You don't need to talk to everyone. This is especially true on social media, but can be true in person too. You don't have to engage with every person. Anytime I post online about gun reform, I get a handful of comments and messages from people who disagree with me. Some of them want to talk or ask me questions. Some of them just want to yell at me and tell me why I'm wrong. It comes with the territory, but it doesn't mean I subject myself to the verbal abuse. I've gotten pretty good at figuring out who wants to talk *with* me and who just wants to talk *at* me. I think it's like a muscle: the more you use it, the stronger it gets. As you engage in these conversations, you'll begin to recognize which conversations may be fruitful and which are a waste of time. Don't feel guilty about setting a boundary. There is nothing wrong with saying, "I don't think we are going to agree here, so I'm going to end the conversation." That's a boundary. And if we are to be in this work for the long haul, boundaries are important. Just because you start a conversation doesn't mean you have to stay in it when it turns harmful. You get to make your own rules.

It's probably going to be uncomfortable and imperfect. This is just the facts. It feels uncomfortable to engage in a controversial conversation. I have had some terrible conversations with people—like, haunted my dreams and tempted me to give up altogether horrible kinds of conversations. It's just how it goes. I believe, though, that in the kingdom of God nothing is wasted. I think the same about these horribly uncomfortable conversations. They aren't wasted. They all teach us something we can use for the next time. You'll replay them over and over in your head and come up with a response you wish you had said at the time, and you know what? You'll remember that next time! Each time is a learning experience and none of them, even the worst ones that haunt your dreams and make you want to crawl into a hole, are wasted.

Lead from your heart. Facts are important. Data is good and helpful. Research? Yes! Give me all the research. But when all the numbers slip your mind and you can't seem to pull a single fact about gun violence out of your head, lead the conversation from your heart. Feelings and facts don't have to be at odds. There is value in saying, "The number of gun deaths and injuries really grieve me, and I'm trying to find out what we can do that may save lives" in lieu of knowing how many people have died in a single year or which law is on the floor of your state senate. I can't count the times I've attempted to state a fact I've stated dozens of times before and then suddenly can't remember my own name, which is one reason why you won't often see me giving speeches to my state lawmakers. Not my calling, friends. It's okay to simply start with your motivation for your beliefs. Then they can share theirs with you. If the other person trusts you and believes in your motivations, there will be plenty of time for facts later. Just start with what you know.

Your conversation will not end gun violence. Read it again. Sometimes when we are engaging in these conversations, we feel that pressure above anything else. It's like all of the sudden if we don't have a successful discussion and change the person's mind forever then we've failed and screwed up any hope of change. The good news is that none of us are that important. Talking to your aunt at Thanksgiving isn't your one chance at reform. Engaging in Facebook comments with an acquaintance from college isn't your only chance. Take the pressure off. You're not going to screw it up. I have to remind myself of this all the time. We are in this together. This isn't a moon landing; we have lots of opportunities and lots of chances to influence people. Each time you try to engage, you become a better advocate, and that's powerful.

People are watching. This is especially true for social media, but can translate to in-person discussions too. In general, the comments section of Facebook posts and Twitter threads can be, as the kids say, a dumpster fire. You will often hear people say that arguing online changes no one's mind. And while I get the sentiment, I actually think a lot of people's minds get changed from arguing online, just maybe not the person you're arguing with. The thing about Facebook and Twitter is that other people can see the comments too. So while you may not change your uncle's mind about guns, someone you grew up with may be following the debate and reconsidering something they believe. Someone may notice a statistic they've never seen before and do a quick internet search to learn more. I can name a few really big issues in which I've become more educated and informed because of the comments sections and the people who are willing to engage in what is sometimes seen as pointless and fruitless debate. Don't engage in harmful discussions, and always end the conversation if it is becoming volatile. But don't discount the fact that people are watching, and you never know who is paying attention.

It doesn't have to end your relationships. One of the biggest concerns I hear when it comes to people sharing how they feel about guns and guns reform is the fear of how it may affect their relationships with loved ones. I am intimately acquainted with this fear and reality. I sit here writing this book about my experience with gun violence and my beliefs about gun reform as a person with entirely different beliefs than her family's. I get it. And yet, I live to tell the tale that speaking up about gun reform doesn't have to end your relationships. Notice that I didn't say that it won't affect your relationships. I think it probably will. It has affected mine. That's a natural result when people grow, learn new information, and change their minds about things. The thing is, though, if this is a concern for you, if you are afraid to speak out about something you care about, then this has already affected your relationships. You're just the only one who knows about it.

It is really difficult to feel like your relationship with loved ones is changing, that they don't support you, or worse—that they don't respect you. And yet, I think some things are worth the risk. For me, I believe so strongly in this work, that the chance that a friend or loved one doesn't support me or thinks I have become an extremist is worth it. More often than not, however, the other person respects me for having strong beliefs, and respects my desire to save lives and end as much suffering as possible. More often than not, they have the same desire, no matter how wide the gap of our disagreement is in how we get to that goal. Even most of my family members and close friends who disagree with me know my heart and are able to respect me for what I am trying to accomplish.

Conversations with friends and family members take extra care because we love these people, but also because we run the risk of getting extra passionate because we want the people we love to be on our team. I have often let my passion and drive explode in these conversations in ways that were not productive. The stakes feel higher with our family members and friends. So we have to remember all the things we've learned here. We need to take extra time to actively listen without planning our next attack, and we need to take extra caution to refrain from making it personal and pressing buttons we know will hurt. We remember that discussing a difference in beliefs is not a zero-sum game, but instead is an opportunity for open communication and under-standing one another. We remember our goal in discussion is to share our beliefs and the reasons we hold them, and to plant seeds for the other person to continue thinking about, once the conversation is over.

It might cost you something. I think about the civil rights movement and the people who were beaten, abused, and killed because they stood up for the equal rights, treatment, and human value of African Americans. Important things and important work come with a per-sonal cost. I think of the 1980s when the AIDS crisis was killing people left and right. I think about the members of ACT UP, the AIDS Co-alition to Unleash Power, who protested the inhumane treatment and intentional perpetuation of suffering of AIDS patients and demanded medical research and action to save lives. They lost jobs, homes, friends, and family—everything they held dear—to fight for some-thing they believed in.

Maybe voicing your beliefs about gun reform costs you some feelings of discomfort or awkwardness at the next family gathering. Maybe it costs you a difficult or frustrating conversation with your dad after the next time you choose to post something on Facebook about gun violence. Maybe it costs you simply feeling judged, anxious, or alone because you chose to speak up and speak out. The thing though, is that the clichés are true. Nothing worth fighting for is free, and changing the world doesn't happen without paying a price.

By the end of this day, one hundred Americans will have died from gun violence. Two hundred more will have been injured and survive.

That includes people who died from suicide, people killed simply for being Black or gay or transgender, women who are abused by their partner, kids who found guns in their homes, and teenagers playing basketball at the neighborhood park. It includes people like you, like your kids, like your family. They are paying the cost for our complacency, our inaction, and our fear of feeling awkward. See, a price is already being paid for gun violence. The question is, are we willing to share in it?

I've had many more conversations about gun reform since that awkward and terrible one with my high school friend. Some have been not so great, and some have been really encouraging. Many, though, have ended up somewhere in between the extremes. Recently I had a conversation with my dad, who by any and all standards, is a responsible gun owner. Conversations with him are easy for me, because he listens to what I say and takes time to try to understand where I'm coming from. Isn't that all we can ask for? I told my dad about some gaps in the background check process—how if a background check isn't returned within three days, the seller is allowed to proceed with the gun sale. My dad told me he hadn't known that until I told him, and he would certainly support closing that loophole through a gun reform law.

It wasn't a world-changing conversation by any means. It was a quick back and forth during a car ride down the street. But it was a conversation between a father and a daughter that ended in a newfound place of common ground. So maybe it was a world-changing conversation after all.

13

BEYOND THOUGHTS AND PRAYERS

WHEN MY HUSBAND AND I lived in East Tennessee, we passed a sign on the side of the interstate every time we drove home to visit our families. The sign reads, "Jesus is Lord" in big red letters. Next to those words, it says, "We buy guns." The sign is on the building for the business Gun Runners USA. We passed this sign often for five years, and it always made my stomach sink when I saw it. I am intimately acquainted with the horror and suffering guns inflict, and even more intimately acquainted with the goodness of God. Nothing in me knows how to make these two things fit together.

The sign, though, is not an anomaly. There is an entire market of products and propaganda using the slogan, "God and Guns." Just do a quick search on Amazon or Etsy and you'll find a plethora of products with images of the cross or a Bible and the image of a gun along with an American flag. I could have a six pack of buttons that say, "God, Guns, and Trump" delivered to my house tomorrow for $12.50. I would be lying if I said I never used a similar phrase—I am certain I did. In America, we have made the love of guns and love of country interchangeable, and if you don't love guns, then you don't love your country. We've gone beyond that though, and created an ideology where guns, country, and God are all intertwined and somehow of equal importance.

Somehow, I don't think God gave his permission to be included in the group. Somehow, I just can't imagine the Jesus I know carrying an AR-15 with a handgun in a hip holster. This image is at odds with the Jesus we see in Matthew 26. There, Jesus is about to be arrested before his crucifixion. His disciple Peter pulls out a sword to defend Jesus from those who seek to harm him and cuts off the ear of the person arresting Jesus. Instead of Jesus welcoming this violent act of defense, he tells Peter, "Put your sword back in its place . . . for all who draw the sword will die by the sword" (Matthew 26:52). Jesus was a peacemaker, devoted to nonviolence even when he knew he would be harmed.

As Christians, we are supposed to not only remind the world of Jesus, but also to be his hands and feet on earth. We are supposed to clothe ourselves with Christ (Colossians 3:12-17), and we are to follow the example of how he lived as a human being in the world. There are verses in Scripture that people use to justify the use of weapons in self-defense or the carrying of weapons to protect other people. Yet when we look beyond words and instead to the actions of Jesus, how he lived his life is indisputable. He lived turning the other cheek and loving his enemies, even when it meant personal harm to himself. In everything we do, we are to be imitators of Christ (Ephesians 5:1), and we should ask ourselves, "Does this look like Jesus? Does this remind people of Jesus?" I will never understand how carrying an AR-15 down the street, like a man did in my town just a few days ago, and justifying it as a God-given right, looks like Jesus. It's not for me to say whether someone is a true believer. However, the holding on to something that causes such destruction and looks so much like this world does not look like Jesus to me. It does not smell like the aroma of Christ. It looks like fear, intimidation, and a quest for power. It looks like clinging to individual liberties and freedoms above the common good.

My friend Stephanie told me a story of a conversation she had with someone in her life who helped her begin to see guns from a different perspective. Here's her story:

> I grew up in a strong pro-gun culture. The first people I heard talk about guns saw themselves as protectors and providers—carrying handguns to protect others from bad guys, and hunting wild game to provide meat for their families.
>
> I took a few self-defense lessons as a teenager, did target practice with handguns and rifles, and planned on getting a concealed carry license as soon as I was old enough. When that opportunity came, my husband and I were living in the guest bedroom of dear friends who constantly amazed us with their everyday generosity.
>
> They shared whatever they had without thinking twice, despite living in one of the most expensive counties in the US on a house-cleaning, web-building budget. They offered folks housing, rides, warm meals, money, and board games. A rag tag group of ski bums and skeptics need a place to hang out and talk Jesus? Their sectional is open every Friday. One of their boys' birth mothers needs help? They show up with food and clothes and a free ride.
>
> When Trevor and I signed up for the concealed carry class, I didn't think twice about how our housemates would react. The community was full of hunters and gun enthusiasts, so when I asked my friend what she thought about guns, her answer surprised me.
>
> "I get why people want a gun, but we're not really interested in owning any ourselves."
>
> "But what about self-defense?" I pressed. "What if someone breaks into your house and hurts your kids?"
>
> She paused, and spoke the next words with gentle conviction. "That would be tragic. But you know, my people know Jesus. We

know where we're headed. I don't know anything about that burglar, and I just don't think there's anything in my house—including my people—that's worth another human being's eternity."

We finished our class, but moves and job changes and babies kept us from ever sending in the paperwork, and it eventually expired. Her words, however, have lived in my heart since the moment she spoke them. There's nothing I have that's worth more than a person's eternity.

The first time Stephanie shared her story with me, I was struck by the powerful words her friend shared with her: "There's nothing in my house that's worth another human being's eternity." I was familiar with the history of pacifism within certain Christian traditions, the belief that any form of violence is incompatible with the Christian faith, even in self-defense. And I was also familiar with the just war perspective, first originating from St. Thomas Aquinas, that qualifies a war as just if it is declared for "noble and right reasons" and "fought in a certain way." It is a war that Christians see as necessary when all other options have failed.[1] This idea, though, the one shared from Stephanie's friend, is different. It may have pacifist roots, sure, but the foundation is different. Her view sees this person's eternity as the most important factor in deciding what self-defense might look like for her and her family. Her view says, a gun has no place here because my life isn't worth more than someone else's.

This is the idea that I have been wrestling with myself over the last few years: Could I use a gun, or any weapon, to kill someone intending to harm me or my family? Am I a pacifist in this regard? Scholars have argued throughout history whether Jesus was a pacifist. I can point you toward Scripture passages that make the case for both sides. In Matthew 5:39-44, Jesus says:

> But I tell you, do not resist an evil person. If anyone slaps you on the right cheek, turn to them the other cheek also. And if anyone wants to sue you and take your shirt, hand over your coat

as well. If anyone forces you to go one mile, go with them two miles. Give to the one who asks you, and do not turn away from the one who wants to borrow from you. "You have heard that it was said, 'Love your neighbor and hate your enemy.' But I tell you, love your enemies and pray for those who persecute you."

We can also look at Scriptures such as Exodus 22:2-3 where God speaks that it is acceptable to defend our home against a thief, or in Luke 11:21 when Jesus says, "When a strong man, fully armed, guards his own house, his possessions are safe."

We can debate the merits of pacifism versus just war theory all day long. I understand people who fall on both sides. I understand people who feel it is not their right to take a life just as much as I understand people who feel that both war and self-defense are often necessary to protect people. My goal is not to convince you one way or another, or convince people that they shouldn't, under any circumstances, use a gun in self-defense. I do not blame or fault people who want to have guns for this purpose and who would use them to protect their families or others who are being harmed. My fear is that we are using the possibility of defensive gun use as an excuse to own exorbitant amounts of guns and ammunition, and we are using self-defense as a cover for fear, anger, and hatred of other people. My fear is that under the guise of self-defense, we are excusing ourselves from loving and praying for our enemies, and we are seeing all human beings as fellow image bearers, made in the image of God, just as we are.

For so long, Americans have been taught to fear people who are not like us, and to fear people that might want to do us harm. I remember the time after the terrorist attacks on September 11, 2001, when anti-Muslim sentiment was at an all-time high, and we feared anyone who looked "foreign." This fear has persisted now for almost twenty years in America and has been held up as justification for discrimination and cruelty against innocent people. The NRA has similar messaging, convincing Americans that we are under a constant state of threat and must always be prepared to defend ourselves, and that we should use a gun to do it. We are taught to be afraid of anyone and anything we don't know. This fear is seen as justification for possessing as many guns as we want because we might need them. This fear of others as a constant threat creates in us a default setting of seeing people as our enemies instead of our neighbors and as fellow human beings. It's why people feel justified in potentially taking a life as punishment for a simple theft, like when a business owner in a town near mine shot a man last week for stealing catalytic converters from his business.[2] When we see people as enemies, it is easy to decide that material possessions are worth more than their lives. I cannot, and would not want to say, that all cases or uses of self-defense are wrong. Maybe the action of self-defense isn't wrong; maybe it's the ideology we use to justify it as always acceptable.

In 2015, Sarah Palin gave a speech to members of the NRA. In her speech, she said, "Gals, you know that nowadays, ammo is expensive. Don't waste a bullet on a warning shot."[3] The crowd cheered and applauded.

After a mass shooting in San Bernardino, California, in 2015, Jerry Falwell Jr., then president of Liberty University, urged students to carry weapons on campus, saying, "I've always thought if more good people had concealed carry permits, then we could end those Muslims before they walked in."[4] In this case too, the crowd cheered and applauded his words. I cannot reconcile the words of these self-proclaimed Jesus followers with the words of Jesus himself in the Sermon on the Mount to "bless those who curse you, do good to those who hate you, and pray for those who spitefully use you and persecute you" (Luke 6:28), or the ones from Genesis where God says that all human beings are made in the image of God (Genesis 1:27).

As humans, even though we have a natural instinct to protect ourselves, our posture toward others as believers in Christ should be one of love and generosity, even toward people who want to harm us. I don't speak from naivety. More than many, I understand how dangerous the world is and how fear can become second nature to us. And yet, I know my call from God is to love others as he does. Jesus consistently showed love and kindness toward people whom he knew would harm him. When we live in a constant state of fear, one that allows us to be ready to do harm, or even encourages us to kill, we are living in a way that is antithetical to the ways of Christ.

Using a gun or any method of lethal force in acts of self-defense should be considered the last possible resort, and one that grieves us deeply. We should not cheer for it, or applaud it, or encourage people to do it under all circumstances of fear. Jesus loves all of us, every single one of us. He loves the person that might break into your home just as much as he loves you. And I'll tell you this—he loves Neil MacInnis, the person who shot me, as much as he loves me. And it should grieve us deeply to think of taking the life of someone whom Jesus loves.

When I began to publicly speak out about gun reform, I expected the backlash and the criticism. What I did not expect were the attacks on my faith and my character from people who claim to follow Jesus. Even though I had spent almost all of my life in a conservative and religious area of the country where many people own firearms, I never grasped just how enmeshed it all is. I was labeled unpatriotic and un-American for wanting to reduce gun violence. I was told that I hate my country, that I should be more grateful to be an American, that I was attacking a God-given right. I have frequently been told that what happened to me is simply a price we pay for freedom. I have been called an angry and emotional woman. I have been accused of using my victimhood to become famous. I have been told that I am selfish— selfish for wanting to take people's rights and guns away. Selfish for telling my own story and having my own beliefs. And selfish for thinking other people should have to make compromises because something bad happened to me. I have been accused of using my story to manipulate people. I have asked people, "If giving up your guns meant saving a life, would you do it?" And they have replied to me, passionately, "No. It's my right." Maybe the worst part of all of this criticism is that when the comments happen online, and I click over to view their profile, I see a line saying that they believe in God.

None of these criticisms or observations about me are true, except for one: I am angry. I am angry about the ways guns have poisoned our country like lead seeping into our water. I am angry that people are taught to cling to their personal freedoms and their individual comforts above caring for real-life humans. I am angry that the God I believe in, the one who teaches us to love our neighbors, to sacrifice our lives for that of our friend, and to consider others more important than ourselves has been turned into a justification for a right he did not bestow and an ideology that looks nothing like him. So, yes, I sure am angry. But more than that, I am sad.

We can debate the context and meaning of the Second Amendment all day long. We can discuss rights and liberty and freedom until our voices grow weak. But at the end of the day, if you are someone who follows Jesus, it just doesn't matter. Maybe it's shocking for you to hear that something in one of our country's foundational documents doesn't matter. Maybe it sounds blasphemous. Let me explain further.

I am thankful to be an American. I recognize the privileges given to me as a citizen of this country from birth, and I'm incredibly grateful for the opportunities afforded to me simply because I was born here. But what I care about more than anything, what I am grateful for more than anything, what I love more than anything, is Jesus. We have been given rights in this country that people in other countries do not have. We should be thankful for that. But if those rights don't serve everyone, if they are misguided, if they are harmful, why do we continue to elevate them as gospel truth? Why have we become so devoted to the twenty-seven words of the Second Amendment that we can close our eyes to the suffering they have inflicted and the lives they've stolen? If you are a follower of Jesus, your inheritance is in Christ. The kingdom of heaven is our home. We are coheirs with Christ in the kingdom of God! That is what the Word of God—the divinely inspired Word of God—tells us. That's what we believe. It is more important than anything on this earth. It is more important than anything any man or woman could write down with quill and ink. That's our gift from God—not some man-made right to own firearms. If I have to choose whether I will pledge my devotion to the kingdom of God or the kingdom of guns? I choose God, every time.

In Matthew 6, Jesus says no one can serve two masters, because we will be devoted to one and despise the other. He's talking about money, I know. We can't serve God and money. He's also talking about the evil that serving money can lead to: loving it so much takes our attention away from more important things, spending so much time and energy thinking about money it becomes our master, controlling us in how we live and make decisions. We can make masters out of anything. We are professionals at making and upholding idols, which is why God made it one of the Ten Commandments. And we have certainly made masters out of our country and out of firearms. When we choose to remain silent and complicit in the 40,000 deaths of our neighbors every year due to gun violence, all in the name of an individual right that has nothing to do with our calling as believers, and then we yell and we scream and we cling desperately to guns when someone so much as mentions the word "reform"—that's a master. That's not Jesus.

In 1 Corinthians 10:23-24, we read, "'I have the right to do anything,' you say—but not everything is beneficial. 'I have the right to do anything'—but not everything is constructive. No one should seek their own good, but the good of others." In America, we have many rights. And yet we should view them through the lens Paul speaks about in these verses. If we exercise a right that does harm to others, we aren't serving anyone, even ourselves. Our freedom is in Christ and Christ alone. Any rights we exercise should align with the ways in which he has asked us to walk.

Gun reform isn't about taking away everyone's guns, or even the right to own one. But I ask you: Even if it were, even if guns were banned tomorrow, why should we be so afraid? If you know and love Jesus and are going to spend eternity in heaven with him, why does the idea of not having guns anymore scare you so much?

When we recite the Lord's Prayer, we say, "Your kingdom come, your will be done, on earth as it is in heaven." There are no guns in heaven. When I pray this prayer, I ask that God would help me bring some of his kingdom to earth. I pray that, in the same way, there would be no gun violence here on earth, just as there is no gun violence in heaven.

Many people own guns for the just-in-case, the maybe, the what-ifs. Meanwhile, I live in a constant state of the reality, the actual, and the absolute. My reality is the same as thousands of others in America who wake up from a nightmare at 3 a.m. and can't sleep. Who operate in a dull state of chronic pain. Who cower at the sound of a car backfiring. Who wonder if the bullet fragments left in their body are poisoning them or damaging their bodies as they move around, inching closer to the surface of their skin. When I log into my online survivors support group I see posts of despair by people who miss their children, their parents, and their friends who were stolen because of gun violence. I see posts from people who are in a state of panic because someone set off fireworks in their neighborhood or who can't stop panicking after seeing reports of a shooting on the news. While some people sit in homes admiring the guns on their nightstand or in their display cases, there's another group of people who are trying their best to figure out how to live in a world where those guns are more important than their lives and the lives of people they love. We don't get to live in the what-if anymore.

The first time I saw gun violence addressed in church was in 2018 when we started attending a Methodist church in Tennessee. A section of the bulletin was dedicated to the topic, with statistics and facts, and an announcement they would be holding a showing of the documentary *The Armor of Light*. Tears streamed down my face as this deep wound in my soul suddenly felt seen and acknowledged by the church. No longer did I feel like a simple casualty of American rights, alone in the desire for change. I felt like people were with me, running on mission alongside me to end this crisis and help alleviate the suffering of thousands of people who live in America. That's when I realized what I had been missing for five years. It's like the link between the church I knew, the America I lived in, and the guns around me was so strong, I never expected it to be talked about in church. It was never even a possibility. When it was, a wall broke down inside my mind, and I could see the things that might be possible if the church would cast aside its connection to guns and would speak up and take a stand against the violence guns help perpetuate.

I want other people to feel the way I did. I want other survivors to know they are seen and known by God and therefore seen and known by us too. I want them to feel supported and held and cared for by us because we are the hands and feet of Jesus on earth. I want to put an end to the days of feeling invisible and forgotten and ignored because our guns are more valued in our country than our lives. Maybe it sounds like hyperbole, but it's not. Ask any survivor or anyone who has lost a loved one in a mass shooting. Ask a parent who lost a child in a school shooting. Ask a mother whose baby was shot and killed while driving in the car through her own neighborhood. Ask what they heard first on the news. Was it, "We need to end gun violence" or was it, "We need more guns!"? Were people quicker to run to protect their guns or their neighbors? Were they quicker to want more rights for themselves or to sacrificially lay down something they hold dear in order to protect someone else?

This morning I saw on the local news that a man was seen walking around our downtown area open carrying an AR-15, simply because he could. I did what I tell myself not to do, and I read the Facebook comments. "It should've been loaded!" one comment said. Another read, "Good for him! Show them they can't take our guns!" I felt my body shaking a little bit, both with anger and sadness. I remembered the pictures of the past few months of heavily armed protestors at the statehouses in Michigan and Virginia. People were walking around with hunting and assault-style rifles as a show of force against people they feel have infringed on their rights. And I'm sad. And I'm angry.

There is not an ounce of empathy or care in those posts for people like me, who have been harmed by the weapons they carry. In those moments, it is all about them and this right that they hold so dearly.

I am not against rights, I promise. I'm against the rights we value above our lives, and our thriving, and our children. I am against this idea that we all just have to keep paying the price for the freedom the Second Amendment supposedly offers while we are dying in our streets and in our classrooms, our churches, our movie theaters, and our homes. We have accepted this as our reality, tossed our hands into the air and said, "Oh well!" And no matter what studies or commentary I read that tell me why this is, I still don't know why this is. There are two sides to the gun reform debate, and they aren't Republican and Democrat. There are those who want to save lives and those who want to save guns. More guns kill more people. We can't be on both sides, and the longer we keep acting like we can, the longer we go on living in this endless cycle of death and suffering, offering only our empty thoughts and our conciliatory prayers.

A lot of Christians blame gun violence on evil, saying no laws can change evil hearts. And they're right. I don't disagree. After my friend Adam was killed on live TV by a man with a gun, I wrote a whole blog post about the cause of gun violence being evil and how we just can't make sense of evil. I still believe that. I just believe other things now too.

People commit acts of gun violence against others because this is a sinful world filled with suffering and strife and yes, evil. What about people who die from firearm suicide? Are they filled with evil? Or are they just suffering from pain that feels too heavy to keep carrying? And then there are the children who find a gun on their dad's nightstand and kill a sibling or a friend thinking it's just a toy. Are they evil? Are their parents evil? Or do they just simply have access to a gun owned by parents who were sold an idea that guns keep their families safer? I believe there is evil in this world. I have seen it up-close and personal standing right in front of me. I have seen it point a gun right at my head. I believe evil makes people do evil things. I just happen to believe we don't have to give guns to the evil.

As believers, we can believe in both things. We can believe there is evil in this world and Satan is constantly attempting to kill, steal, and destroy. We can also believe in the power of laws and action as a form of loving and serving our neighbor.

In Luke 10, Jesus tells the story of the Good Samaritan to a law expert who asked him, "What must I do to inherit eternal life?" Jesus tells him the story of a man who was attacked by robbers and was left on the side of the road half-dead. A priest and a Levite both passed him on the opposite side of the road. But then, the Samaritan came along and took pity on this broken and beaten man. He bandaged his wounds and poured oil and wine on them. He took the man to an inn and cared for him. Jesus asked the people listening to the story, "Which of these three do you think was a neighbor to the man who fell into the hands of robbers?" The expert in the law replied, "The one who had mercy one him." And Jesus said to him, "Go and do likewise."

I am constantly struck by the context of the telling of this story. The story of the Good Samaritan in itself is good and helpful. But it's why Jesus told this story that gets me. The beginning of the story reads:

> On one occasion an expert in the law stood up to test Jesus. "Teacher," he asked, "what must I do to inherit eternal life?"
>
> "What is written in the Law?" he replied. "How do you read it?"
>
> He answered, "'Love the Lord your God with all your heart and with all your soul and with all your strength and with all your mind'; and, 'Love your neighbor as yourself.'"
>
> "You have answered correctly," Jesus replied. "Do this and you will live." (Luke 10:25-28)

Jesus says to inherit eternal life we must love God, and we must love our neighbor. Then he tells us what loving our neighbor looks like. He says go and do. Imagine a scenario in which the Good Samaritan passed by the man dying on the side of the road and stopped down to offer his thoughts and prayers and then go on his merry way. This man is called good because he cared for this man's physical needs, because he showed this man mercy, not because he simply prayed for this man to be helped. Jesus says this is what loving our neighbor is. It is seeing their needs and taking care of them the way we take care of our own.

I believe in the power of prayer. I believe in praying for others and I am thankful everyday for the people who have and continue to pray for me. Every time I see a shooting on the news, I pause to pray, every time. Every month in my prayer journal I write a line for gun violence. It's not the thoughts and prayers I'm tired of. It's pretending the thoughts and prayers are all we have to do and all we have to offer.

I can't make people change their minds about gun reform. I can't force people to believe the data, the studies, and the stories. All I can do is offer these up for consideration. I can remind us of the words of Jesus many of us have read in the Bible since childhood. I can offer a picture of what the world might look like if Christians fought to save lives lost at the hands of gun violence as they do for those lost in abortion. I can ask all of us to imagine a world where we lay down the weapons of this world and try out the ways of Jesus for a change. The worst that could happen? We end up more like him and less like this world.

We have so much more to offer this world than thoughts and prayers. We know a Savior who redeem, rescues, and gives of himself to save others. A Savior who leaves the ninety-nine to find the one who is lost. We know a Savior who has taught us how to love one another. This is what we have to offer this world. This is what I want us to see.

We are clinging so tightly to this thing that the world gave us, instead of walking in the ways that Jesus offers to us.

I want to end gun violence. I want no one else to have to suffer as a result of this horrific crisis. But what I want even more than that, is for Christians to take up their place in this fight. I want them to finally open their eyes to this injustice all around them, and to show the world we are here and we care and we will work to protect each other. I want us to stop enabling violence and instead seek peace, even if it costs us something. We have the ability to bring the kingdom of God to this earth with our hands and our feet. If the goal of being a follower of Jesus is to be more like him and to invite other people into his kingdom, then this would be a great place to start.

We can't keep trying to serve two masters. We can't keep passing the dying man on the side of the road. We've desperately tried for decades to hold a Bible in one hand and a gun in the other and we have no hands left to serve each other, or Jesus. We have to choose. We have to lay one down. So I ask, who will you serve this day?

EPILOGUE

A FEW DAYS AGO, I stood at my kitchen sink, washing dishes with my hands, one of them still wounded and scarred, while tears ran down my cheeks. Over and over again, I whispered to myself it's only fireworks, it's not gunshots. I said it until I believed it, and then again at 2 a.m. when the sound of someone else's Fourth of July celebration woke me up and put me back into my worst nightmare. The next morning, amidst the sounds that accompany a toddler's existence—the banging of blocks and the whining sounds he uses to try to express feelings he doesn't quite yet have words for—I felt on edge. I felt like the insides of myself were scratching against sandpaper, making me want to crawl out of my skin. For me, right now, living in the seventh year after the shooting, this is PTSD.

When I have trouble holding Henry in my hands because one doesn't work like I need it to work, I grow frustrated, and I imagine what life would be like if I didn't have bullet fragments in my body, and I cry. For me, right now, that is grief. Sometimes on good days when I don't feel much physical pain and I don't feel hindered by my limitations, it feels like the shooting was a lifetime ago, like it was then, and not now. But later, some pain sends aches through my body or a bad dream wakes me up, and I remember that after a shooting the then is always the now. It changes and it doesn't change at the same time.

My life is good. Even when it is filled with hard things, traumatic memories, and physical pain—it is so good. I wake up every morning next to a husband who has loved me through the hardest moments. I pour my coffee and take a few minutes to read Scripture while the day is still quiet and new. I hear my son being chatty from his room, and I walk in to see him smiling at me. I get to clean the counters and fold the laundry and sip the good wine. I get to take deep breaths of fresh air while I walk my dog who has been a faithful friend to me. I get to feel the sun on my face and the waves wash over my feet. I am here for the normal, everyday things that were almost taken from me. I get to do work that matters and pushes me to make the world a better place. The shooting changed me and my life in so many ways. And it would be dishonest to not admit to the ways in which it changed me for the better.

Sometimes acknowledging the ways the shooting has made my life better feels like a surrender, like I am saying I am thankful I was shot, or that it's okay. It's not okay that I was shot. And yet, so much of who I am has been made better through what God has done in my life in the aftermath of the worst day of my life.

I am a more empathetic person than I was before. I am a better friend and a better advocate for people who are suffering. I am no longer blinded to injustice and inequality in the world. I don't feel weak in the ways I felt weak before. I know how to fight now, for myself and for others. I learned how strong I am, because of how strong God is in me.

I am proud of the work I did to recover, the tears I cried, and the pain I pushed through to get where I am. I am thankful to God every day for rescuing me, interceding for me, and for never leaving my side even when the darkness of night felt like it would never make way for the light of day to breakthrough. God has made much beauty out of my ashes. Even now as I am experiencing new complications from my injuries almost eight years later, and I wonder what my life will look like as daily life takes its toll on my bones and my joints, I will shout from the rooftops that God is faithful to me. Even when I am not. He continues to turn my mourning into dancing and my tears into laughter. And the best part? It's not a one-time deal.

I get to experience God doing this for me day in and day out. When I cry at the sink because the loud booms rattle my body, he is there with his mighty hand to calm my spirit. When fear fills my mind and tries to keep me trapped in my anxieties, he is there bringing a peace that surpasses my understanding. When I feel inadequate and defective because I can't get my child's shoes on or open a jar by myself, he reminds me I am made in his image and held in his hand. When I imagine the worst happening to my husband or my son, he brings me back to the safety of his arms.

Today Henry cried because he wanted me to help him put his rain boots on. We sat on the floor together as I attempted to pull them on, not being able to maneuver my hand to hold them steady enough to slide his foot into. "I'm so sorry, Momma can't do it," I told him. "I'm so sorry, I wish I could get them on for you." And we both sat in the floor crying. Because he just wanted to wear his rain boots, and he can't understand why his momma can't help him do it, and she doesn't ever want to have to explain to him why.

I will have to explain it to him, though. Someday Eric and I will sit down with him and explain to him why his mom has scars on her hand and her chest. When he goes to school and has to practice hiding in his classroom closet, he will understand that gun violence has already touched his life more than other kids at school. He'll understand no one is exempt.

Since he was born, I've had this horrible vision in my head: a school shooting comes across the news and Henry asks me, "Why didn't you do anything to stop it?" In everything I write and speak about gun violence, this is what drives me: the future of my child, my nieces and nephews, my friend's kids, your kids—all of our kids. My generation and the ones after mine deserve better than what we got, and I want better for our kids. It seems like the least we can do for our kids is do everything we can to prevent them from getting murdered at school. We may not be able to pay their college tuition, but at least they'll be alive to go.

I want Henry to know his mom did everything she could to protect him, to keep him safe, and to make sure he doesn't have to ever experience what she did. Maybe it seems like a pipe dream, an uphill battle, and an impossibility. I'll keep taking the hateful comments and the threatening direct messages. I'll receive the judgmental glances and hear the whispers behind my back of how I've changed, how I've fallen so far from who I was, how I'm deceived.

I'll keep working for peace and for life. He's worth it. I'm worth it. We are worth it.

People tell me new laws won't work and new restrictions won't save lives. I say, let's try and see. I'm willing to be wrong. I'm not willing to not try.

Sometimes it all feels too big and too far gone. I feel like one person trying to pull a sinking ship to shore. But then I feel the tension lessen and I look over my shoulder to find someone new helping me pull the rope, and I think, maybe we can do this.

Maybe we can do it together.

ACKNOWLEDGMENTS

TO ERIC: IT WOULD BE impossible for me to describe here the things you sacrificed, the work you did, the time you spent helping me recover, and the ways you have supported me since the shooting. Our first years of marriage were not like either one of us expected, but you gave up so much to make sure I got the care, the support, and the help that I needed to heal and to recover. You sacrificed without complaint and did thankless work for me that no one else ever saw. While I sometimes wish we didn't go through all the things we did, I am thankful we entered into our marriage knowing what is really important in life. We have faced things in our ten years together that most people will never have to, and I know that we are as solid as we are because of it. When I was trapped inside that supply closet, I was so scared I would never see you again and that we would never get to get married, have children, or grow old together. Every day, I'm thankful that we do. I love you.

To Henry: One day you'll read this book. You won't remember all the days of me writing it in the corner of the room while you played, or stealing away into the kitchen for a few moments just to get another three words written. You may not understand how you were the driving force in my writing these words even when it felt impossible. But you, my little buddy, are the reason I wrote this book. When I feel defeated about changing anyone's mind or hopeless at the prospect of ending gun violence, I just look at you. You were born into this world that you did not create. For too long, the grownups in the room have abdicated our responsibility and passed on our problems to our kids.

I want to be a better kind of grown up. I want to make the world safer, happier, better, and more just for you—and for every other child. I love you more than anything in the whole world.

To my parents, Brenda and Gerry, the people who always knew I would write a book someday: I know this isn't quite the one we imagined. Thank you for raising me to be kind and compassionate, and never making me feel like my empathy was a weakness. Thank you for teaching me about Jesus and to love my neighbors well. Thank you for creating a safe and loving home for Kelley and me. It would be nearly impossible for me to express how grateful I am to you both for everything you have done and continue to do for me, but I'll try. Thank you for always allowing me to be myself and to pursue things that made me happy. Dad, thank you for always encouraging me to become a writer. You never let me think it might be too hard or too frivolous to try. I always believed I could do it, and I know that's because of you. Mom, you always believed I would do great things in my life. Thank you for praying for me daily, and for teaching me the things that matter most in life: loving God and loving people. I love you both so very much.

To my sister, Kelley: Thank you for always making me laugh and being a bright spot on days that felt too hard and too heavy. I will never forget how you learned how to do my finger exercises so that I could go to my bachelorette party, and all the days you helped me fix my hair or do my makeup so I could feel just a little bit normal. I will never know what it was like for you to experience the day of the shooting and the ones that came after, but I'm thankful that you were there with me, and I'm always thankful that you are my sister. Through thick and thin, I love you lots.

To my Hype Squad: Lauryn, Bekkah, and Stephanie. There is no way this book would've gotten written if not for you all encouraging me, cheering me on, praying for me, and celebrating each step in the process with me. Each of you ran toward me during days where other people were running away from me. You entered into a relationship with me when I was in a dark season, and you each have been the hands and feet of Jesus to me here on earth. You answered panicked texts with encouragement and let me vent and process when I needed to. You are my dearest friends, and I am so incredibly thankful for you all.

To Sophie: Where to begin? You were there in the minutes right after the shooting, and you never left. Thank you for picking the pieces of wood shrapnel out of my hair and making sure I had the appropriate feminine hygiene products because, as it turns out, one is not immune from a period just because she got shot. Thank you for sitting with me in my pain and my grief and allowing me to be real and honest. Thank you for never forgetting and never making me feel forgotten or left behind. You are a once in a lifetime best friend. And I am so glad you are mine.

To my dear friend and sister-in-love, Kathryn: I love you a lot. I'm so thankful for you and how well you loved and supported both Eric and myself in the days following the shooting and every day since. Thank you for planning such fun things for us to do together—from our pumpkin spice tours to furniture shopping and everything in between. Thank you for always supporting me, encouraging me, praying for me, and cheering me on. Love you dearly.

To my second family, Dave, Susy, Matt, Chris, Elizabeth, Katie, and Kevin: When I met you all, I was immediately excited to be part of the family. I couldn't have known then how important it would be to have such a strong support system full of love, prayer, support, and joy. You all took me into the family as if I had always been a part. On the darkest of days, you helped to carry Eric and me with strength and resolve. You made us laugh when things were heavy and celebrated with us when things were good. I am forever grateful to you all. Thank you.

To Martha: I would not be who I am today without you. I am so very grateful that my family kidnapped me and brought me to see you, even when I did not want to go. You taught me about God and grief, pain and joy. You sat with me in my suffering and my sadness, and helped me find a way through it. You prayed for me and helped me find a way back to myself. I am forever grateful for you, your kindness, and support. Thank you.

To Patti: I still get teary eyed when I think about how terrified I was in the days after the shooting and how coming into your office for therapy was somehow always calming to me, even though I knew there would be pain involved. I am grateful to no end that God placed you in my path and allowed me to spend a year sitting across the table from you. You helped bring my hand back to life and helped bring me back to life too. I will never forget the kindness and tenderness with which you treated me, even on the hardest and most painful days. Thank you for everything. I will never forget it.

To Holly: In 2015 you asked me to go a writer's conference with you, and the rest is history. Everything I learned that weekend, and the encouragement from you, gave me the confidence to call myself a writer and to say out loud that I wanted to write a book. This book, I feel confident saying, wouldn't have happened without you. Thank you.

To KJ: Thank you for mentoring me, not just in writing, but in how to be a fully embodied human and follower of Jesus. Thank you for all of your encouragement, your wisdom, and your kindness.

To my Twitter fam: I don't know how it happened, but I managed to become part of the most kind, supportive, and fun place on that website. There are too many of you to name here, and too many ways you've helped and encouraged me to list. You have sent encouraging messages, prayed, sent snacks, coffee money, and delightful skincare products to get me through the darkest days of writing. You've held my story with kindness, care, and openness. And maybe most importantly, you made sure I knew that the world needed my words. I truly cannot express enough gratitude to you all. Thank you.

To Randy and Keith: Thank you for everything you did to support me and my family in the days and years following the shooting. I felt such peace knowing you were on our side. Randy, thank you for reaching out to me every year on the anniversary of the shooting and letting me know I am not forgotten. It means everything. Thank you.

To Jess Connolly: Thank you for being my hype man whenever I needed one. Thank you for reminding me daily why I do what I do, and how impactful it is to the world. Thank you for speaking life into my heart and calling me up into the work God gave me to do. I am so grateful for you and your friendship.

To Joy Beth Smith: Thank you for believing in me and seeing what I could accomplish even before I could. You helped me start believing that I really did have books in me, and helped me make it happen. I am so incredibly grateful to and for you. Thank you.

To my church family at Bright City: Thank you for welcoming us into your community and supporting me in so many different ways as I wrote this book. Your love and support has been invaluable.

To my agent, Keely: This book exists in large part because of you. Thank you for taking a chance on someone you randomly encountered on Twitter, and for believing in me and in this book. You worked so hard to help me get this book into the world—helping me craft the best book proposal I could write, and being my strongest advocate for what I wanted this book to be. I can never thank you enough.

To my editor, Al, and the team at IVP: Thank you for believing in me and in this book. Thank you for helping bring my story and my words to life. I am forever grateful.

DISCUSSION GUIDE

INTRODUCTION

- Give yourself a moment to consider how you're feeling about reading this book. What are the words you would use to describe your emotional state, thought process, and even the way you feel in your body?

- What have your conversations about guns been like in the past? Do you come from a background where many people shared a opinion on guns or gun reform, or have you had experience with diverse approaches to guns and gun reform?

- Think about an event in your life that changed the way you experienced later events. It could be positive: a new job, the birth of a child, a graduation; or it could be negative: a traumatic event like a death or tragedy, the loss of a relationship, or an illness. How has that event not merely stayed in the past for you but stuck with you as you continue on in your life?

CHAPTER ONE

- What was it like for you to read Taylor's story?

- Which parts of the story did you find yourself continuing to think about after you finished the chapter?

- Did this chapter remind you of any traumatic events in your own life? Perhaps you've been the beloved one in the hospital, or you've been the one standing in the hallway as you wait on the news of a surgery's outcome. What memories come to mind, and how can you take steps to acknowledge the feelings they conjure and process them as you carry on in your reading?

CHAPTER TWO

- Taylor writes, "There is a special cruelty in experiencing an intense trauma at the hands of someone else and then realizing that you'll be paying for it the rest of your life." What is an example of this in your own life or the life of someone you know?

- Have you ever anticipated a "victory story" or miracle in your life? What happened? How did the outcome shape your view of God and yourself?

- How would you answer Taylor's question, "Where [does] a story of a lack of healing fit into the kingdom?"

CHAPTER THREE

- Taylor wondered why she couldn't just "be grateful" at her bridal shower. Have you ever been in a situation where you felt guilty for your lack of gratitude, but simply couldn't conjure it? What was that like?

- This chapter details some of the ways that Taylor's relationships changed after the shooting. How have you experienced shifts in your friendships or romantic relationships after one of you experienced something unexpected?

- "I began allowing myself to grieve without guilt. It allowed me to identify the parts of me that were hurting, and it brought the freedom to invite the people around me into my experience," Taylor writes. How does acknowledging our pain open us up to deeper relationships?

CHAPTER FOUR

- Have you ever experienced posttraumatic stress or do you know someone who has? How has that experience—whether your own or that of someone you love—shaped your life?

- Taylor writes that she "couldn't figure out how the world kept going and seemingly everyone else could go back to their normal lives, but I was stuck here." How does that statement resonate with your own experiences, or how does it shape your perspective on the experiences of others?

- What's your worst-case scenario? How might playing it out in your mind bring it "out of the darkness and [give] you the power back" from fear of the possibility?

CHAPTER FIVE

- Taylor explains some of the legal proceedings that took place in the days, weeks, and months after the shooting. What did you learn from her story about the way the criminal justice system responds to shootings?

- Eric, Taylor's husband, once said to her, "Taylor, if we wait until justice is done on earth to move on, we will never move on." What is a personal experience or world event that caused you to long for justice on earth? How would you respond to Eric's statement?

- What were some of your reactions to some of the components of the courtroom testimony, such as the shooter's experience of buying a gun and his online post?

CHAPTER SIX

- Have you ever assumed that God had something "big" planned for you but it turned out that he had something else for you? What was that experience like?

- Taylor says that she felt like "God saved the wrong person" because she wasn't telling her story the way that she thought she should be. When have you wondered if you were disappointing God or others?

- How do Taylor's experiences with statements like "well, if anyone you can handle it, you can" and "everything happens for a reason" coincide with or challenge your perspective on such maxims? How about the idea of God wanting her to rest in him?

CHAPTER SEVEN

- Taylor asks, "If I stayed silent, despite not feeling ready to wade into the public discourse around gun violence, was I contributing to the suffering of others?" How would you respond to her?

- How have you seen your views—political or otherwise—shift over time due to personal experiences in your life?

- Taylor writes that she felt abandoned by her fellow believers. Have you ever felt that way? Have you ever, even unintentionally, acted in a way that could make someone else feel that way? How can you take a step toward suffering with those who suffer, or allowing others to suffer with you?

PART 2

- Take some time to digest what you've read so far. How are you feeling? What are you thinking? What have you learned? What will you continue to ponder?

- Think about a trauma you or someone you know has experienced. Talk through, or even write down, the people who were affected, like Taylor does when she describes the ripple effects of a shooting for family members, coworkers, bystanders, and first responders. How many people, or groups of people, may that trauma have touched?

- Take stock of what you know going into this section about violence from past reading, experiences, or news consumption. Did the fact that one hundred people are shot and killed and two hundred ten people survive gunshot injuries in the United States surprise you in any way? Give yourself some time to assess your position on guns, what informs it, and how you're feeling going into part two of the book.

CHAPTER EIGHT

- What did you learn about intimate-partner gun violence? What are your thoughts on reforms laws pertaining to domestic gun violence, specifically those recommended in this chapter?

- What is your reaction to the idea of firearm suicide being a type of gun violence?

- Choose one of the recommended reforms (permit-to-purchase, red flag, mandatory waiting periods, safe storage) and, as an exercise, make an argument for and against the reform. What's natural for you to argue? What's more difficult?

CHAPTER NINE

- How old were you when the Columbine High School shooting happened (1999)? How did that event, or any other school shooting, affect you?

- Taylor shares how her perspective on active-shooter drills changed as she learned about their effect on children. What are your thoughts on active-shooter drills?

- What is something you learned about the ways mass shootings are categorized and defined? What are your thoughts on legal possibilities such as limiting assault-style weapons and high-capacity magazines, taxing assault-style weapons and ammunition, and extreme risk protection orders?

CHAPTER TEN

- Polarized conversations about guns often tend to create the impression that people who are pro-gun reform are anti-police, but the evidence demonstrates that "limiting the number of guns in the hands of civilians would not only reduce fatal police shootings, but would save police officers as well." How does that information influence your perspective on gun ownership, gun violence, and gun reform?

- What did you learn about the intersection of race, gun violence, and police violence from this chapter?

- What's one step you could take toward a deeper understanding of the relationship between systemic and structural racism in America and urban gun violence?

CHAPTER ELEVEN

- Do you, or did you, believe any of the talking points Taylor disputes as myths? If so, how could you learn more and pursue the truth?

- Do you find yourself drawn to any of the suggestions in the "What can I do to help?" or "What can churches do to help?" sections? If so, which one? What's one step you can take toward taking that action?

- Who in your life could be a safe person for you to process your thoughts about gun violence and reform?

CHAPTER TWELVE

- How comfortable are you with saying, "I don't know"?

- How can you become a person who can change their mind, and is a safe person for others to engage with about changing their minds?

- What are the potential points of discomfort in your relationships if you engage in conversations about gun violence? How does that feel? How can you both engage in difficult conversations and re-member that you are not solely responsible to solve gun violence?

CHAPTER THIRTEEN

- What are the differences between respecting a right and being mastered by it?

- How do you understand the role of prayer when it comes to gun violence?

- Based on what you've learned and considered while you've read, what are one to three action steps you want to take?

NOTES

INTRODUCTION

[1]"Statistics," Giffords Law Center to Prevent Gun Violence, September 18, 2020, https://giffords.org/gun-violence-statistics/.

[2]"Firearm Suicide in the United States," Everytown Research & Policy, August 11, 2020, https://everytownresearch.org/firearm-suicide/.

[3]"Gun Violence in America," Everytown Research & Policy, August 3, 2020, https://everytownresearch.org/gun-violence-america/.

3. GRIEVING WHAT SHOULD HAVE BEEN

[1]Bessel van der Kolk, *The Body Keeps the Score: Brain, Mind, and Body in the Healing of Trauma* (New York: Penguin Books, 2015), 53.

8. DOMESTIC VIOLENCE, FAMILY FIRE, AND FIREARM SUICIDE

[1]"Gun Violence in America," Everytown Research & Policy, May 19, 2020, https://everytownresearch.org/report/gun-violence-in-america/.

[2]Ryan J. Foley, "States Taking Action to Keep Guns out of Abusers' Hands," *Des Moines Register*, February 7, 2016, www.desmoinesregister.com/story/news/2016/02/07/states-taking-action-keep-guns-out-abusers-hands/79975478/.

[3]"Guns and Violence Against Women: America's Uniquely Lethal Intimate Partner Violence Problem, 10.17.2019," Everytown Research & Policy, October 17, 2019, https://everytownresearch.org/report/guns-and-violence-against-women-americas-uniquely-lethal-intimate-partner-violence-problem/.

[4]"Guns and Violence Against Women."

[5]"Guns and Violence Against Women."

[6]"Guns and Violence Against Women."

[7]Maura Ewing, "An Estimated 4.5 Million Women Have Been Bullied With Guns By Abusive Partners," *The Trace*, October 5, 2016, www.thetrace.org/2016/10/nonfatal-gun-use-domestic-violence/.

[8]Jennifer Mascia, "When Men Use Guns to Abuse Women, Without Pulling the Trigger," *The Trace*, March 25, 2019, www.thetrace.org/2018/09/guns-domestic-violence-coercive-control/.

[9]"Guns and Violence Against Women."

[10]"Guns and Violence Against Women."

[11]"Guns and Violence Against Women."

[12]"Domestic Violence & Firearms," Giffords Law Center to Prevent Gun Violence, October 29, 2020, https://giffords.org/lawcenter/gun-laws/policy-areas/who-can-have-a-gun/domestic-violence-firearms/.

[13]"Guns and Violence Against Women."

[14]"Domestic Violence & Firearms."

[15]AZ, CA, CO, DE, HI, IL, IN, MA, MN, MD, NJ, NM, NY, OR, PA, RI, SC, TX, VT, WI, and Washington, DC.

[16]CA, CT, DE, HI, IL, IN, KS, MA, ME, MD, MN, NE, NJ, NM, NY, OR, RI, VT, WA, WV, and Washington, DC.

[17]CA, CT, DE, HI, IL, LA, MA, MD, MN, NC, NH, NJ, NM, NY, OR, PA, RI, TX, WA, WI, WV, and Washington, DC.

[18]"Guns and Violence Against Women."

[19]"Guns and Violence Against Women."

[20]"Guns and Violence Against Women."

[21]U.S. Government Accountability Office, "Gun Control: Analyzing Available Data Could Help Improve Background Checks Involving Domestic Violence Records," July 5, 2016, www.gao.gov/products/GAO-16-483.

[22]"Gun Control."

[23]CA, CO, CT, HI, IA, LA, MD, MA, MN, NV, NJ, NY, OR, PA, RI, and TN.

[24]"Firearm Relinquishment," Giffords Law Center to Prevent Gun Violence, October 23, 2020, https://giffords.org/lawcenter/gun-laws/policy-areas/who-can-have-a-gun/firearm-relinquishment/.

[25]Jennifer Mascia, "Domestic Violence Offenders Abusers Frequently Get to Keep Their Guns. Here Are the Big Reasons Why," *The Trace*, October 2, 2018, www.thetrace.org/2015/10/domestic-abuse-guns-boyfriend-loophole/.

[26]"Domestic Abuse Protective Orders and Firearm Access in Rhode Island," Everytown Research & Policy, June 15, 2015, https://everytownresearch.org/report/domestic-abuse-protective-orders-and-firearm-access-in-rhode-island/.

[27]"Guns and Violence Against Women."

[28]"Gun Control."

[29]"Key Statistics," Brady Campaign to End Gun Violence, accessed January 4, 2021, www.bradyunited.org/key-statistics.

[30]Nora Biette-Timmons, "Roughly 4.6 Million American Kids Live in Homes With Unlocked, Loaded Guns," *The Trace*, May 21, 2018, www.thetrace.org/rounds/study-american-children-unlocked-loaded-gun-storage/.

[31]"Unload, Lock, and Separate: Secure Storage Practices to Reduce Gun Violence," Everytown Research & Policy, September 3, 2019, https://everytown research.org/report/unload-lock-and-separate-secure-storage-practices-to -reduce-gun-violence/.

[32]"Unload, Lock, and Separate."

[33]"Unload, Lock, and Separate."

[34]CBS News, "3 Out of 4 Children in Homes with Guns Know Where the Firearms Are Kept," CBS Interactive, March 19, 2018, www.cbsnews.com /news/3-out-of-4-children-in-homes-with-guns-know-where-the-firearms -are-kept/.

[35]CA, DC, MA, MN, NV, NY, and VA.

[36]"Unload, Lock, and Separate."

[37]CT, DE, FL, HI, IA, IL, MD, NC, NH, NJ, RI, TX, WA, and WI.

[38]"Unload, Lock, and Separate."

[39]"Unload, Lock, and Separate."

[40]"Unload, Lock, and Separate."

[41]Shannan Catalano, "Victimization During Household Burglary," Bureau of Justice Statistics (BJS), September 30, 2010, www.bjs.gov/index.cfm?ty=pbdetail.

[42]Catalano, "Victimization During Household Burglary."

[43]"Unload, Lock, and Separate."

[44]Therese Apel and Harold Gator, "13-Year-Old Girl Dead after 9-Year-Old Brother Shoots Her over Video Game, Sheriff Says," *Mississippi Clarion Ledger*, March 18, 2018, www.clarionledger.com/story/news/local/2018/03/18/video -game-argument-shooting/436364002/.

[45]"Firearm Suicide in the United States," Everytown Research & Policy, August 20, 2019, https://everytownresearch.org/report/firearm-suicide-in-the-united-states/.

[46]"Firearm Suicide in the United States."

[47]"Firearm Suicide in the United States."

[48]"Firearm Suicide in the United States."

[49]Segen's Medical Dictionary, s.v. "Means Substitution," retrieved November 2, 2020, https://medical-dictionary.thefreedictionary.com/Means+Substitution.

[50]Sara B Vyrostek, Joseph L Annest, and George W Ryan, "Surveillance for Fatal and Nonfatal Injuries—United States, 2001," morbidity and mortality weekly report, surveillance summaries, Washington, DC: 2002, *U.S. National Library of Medicine*, September 3, 2004, https://pubmed.ncbi.nlm.nih.gov/15343143/.

[51]Madeline Drexler, "Guns & Suicide," *Harvard Public Health Magazine*, December 1, 2016, www.hsph.harvard.edu/magazine/magazine_article/guns-suicide/.

[52]"Firearm Suicide in the United States."

[53]Matthew Miller and David Hemenway, "Guns and Suicide in the United States: NEJM," *New England Journal of Medicine*, October 8, 2020, www.nejm.org/doi /full/10.1056/NEJMp0805923.

[54]Andrew Anglemyer, Tara Horvath, and George Rutherford, "The Accessibility of Firearms and Risk for Suicide and Homicide Victimization Among Household Members," *Annals of Internal Medicine* 160, no. 2 (2014): 101-10, https://doi.org/10.7326/m13-1301.

[55]Kate Masters, "A Psychiatrist Debunks the Biggest Myths Surrounding Gun Suicides," *The Trace*, May 14, 2018, www.thetrace.org/2015/11/gun-suicides -mental-illness-statistics/.

[56]CT, HI, IL, IA, MD, MA, NJ, NY, NC, and Washington, DC.

[57]Ryan Lindsay, "Study: Permit-To-Purchase Laws, Not Background Checks, More Effective In Decreasing Gun Violence," WAMU 88.5—American University Radio, August 13, 2019, https://wamu.org/story/19/08/13 /researchers-say-permit-to-purchase-laws-not-background-checks-more -effective-in-decreasing-gun-vio/.

[58]"Suicide-By-Firearm Rates Shift in Two States After Changes in State Gun Laws," Johns Hopkins Bloomberg School of Public Health, September 1, 2015, www.jhsph.edu/news/news-releases/2015/suicide-by-firearm-rates-shift-in -two-states-after-changes-in-state-gun-laws.html.

[59]Cassandra K. Crifasi et al., "Effects of Changes in Permit-to-Purchase Handgun Laws in Connecticut and Missouri on Suicide Rates," *Preventive Medicine* (Academic Press, July 23, 2015), www.sciencedirect.com/science/article/abs/pii /S0091743515002297.

[60]Crifasi, "Effects of Changes in Permit-to-Purchase Handgun Laws in Connecticut and Missouri on Suicide Rates."

[61]Aaron J. Kivisto and Peter Lee Phalen, "Effects of Risk-Based Firearm Seizure Laws in Connecticut and Indiana on Suicide Rates, 1981–2015," *Psychiatric Services* 69, no. 8 (June 1, 2018): 855-62, https://doi.org/10.1176/appi.ps.201700250.

[62]States with Extreme Risk Laws: CA, CT, DE, D.C., FL, IL, IN, MD, MA, NJ, NY, OR, RI, VT, and WA.

[63]"Extreme Risk Laws Save Lives," Everytown Research & Policy, October 6, 2020, https://everytownresearch.org/report/extreme-risk-laws-save-lives/.

[64]"Extreme Risk Laws Save Lives."

[65]Terry Spencer, "Florida 'Red Flag' Gun Law Used 3,500 Times since Parkland," Associated Press, February 14, 2020, https://apnews.com/article/6560501986 455adcb0ef57fdb370035a.

[66]"Firearm Suicide in the United States."

[67]"Firearm Suicide in the United States."

[68]April M. Zeoli, Jon S. Vernick, and Daniel W Webster, "Association Between Youth-Focused Firearm Laws and Youth Suicides—Correction," *Jama* 292, no. 10 (August 2004): 1178, https://doi.org/10.1001/jama.292.10.1178-a.

[69]"Firearm Suicide in the United States."

[70]"Lung Cancer Fact Sheet," American Lung Association, May 27, 2020, www .lung.org/lung-health-diseases/lung-disease-lookup/lung-cancer/resource -library/lung-cancer-fact-sheet.

[71]"What Are the Risk Factors for Lung Cancer?," Centers for Disease Control and Prevention, September 22, 2020, www.cdc.gov/cancer/lung/basic_info /risk_factors.htm.

[72]Emma Kennedy, "Tate Student's AR-15, Father's 54 Guns Removed under New Red Flag Law," *Pensacola News Journal*, July 9, 2018, www.pnj.com/story/news /crime/2018/07/09/red-flag-law-ecso-has-filed-2-petitions-remove-guns -since-parkland/762699002/.

9. SCHOOL AND MASS SHOOTINGS

[1]John Woodrow Cox et al., "Analysis: More than 240,000 Students Have Experienced Gun Violence at School since Columbine," *Washington Post*, January 24, 2020, www.washingtonpost.com/graphics/2018/local/school-shootings -database/.

[2]"Keeping Our Schools Safe: A Plan for Preventing Mass Shootings and Ending All Gun Violence in American Schools," Everytown Research & Policy, July 31, 2020, https://everytownresearch.org/report/a-plan-for-preventing-mass -shootings-and-ending-all-gun-violence-in-american-schools/.

[3]Allyson Chiu, "'Shut the Lights off, Say No More': Nursery Rhyme Prepares Kindergartners for Lockdowns," *Washington Post*, April 29, 2019, www .washingtonpost.com/news/morning-mix/wp/2018/06/08/lockdown -lockdown-is-a-kindergarten-nursery-rhyme-at-massachusetts-school/.

[4]Sylvia Varnham O'Regan, "The Company Behind America's Scariest School Shooter Drills," *The Trace*, December 16, 2019, www.thetrace.org/2019/12 /alice-active-shooter-training-school-safety/.

[5]O'Regan, "The Company Behind America's Scariest School Shooter Drills."

[6]Arika Herron, "'It Hurt so Bad': Indiana Teachers Shot with Plastic Pellets during Active Shooter Training," *The Indianapolis Star*, March 22, 2019, www .indystar.com/story/news/politics/2019/03/21/active-shooter-training-for -schools-teachers-shot-with-plastic-pellets/3231103002/.

[7]Elizabeth Williamson, "When Active-Shooter Drills Scare the Children They Hope to Protect," *New York Times*, September 4, 2019, www.nytimes.com /2019/09/04/us/politics/active-shooter-drills-schools.html.

[8]Elizabeth Chuck, "Active Shooter Drills Are Scaring Kids and May Not Protect Them. Some Schools Are Taking a New Approach," NBCNews.com, April 18, 2019, www.nbcnews.com/news/us-news/active-shooter-drills-are-scaring-kids -may-not-protect-them-n992941.

[9]"Keeping Our Schools Safe."

[10]Moriah Balingit, "Teacher Unions, Gun-Control Advocates Urge Changes to Active-Shooter Drills, Citing Student Trauma," *Washington Post*, February 12, 2020, www.washingtonpost.com/local/education/teacher-unions-gun-control -advocates-urge-changes-to-active-shooter-drills-citing-student-trauma /2020/02/11/732e419e-4d09-11ea-bf44-f5043eb3918a_story.html.

[11]O'Regan, "The Company Behind America's Scariest School Shooter Drills."

[12]Ken Ritter, "Las Vegas Marks 3rd Year since Deadliest US Mass Shooting," Associated Press, October 2, 2020, https://apnews.com/article/virus-outbreak -las-vegas-las-vegas-mass-shooting-nevada-shootings-ea1ab5537d62f9e3e52 bb4f770910452.

[13]Marisa Booty et al., "Describing a 'Mass Shooting': the Role of Databases in Understanding Burden," *Injury Epidemiology* 6, no. 1 (December 3, 2019), https://doi.org/10.1186/s40621-019-0226-7.

[14]"Active Shooter Incidents in the United States in 2019," FBI, April 8, 2020, www.fbi.gov/file-repository/active-shooter-incidents-in-the-us-2019-042820 .pdf/view.

[15]"Active Shooter Incidents in the United States in 2019."

[16]"Gun Violence Archive," Gun Violence Archive, November 2, 2020, www.gun violencearchive.org/past-tolls.

[17]Booty, "Describing a 'Mass Shooting': the Role of Databases in Understanding Burden."

[18]"Ten Years of Mass Shootings in the United States," Mass Shootings in America 2009-2019, Everytown for Gun Safety Support Fund, November 21, 2019, https://maps.everytownresearch.org/massshootingsreports/mass-shootings-in -america-2009-2019/.

[19]"Ten Years of Mass Shootings in the United States."

[20]"Ten Years of Mass Shootings in the United States."

[21]"Ten Years of Mass Shootings in the United States."

[22]"Ten Years of Mass Shootings in the United States."

[23]Daniel W. Webster et al., "Evidence Concerning the Regulation of Firearms Design, Sale, and Carrying on Fatal Mass Shootings in the United States," *Criminology & Public Policy* 19, no. 1 (2020): 171-212, https://doi.org/10.1111 /1745-9133.12487.

[24]Webster, "Evidence Concerning the Regulation of Firearms Design, Sale, and Carrying on Fatal Mass Shootings in the United States."

[25]"Assault Weapons and High-Capacity Magazines," Everytown Research & Policy, September 8, 2020, https://everytownresearch.org/report/assault -weapons-and-high-capacity-magazines/.

[26]Meghan Keneally, "Understanding the 1994 Assault Weapons Ban and Why It Ended," ABC News, September 13, 2019, https://abcnews.go.com/US /understanding-1994-assault-weapons-ban-ended/story?id=65546858.

[27]Charles Dimaggio et al., "Changes in US Mass Shooting Deaths Associated with the 1994–2004 Federal Assault Weapons Ban," *Journal of Trauma and Acute Care Surgery* 86, no. 1 (January 2019): 11-19, https://doi.org/10.1097/ta.0000 000000002060.

[28]Dimaggio, "Changes in US Mass Shooting Deaths Associated with the 1994– 2004 Federal Assault Weapons Ban."

[29]John Donohue and Theodora Boulouta, "That Assault Weapon Ban? It Really Did Work," *New York Times*, September 4, 2019, www.nytimes.com/2019/09/04 /opinion/assault-weapon-ban.html.

[30]Alex Yablon, "Diving Into the Data on Assault Weapons Bans," *The Trace*, August 17, 2019, www.thetrace.org/2019/08/what-the-data-says-asssault-weapons-bans/.

[31]CA, CT, HI, MD, MA, NJ, NY, and Washington, DC.

[32]"Assault Weapons and High-Capacity Magazines."

[33]Saul Cornell, "Don't Ban Assault Weapons—Tax Them," *Atlantic*, August 14, 2019, www.theatlantic.com/ideas/archive/2019/08/taxing-assault-weapons -old-solution-modern-problem/596047/.

[34]Rocco Pallin et al., "Assessment of Extreme Risk Protection Order Use in California From 2016 to 2019," JAMA Network Open 3, no. 6 (2020), https://doi .org/10.1001/jamanetworkopen.2020.7735.

[35]Garen J. Wintemute et al., "Extreme Risk Protection Orders Intended to Prevent Mass Shootings," *Annals of Internal Medicine* 171, no. 9 (2019): 655, https://doi. org/10.7326/m19-2162.

[36]"Keeping Our Schools Safe: A Plan for Preventing Mass Shootings and Ending All Gun Violence in American Schools," Everytown Research & Policy, July 31, 2020, https://everytownresearch.org/report/a-plan-for-preventing-mass -shootings-and-ending-all-gun-violence-in-american-schools/.

[37]U.S. Government Accountability Office, "Gun Control: Analyzing Available Data Could Help Improve Background Checks Involving Domestic Violence Records," July 5, 2016, www.gao.gov/products/GAO-16-483.

10. THE COSTS OF GUN VIOLENCE IN OUR COMMUNITIES

[1]Michelle Singletary, "Perspective: The Enormous Economic Cost of Gun Violence," *Washington Post*, March 31, 2019, www.washingtonpost.com/news/get-there/wp/2018/02/22/the-enormous-economic-cost-of-gun-violence/.

[2]U.S. Congress Joint Economic Committee Democratic Staff, "A State-by-State Examination of the Economic Costs of Gun Violence," Congresswoman Carolyn Maloney, September 18, 2019, www.jec.senate.gov/public/_cache/files/b2ee3158-aff4-4563-8c3b-0183ba4a8135/economic-costs-of-gun-violence.pdf.

[3]U.S. Congress Joint Economic Committee, "A State-by-State Examination of the Economic Costs of Gun Violence."

[4]U.S. Congress Joint Economic Committee, "A State-by-State Examination of the Economic Costs of Gun Violence."

[5]U.S. Congress Joint Economic Committee, "A State-by-State Examination of the Economic Costs of Gun Violence."

[6]Yasemin Irvin-Erickson et al., "Gun Violence Affects the Economic Health of Communities," Urban Institute, July 12, 2018, www.urban.org/research/publication/gun-violence-affects-economic-health-communities.

[7]Aaron Karp, "Small Arms Survey," SmallArmsSurvey.Org, June 2018, www.smallarmssurvey.org/fileadmin/docs/T-Briefing-Papers/SAS-BP-Civilian-Firearms-Numbers.pdf.

[8]"Fatal Force: Police Shootings Database," *Washington Post*, January 22, 2020, www.washingtonpost.com/graphics/investigations/police-shootings-database/.

[9]"Police Shootings," Giffords Law Center to Prevent Gun Violence, September 6, 2020, https://giffords.org/issues/police-shootings/.

[10]German Lopez, "Police Shootings Are Also Part of America's Gun Problem," Vox, April 9, 2018, www.vox.com/2018/4/9/17205256/gun-violence-us-police-shootings.

[11]Christopher Ingraham, "More Police Officers Die on the Job in States with More Guns," *Washington Post*, April 29, 2019, www.washingtonpost.com/news/wonk/wp/2016/07/08/more-police-officers-die-on-the-job-in-states-with-more-guns/.

[12]Kirsten Weir, "Policing in Black & White," *Monitor on Psychology*, American Psychological Association, December 2016, www.apa.org/monitor/2016/12/cover-policing.

[13]German Lopez, "Unarmed People Are Much More Likely to Be Killed by Police When They're Not White," Vox, June 2, 2015, www.vox.com/2015/6/2/8713247/police-shootings-racist.

[14]Phillip Atiba Goff et al., "The Essence of Innocence: Consequences of Dehumanizing Black Children.," *Journal of Personality and Social Psychology* 106, no. 4 (February 24, 2014): 526-45, https://doi.org/10.1037/a0035663.

[15]Lopez, "Police Shootings Are Also Part of America's Gun Problem."

[16]Champe Barton, "Police, Power, and the Specter of Guns," *The Trace*, June 12, 2020, www.thetrace.org/2020/06/police-power-guns-george-floyd/.

[17]A sociologist at Rutgers, Frank Edwards, calls this the "ceiling effect."

[18]German Lopez, "More Police Officers Are Killed on Duty in States with More Guns," Vox, August 15, 2015, www.vox.com/2015/8/15/9157087/police -officers-guns-homicides.

[19]David Brancaccio, Rose Conlon, and Candance Manriquez Wrenn, "How Police Departments Got Billions of Dollars of Tactical Military Equipment," Marketplace, June 12, 2020, www.marketplace.org/2020/06/12/police-depart ments-1033-military-equipment-weapons/.

[20]"Demilitarizing America's Police: A Constitutional Analysis," Constitution Project, The Constitution Project Committee on Policing Reforms, August 2016, https://archive.constitutionproject.org/wp-content/uploads/2016/08 /Demilitarizing-Americas-Police-August-2016-FINAL.pdf.

[21]"US Law Enforcement Violated Black Lives Matter Protesters' Human Rights," Amnesty International, accessed November 3, 2020, www.amnesty.org/en/ latest/news/2020/08/usa-law-enforcement-violated-black-lives-matter-pro testers-human-rights/.

[22]Rick Noack, "5 Countries Where Most Police Officers Do Not Carry Firearms— and It Works Well," *Washington Post*, April 19, 2019, www.washingtonpost.com /news/worldviews/wp/2015/02/18/5-countries-where-police-officers-do-not -carry-firearms-and-it-works-well/.

[23]Mélissa Godin, "What the U.S Can Learn from Countries Where Cops Are Unarmed," *TIME*, June 19, 2020, https://time.com/5854986/police-reform -defund-unarmed-guns/.

[24]"Officers Feloniously Killed," FBI, April 26, 2019, https://ucr.fbi.gov /leoka/2019/topic-pages/officers-feloniously-killed.

[25]"The United Kingdom's Police Roll Of Honour," Police Roll Of Honour Trust, accessed November 3, 2020, https://policememorial.org.uk/rollofhonour.php.

[26]Lucy Clarke-Billings, "Britain's Gun Laws: Who Can Own a Firearm?," Newsweek, June 22, 2016, www.newsweek.com/britains-gun-laws-who-can -own-firearm-471473.

[27]"104 Shot, 15 Fatally, over Father's Day Weekend in Chicago," *Chicago Sun-Times*, June 22, 2020, https://chicago.suntimes.com/crime/2020/6/20

/21297470/chicago-fathers-day-weekend-shootings-homicide-gun-violence
-june-19-22-104-shot.

[28]Annie McCormick, "32 Victims from Weekend Gun Violence in Philadelphia,"
WPVI-TV, Philadelphia, June 17, 2019, https://6abc.com/32-victims-from
-weekend-gun-violence-in-the-city/5350387/.

[29]John Gramlich and Drew DeSilver, "Despite Recent Violence, Chicago Is Far
from the U.S. 'Murder Capital,'" Pew Research Center, May 30, 2020, www
.pewresearch.org/fact-tank/2018/11/13/despite-recent-violence-chicago-far
-from-u-s-murder-capital/.

[30]"A Nation of Survivors: The Toll of Gun Violence in America," Everytown
Research & Policy, July 31, 2020, https://everytownresearch.org/report
/a-nation-of-survivors-the-toll-of-gun-violence-in-america/.

[31]Howard Schubiner, Richard Scott, and Angela Tzelepis, "Exposure to Violence
among Inner-City Youth," *Journal of Adolescent Health* 14, no. 3 (1993): 214-19,
https://doi.org/10.1016/1054-139x(93)90008-d.

[32]"Black Children and Teens Are 14 Times More Likely than White Children and
Teens of the Same Age to Die by Gun Homicide," Everytown Research &
Policy, August 18, 2020, https://everytownresearch.org/stat/black-children
-and-teens-are-14-times-more-likely-than-white-children-and-teens-of-the
-same-age-to-die-by-gun-homicide/.

[33]Yolanda T. Mitchell and Tiffany L. Bromfield, "Gun Violence and the Minority
Experience National Council on Family Relations, January 10, 2019, www.ncfr
.org/ncfr-report/winter-2018/gun-violence-and-minority-experience.

[34]Sam Bieler, "Raising the Voices of Gun Violence," Raising the Voices of Gun
Violence, accessed November 3, 2020, https://apps.urban.org/features/Raising
theVoicesofGunViolence/.

[35]Sarah Ryley, Jeremy Singer-Vine, and Sean Campbell, "5 Things to Know About
Cities' Failure to Arrest Shooters," *The Trace*, January 24, 2019, www.thetrace
.org/2019/01/gun-murder-solve-rate-understaffed-police-data-analysis/.

[36]Thomas Abt, "We Can't End Inequality Until We Stop Urban Gun Violence,"
The Trace, July 12, 2019, www.thetrace.org/2019/07/we-cant-end-inequality
-until-we-stop-urban-gun-violence/.

[37]German Lopez, "How to Dramatically Reduce Gun Violence in American
Cities," Vox, July 12, 2019, www.vox.com/policy-and-politics/2019/7/12
/20679091/thomas-abt-bleeding-out-urban-gun-violence-book-review.

[38]Mitchell and Bromfield, "Gun Violence and the Minority Experience."

[39]Aliza Aufrichtig et al., "Want to Fix Gun Violence in America? Go Local," *The
Guardian*, accessed November 3, 2020, https://www.theguardian.com/us-news
/ng-interactive/2017/jan/09/special-report-fixing-gun-violence-in-america.

[40]Michael Siegel et al., "The Impact of State Firearm Laws on Homicide Rates in Suburban and Rural Areas Compared to Large Cities in the United States, 1991–2016," *The Journal of Rural Health* 36, no. 2 (July 30, 2019): 255-65, https://doi.org/10.1111/jrh.12387.

[41]Mike McLively and Brittany Nieto, "A Case Study in Hope: Lessons from Oakland's Remarkable Reduction in Gun Violence," Giffords Law Center to Prevent Gun Violence, April 2010, https://giffords.org/wp-content/uploads/2019/05 /Giffords-Law-Center-A-Case-Study-in-Hope.pdf.

[42]McLively and Nieto, "A Case Study in Hope."

[43]Lopez, "How to Dramatically Reduce Gun Violence in American Cities."

[44]"Projects Reducing Violence and Increasing Graduation," *Becoming a Man*, UChicago Urban Labs, accessed November 4, 2020, https://urbanlabs .uchicago.edu/projects/becoming-a-man.

[45]Sara F. Jacoby et al., "The Enduring Impact of Historical and Structural Racism on Urban Violence in Philadelphia," *Social Science & Medicine* 199 (May 19, 2017): 87-95, https://doi.org/10.1016/j.socscimed.2017.05.038.

[46]Paige Fernandez, "Defunding the Police Will Actually Make Us Safer," American Civil Liberties Union, June 11, 2020, www.aclu.org/news/criminal -law-reform/defunding-the-police-will-actually-make-us-safer/.

[47]Christy Lopez, "Opinion: Defund the Police? Here's What That Really Means," *Washington Post*, July 6, 2020, www.washingtonpost.com/opinions/2020/06/07 /defund-police-heres-what-that-really-means/.

11. COMMON ARGUMENTS AGAINST GUN REFORM

[1]Kitty Felde, "California Gun Laws Prevented Pentagon Gunman from Buying Gun," Southern California Public Radio, April 19, 2010, www.scpr.org /news/2010/04/19/14261/california-gun-laws-prevented-pentagon-gunman -john/.

[2]Caroline Wolf Harlow, "Firearm Use by Offenders," Bureau of Justice Statistics, US Department of Justice, February 4, 2002.

[3]Harlow, "Firearm Use by Offenders."

[4]Defilippis and Hughes, "New Study Finds No Advantages to Defensive Gun Use," *The Trace*, April 20, 2018, www.thetrace.org/2015/07/defensive-gun-use-myth/.

[5]Defilippis and Hughes, "New Study Finds No Advantages to Defensive Gun Use."

[6]Timothy Johnson, "NRA Commentary Admits The Odds Of Needing A Gun To Defend Yourself Are Infinitesimal," Media Matters for America, October 21, 2015, www.mediamatters.org/national-rifle-association/nra-commentary -admits-odds-needing-gun-defend-yourself-are-infinitesimal.

[7]Arthur L. Kellermann et al., "Injuries and Deaths Due to Firearms in the Home," *The Journal of Trauma: Injury, Infection, and Critical Care* 45, no. 2 (August 1998): 263-67, https://doi.org/10.1097/00005373-199808000-00010.

[8]"Guns and Violence Against Women: America's Uniquely Lethal Intimate Partner Violence Problem 10.17.2019," Everytown Research & Policy, October 17, 2019, https://everytownresearch.org/report/guns-and-violence-against -women-americas-uniquely-lethal-intimate-partner-violence-problem/.

[9]Andrew Anglemyer, Tara Horvath, and George Rutherford, "The Accessibility of Firearms and Risk for Suicide and Homicide Victimization Among Household Members," *Annals of Internal Medicine* 160, no. 2 (2014):101-10, https://doi.org/10.7326/m13-1301.

[10]"Universal Background Checks," Giffords Law Center to Prevent Gun Violence, October 28, 2020, https://giffords.org/lawcenter/gun-laws/policy -areas/background-checks/universal-background-checks/.

[11]Kellermann, "Injuries and Deaths Due to Firearms in the Home."

[12]"The Impact of Gun Violence on Children and Teens," Everytown Research & Policy, August 17, 2020, https://everytownresearch.org/report/the-impact -of-gun-violence-on-children-and-teens/.

[13]Adrian D. Sandler, "Seeing Is Believing: What Do Boys Do When They Find a Real Gun?," *Journal of Developmental & Behavioral Pediatrics* 22, no. 6 (June 2001): 452, https://doi.org/10.1097/00004703-200112000-00035.

[14]"Guns and Violence Against Women."

[15]Dylan Matthews, "Living in a House with a Gun Increases Your Odds of Death," Vox, October 1, 2015, www.vox.com/2015/10/1/18000520/gun-risk-death.

[16]Dave Gilson, "10 Pro-Gun Myths, Shot Down," *Mother Jones*, January 31, 2013, www.motherjones.com/politics/2013/01/pro-gun-myths-fact-check/.

[17]Evan Defilippis and Devin Hughes, "The Myth Behind Defensive Gun Ownership," *POLITICO Magazine*, January 14, 2015, www.politico.com/magazine /story/2015/01/defensive-gun-ownership-myth-114262.

[18]Defilippis and Hughes, "The Myth Behind Defensive Gun Ownership."

[19]"Gun Violence Archive," Gun Violence Archive, November 2, 2020, www.gun violencearchive.org/past-tolls.

[20]Eugenio Weigend Vargas, "Gun Violence in America: A State-by-State Analysis," Center for American Progress, November 20, 2019, www.american progress.org/issues/guns-crime/news/2019/11/20/477218/gun-violence -america-state-state-analysis/.

[21]Harvard School of Public Health, "States With Higher Levels Of Gun Ownership Have Higher Homicide Rates," ScienceDaily, accessed November 2, 2020, www.sciencedaily.com/releases/2007/01/070111181527.htm.

[22]Richard Florida, "The Geography of Gun Deaths," *Atlantic*, January 13, 2011, www.theatlantic.com/national/archive/2011/01/the-geography-of-gun-deaths/69354/.

[23]Danielle Kurtzleben, "Fact Check: Is Chicago Proof That Gun Laws Don't Work?," NPR (NPR, October 5, 2017), www.npr.org/2017/10/05/555580598/fact-check-is-chicago-proof-that-gun-laws-don-t-work.

[24]University of Pennsylvania School of Medicine, "States with strict gun laws see more homicides when they border states with lax ones: Over a 5-year period, most guns found in states with strict gun laws were obtained from less restrictive states," ScienceDaily, accessed November, 4, 2020, www.sciencedaily.com/releases/2019/03/190306110629.htm.

13. BEYOND THOUGHTS AND PRAYERS

[1]"The Just War Tradition in Christianity and Its Continuing Relevance—Modern Warfare—CCEA—GCSE Religious Studies," BBC News, accessed November 4, 2020, www.bbc.co.uk/bitesize/guides/zrndpg8/revision/2.

[2]Staff, "Deputies: Man Shot While Attempting to Steal Catalytic Converter from Berkeley Co. Auto Dealer," Live 5 News, Charleston, SC, October 27, 2020, www.live5news.com/2020/10/27/deputies-shooting-sparked-by-attempted-theft-auto-dealer/.

[3]Joe Coscarelli, "Sarah Palin Out-Palins Herself at NRA Convention: 'Waterboarding Is How We Baptize Terrorists,'" *Intelligencer*, April 28, 2014, https://nymag.com/intelligencer/2014/04/palin-waterboarding-how-we-baptize-terrorists-nra-video.html.

[4]Associated Press, "Liberty University President Urges: 'End Those Muslims' via Concealed Gun Carry," *The Guardian*, December 5, 2015, www.theguardian.com/us-news/2015/dec/05/liberty-university-president-san-bernardino-shooting-concealed-weapons-carry-muslims.

RESOURCE INDEX

Gun Violence Prevention Organizations

Everytown for Gun Safety
https://everytown.org

Moms Demand Action for Gun Sense in America
https://momsdemandaction.org

Brady United
www.bradyunited.org

Giffords Law Center to Prevent Gun Violence
https://giffords.org/lawcenter/gun-laws

Coalition to Stop Gun Violence
www.csgv.org

Violence Policy Center
https://vpc.org

New Yorkers Against Gun Violence
https://nyagv.org

Women Against Gun Violence
https://wagv.org/get-involved

The Educational Fund to Stop Gun Violence
https://efsgv.org

Guns Down America
https://gunsdownamerica.org

End Family Fire
www.endfamilyfire.org

Gun Owners for Responsible Ownership
www.responsibleownership.org

Gun Violence Research

Johns Hopkins Center for Gun Policy and Research
www.jhsph.edu/research/centers-and-institutes/johns-hopkins-center-for-gun-policy-and-research

Gun Violence Archive
www.gunviolencearchive.org

New Jersey Gun Violence Research Center
    https://gunviolenceresearchcenter.rutgers.edu

The National Gun Violence Research Center
    https://gunresearch.org

Keeping Kids Safe from Guns

Be SMART Campaign
    https://besmartforkids.org

Asking Saves Kids
    www.bradyunited.org/program/end-family-fire/asking-saves-kids

Survivor Resources

The Rebels Project
    www.therebelsproject.org

Survivors Lead
    www.survivorslead.com

Moments that Survive Resources
    https://momentsthatsurvive.org/resources

Gun Violence Survivors Foundation
    http://gvsfoundation.org

Books

Beating Guns, Shane Claiborne and Michael Martin

Collateral Damage: Changing the Conversation about Firearms and Faith, James A. Atwood

Films

The Amor of Light
    www.armoroflightfilm.com

Under the Gun
    https://underthegunmovie.com

Studies

"Kingdom Dreams, Violent Realities"
    www.umcjustice.org/news-and-stories/kingdom-dreams-violent-realities-
    bible-study-412